Entrepreneurial Journalism

Entrepreneurial journalism has emerged as a 'hot topic' for 21st century journalism, not just in the industry itself, but also in the academic community. This timely book seeks to make sense of the dramatic transformation of journalism, with a specific focus on what entrepreneurialism means for the world of journalism.

The volume brings together leading international scholars to examine critical topics including the ethics underpinning new funding models such as crowdfunding; best practices in entrepreneurial journalism education; the implications of the emergence of a start-up culture; and differing interpretations of what is understood by the term 'entrepreneurialism' in the field of journalism. The collection analyses and discusses the future of journalism from the perspective of entrepreneurial culture drawing on relevant case studies from the United Kingdom, Belgium, France, Spain, Greece, Denmark, Canada, and the United States.

This book was originally published as a special issue of *Journalism Practice*.

Kevin Rafter is Professor of Political Communication at Dublin City University, Ireland. He has published widely on topics related to media and politics. His recent volumes include *Political Advertising in the 2014 European Parliament Elections* (with Christina Holtz-Bacha and Edoardo Novelli, 2017), and *Media and Elections in Ireland since 1969* (forthcoming). He is a former political journalist with the *Irish Times* and RTÉ, the Irish public broadcaster.

Journalism Studies: Theory and Practice

Series editor: Bob Franklin, Cardiff School of Journalism, Media and Cultural Studies, Cardiff University, UK

The journal *Journalism Studies* was established at the turn of the new millennium by Bob Franklin. It was launched in the context of a burgeoning interest in the scholarly study of journalism and an expansive global community of journalism scholars and researchers. The ambition was to provide a forum for the critical discussion and study of journalism as a subject of intellectual inquiry but also an arena of professional practice. Previously, the study of journalism in the UK and much of Europe was a fairly marginal branch of the larger disciplines of media, communication and cultural studies; only a handful of Universities offered degree programmes in the subject. *Journalism Studies* has flourished and succeeded in providing the intended public space for discussion of research on key issues within the field, to the point where in 2007 a sister journal, *Journalism Practice,* was launched to enable an enhanced focus on practice-based issues, as well as foregrounding studies of journalism education, training and professional concerns. Both journals are among the leading ranked journals within the field and publish six issues annually, in electronic and print formats. More recently, 2013 witnessed the launch of a further companion journal *Digital Journalism* to provide a site for scholarly discussion, analysis and responses to the wide ranging implications of digital technologies for the practice and study of journalism. From the outset, the publication of themed issues has been a commitment for all journals. Their purpose is first, to focus on highly significant or neglected areas of the field; second, to facilitate discussion and analysis of important and topical policy issues; and third, to offer readers an especially high quality and closely focused set of essays, analyses and discussions.

The *Journalism Studies: Theory and Practice* book series draws on a wide range of these themed issues from all journals and thereby extends the critical and public forum provided by them. The Editor of the journals works closely with guest editors to ensure that the books achieve relevance for readers and the highest standards of research rigour and academic excellence. The series makes a significant contribution to the field of journalism studies by inviting distinguished scholars, academics and journalism practitioners to discuss and debate the central concerns within the field. It also reaches a wider readership of scholars, students and practitioners across the social sciences, humanities and communication arts, encouraging them to engage critically with, but also to interrogate, the specialist scholarly studies of journalism which this series provides.

Recent titles in the series:
(for full list, see: www.routledge.com/Journalism-Studies/book-series/JOURNALISM)

Journalism, Democracy and Civil Society in India
Edited by Shakuntala Rao and Vipul Mudgal

Photojournalism and Citizen Journalism
Edited by Stuart Allan

Entrepreneurial Journalism
Edited by Kevin Rafter

Rethinking Research Methods in an Age of Digital Journalism
Edited by Michael Karlsson and Helle Sjøvaag

Entrepreneurial Journalism

Edited by
Kevin Rafter

Routledge
Taylor & Francis Group
LONDON AND NEW YORK

First published 2018 by Routledge

2 Park Square, Milton Park, Abingdon, Oxfordshire OX14 4RN
52 Vanderbilt Avenue, New York, NY 10017

Routledge is an imprint of the Taylor & Francis Group, an informa business

First issued in paperback 2019

British Library Cataloguing in Publication Data
A catalogue record for this book is available from the British Library

ISBN 13: 978-1-138-07029-5 (hbk)
ISBN 13: 978-0-367-26462-8 (pbk)

Typeset in Myriad Pro
by RefineCatch Limited, Bungay, Suffolk

Publisher's Note
The publisher accepts responsibility for any inconsistencies that may have arisen during the conversion of this book from journal articles to book chapters, namely the possible inclusion of journal terminology.

Contents

Citation Information

The chapters in this book were originally published in *Journalism Practice*, volume 10, issue 2 (March 2016). When citing this material, please use the original page numbering for each article, as follows:

Introduction

Understanding where entrepreneurial journalism fits in
Kevin Rafter
Journalism Practice, volume 10, issue 2 (March 2016), pp. 140–142

Chapter 1

Media Discourse about Entrepreneurial Journalism: Implications for journalistic capital
Tim P. Vos and Jane B. Singer
Journalism Practice, volume 10, issue 2 (March 2016), pp. 143–159

Chapter 2

Ideology as Resource in Entrepreneurial Journalism: The French online news startup Mediapart
Andrea Wagemans, Tamara Witschge, and Mark Deuze
Journalism Practice, volume 10, issue 2 (March 2016), pp. 160–177

Chapter 3

Entrepreneurialism or Cooperativism? An exploration of cooperative journalistic enterprises
Eugenia Siapera and Lambrini Papadopoulou
Journalism Practice, volume 10, issue 2 (March 2016), pp. 178–195

Chapter 4

Accountability and Transparency of Entrepreneurial Journalism: Unresolved ethical issues in crowdfunded journalism projects
Colin Porlezza and Sergio Splendore
Journalism Practice, volume 10, issue 2 (March 2016), pp. 196–216

Chapter 5

"It's Like Having a Second Full-Time Job": Crowdfunding, journalism and labour
Andrea Hunter
Journalism Practice, volume 10, issue 2 (March 2016), pp. 217–232

Chapter 6

Discourses of Enterprise in Hyperlocal Community News in the UK
Dave Harte, Jerome Turner, and Andy Williams
Journalism Practice, volume 10, issue 2 (March 2016), pp. 233–250

Chapter 7

Freelancing in Flemish News Media and Entrepreneurial Skills as Pivotal Elements in Job Satisfaction: Perspectives of masters or servants?
Rozane De Cock and Hedwig de Smaele
Journalism Practice, volume 10, issue 2 (March 2016), pp. 251–265

Chapter 8

Towards a Broader Conception of Entrepreneurial Journalism Education: Starting with everyday practice
Kirsten Sparre and Helle Meibom Færgemann
Journalism Practice, volume 10, issue 2 (March 2016), pp. 266–285

Chapter 9

The Journalists of the Future meet Entrepreneurial Journalism: Perceptions in the classroom
Andreu Casero-Ripollés, Jessica Izquierdo-Castillo, and Hugo Doménech-Fabregat
Journalism Practice, volume 10, issue 2 (March 2016), pp. 286–303

Notes on Contributors

Andreu Casero-Ripollés is Associate Professor of Journalism in the Department of Communication Science at Universitat Jaume I de Castelló, Spain. His research focuses on political communication, the structure of the digital media industry, the future of journalism in a digital age, and the professional relationship between journalists and politicians.

Rozane De Cock is Professor and Director of the Brussels Centre for Journalism Studies, KU Leuven, Belgium. Her research focuses on news production and research, quantitative and qualitative research, content analysis, innovative research designs, the problems of internet usage, and coverage of the courts and criminal justice news.

Hedwig de Smaele is Professor and Program Director of the Master's in Journalism at the Brussels Centre for Journalism Studies, KU Leuven, Belgium. Her research interests centre on journalism research methods, new media, Russian language and culture, communications theory, political communication, and media policy.

Mark Deuze is Professor of Media Studies at the University of Amsterdam, The Netherlands. His research reflects on the interaction which society has with forms of new media, particularly with regards to professional media production. He has written extensively on subjects including internet journalism and digital culture. He is the author of *Media Life* (2012) and the editor of *Managing Media Work* (2010).

Hugo Doménech-Fabregat is Professor in the Department of Communication Science at Universitat Jaume I de Castelló, Spain. His research interests focus on photojournalism and issues related to Web 2.0 and its repercussions on journalism. His work has appeared in journals including *Journalism Practice* and *Textual & Visual Media.*

Helle Meibom Færgemann is a Development Consultant in the Centre for Teaching Development and Digital Media at Aarhus University, Denmark, where she develops, teaches, and evaluates courses on innovation and entrepreneurship. Her work has appeared in the international journals *Journalism Practice* and *International Journal of Entrepreneurship and Small Business.*

Dave Harte is Senior Lecturer in Media and Communication at Birmingham City University, UK. He researches the emerging trend of local community 'hyperlocal' news websites, and has published widely on the subject. In the past he has worked with local media companies to support the growth of the creative economy. For many years he has worked closely with Birmingham's vibrant digital media sector acting as a link between the public sector and the business community.

Andrea Hunter is Assistant Professor in the Department of Journalism at Concordia University, Montreal, Canada. Her current research examines the ethical and labour issues involved in crowdfunding and journalism. She has worked as a producer, reporter, on-air contributor, and host for national and regional radio shows on CBC Radio.

Jessica Izquierdo-Castillo is Professor in the Department of Communication Science at Universitat Jaume I de Castelló, Spain. Her research focuses on business models of communication companies, the transformation of these companies in the digital age, and communicative structures. Her work has been published in journals including *Journal of Media Business Studies, The Information Professional, Journalism Practice*, and the *Latin Journal of Social Communication.*

Lambrini Papadopoulou is a Greek journalist and a Ph.D. candidate in the Department of Communication, Media and Culture at the Panteion University of Athens, Greece. Her research and thesis explore alternative media business models and media cooperatives. Her academic interests are focused on radical journalism, alternative media business models, and media crisis.

Colin Porlezza is Assistant Professor in the Institute for Media Studies and Media Research at the University of Zurich, Switzerland. His research focuses on journalism research, media accountability and transparency, and crowdfunding. He is the co-editor of *Journalists and Media Accountability: An International Study of People in the Digital Age* (with Fengler, Mazzoleni, Eberwein, and Russ-Mohl, 2013).

Kevin Rafter is Professor of Political Communication at Dublin City University, Ireland. He has published widely on topics related to media and politics. His recent volumes include *Political Advertising in the 2014 European Parliament Elections* (with Christina Holtz-Bacha and Edoardo Novelli, 2017), and *Media and Elections in Ireland since 1969* (forthcoming). He is a former political journalist with the *Irish Times* and RTÉ, the Irish public broadcaster.

Eugenia Siapera is Senior Lecturer in the School of Communications at Dublin City University, Ireland. Her current research looks at the future of journalism from the perspective of journalists and how their professional practices, perception of their roles, and their roles themselves are changing in a rapidly shifting media landscape. She is the author of *Understanding New Media* (2011) and *Cultural Diversity and Global Media: The Mediation of Difference* (2010).

Jane B. Singer is Director of Research and Professor of Innovation Journalism in the Department of Journalism at City University, London, UK. A former print and online journalist, she has been studying journalists' responses to digital technologies since the mid-1990s, and is especially interested in the impact of digital media on journalists' roles, norms, practices, and products. She is the co-author of *Participatory Journalism* (2011) and *Online Journalism Ethics* (2007).

Kirsten Sparre is Assistant Professor in the School of Communication and Culture at Aarhus University, Denmark. Her work has appeared in international journals including the *Harvard Journal of Press/Politics, Studies in Communication Sciences, Journalism Practice*, and *Nordicom Review.* She is currently involved in a research project investigating the success of exported Danish television drama series.

Sergio Splendore is Adjunct Professor in the Department of Social and Political Sciences at the University of Milan, Italy. His research focuses on media production, both in journalism and in the entertainment industry. He has written for a number of international journals, including *Sociology Compass*, *Journalism Practice*, *Journalism*, *Current Politics and Economics of Europe*, the *European Journal of Communication*, and the *Journal of Popular Television*.

Jerome Turner is a Research Assistant in the School of Media at Birmingham City University, UK, where he worked on the Research Council-funded project 'Community, Media and the Creative Citizen'. He is currently completing his ethnographic study of online local community media audiences for Ph.D. submission.

Tim P. Vos is Associate Professor and Chair of the Journalism Studies faculty at the University of Missouri, USA. His research involves roles of journalism, media sociology and gatekeeping, media history, and media policy. He is the editor of *Gatekeeping in Transition* (with F. Heinderyckx, 2015) and the author of *Gatekeeping Theory* (with P.J. Shoemaker, 2009). He is a former broadcast journalist, interviewing nearly every major party candidate for U.S. President in that role.

Andrea Wagemans is a Lecturer at the Université Sorbonne Nouvelle – Paris 3, France, where she is studying for a Ph.D. in Communication and Media Studies, and teaches both cultural studies and journalism writing. She is also a freelance editor, researcher, and translator. She was formerly based at the University of Amsterdam, The Netherlands, where she studied for a Master's Degree in Journalism.

Andy Williams is a Lecturer in the School of Journalism, Media and Cultural Studies at Cardiff University, UK. His current major research interests relate to news sources and the influence of public relations on the UK media, especially in the area of science, health, and environment news. He is a regular contributor to a number of national and regional press and broadcast media outlets in the UK.

Tamara Witschge is Associate Professor and Rosalind Franklin Fellow at the University of Groningen, The Netherlands. Her research explores the ways in which technological, economic, and social change is reconfiguring journalism, with a particular focus on innovation and entrepreneurship in journalism and media. She is the author of *Changing Journalism* (with Lee-Wright and Phillips, 2011) and editor of the *Sage Handbook of Digital Journalism* (with Hermida and Domingo, 2016).

INTRODUCTION
Understanding where entrepreneurial journalism fits in

Kevin Rafter

Entrepreneurial journalism has emerged as a "hot topic" for the twenty-first-century journalism industry with the academy—in research and in the classroom—now playing catch-up. Explanations for this interest are all too obvious in an industry that has undergone—and continues to undergo—huge transformation. Yet, despite the speed and scale of the contemporary reordering of journalism, there is a historical lineage. In 1850, fewer than 20 newspapers were published in South Africa, by 1900 that figure had increased to over 140 publications. Some 9000 miles away on the west coast of Ireland, Castlebar, a town with a population of 3558 people, sustained five local newspapers alongside a reading public which had on order from local newsagents a mixture of Irish and British-produced magazines, and popular and quality papers (Legge 1998). Nineteenth-century entrepreneurs—as owners, editors and reporters—started new businesses taking full advantage of the modernisation of the postal service, developments in the railway network and, in particular, the advance of the telegraph, as this new technology reconfigured time and changed how people communicated information (Chalaby 1998). With our contemporary focus on Google, Buzzfeed and a plethora of other digital media start-ups, we should not forget that the history of journalism is marked by entrepreneurial spirit.

Indeed, it may well be that the dominance of big media enterprises in the twentieth-century model of journalism comes in time to be seen as an interregnum between two start-up cultures spawned by specific communication technology innovations, the telegraph and the internet. Yet, that interregnum is important because for many decades the accepted model of journalism saw finance and editorial divorced from each other. In many media outlets, such normative demarcations between editorial and commercial were evident in having the two divisions on different floors of the same building; interdependent but separate. The contemporary "crisis" in the journalism industry has necessitated a re-evaluation of this relationship between editorial and finance. In particular, with the (re) emergence of entrepreneurialism in journalism we increasingly see content producers and distributors acting as revenue generators. One consequence is a challenge to these traditional normative demarcations with, as yet, unclear consequences.

Courses in news management and the business of media have had their place in the teaching of journalism. But disruption in the twentieth-century business model of journalism has refocused minds, especially with changes in employment opportunities and career structures. As Jeff Jarvis, a leading figure in debates about the future of journalism, has observed, "journalists must now take on the urgent responsibility of building the future of news" and with that work occurring in "new entrepreneurial ventures" (Jarvis 2012, xv).

The concept of entrepreneurial journalism is not just of interest to those in industry; it has also caught the attention of scholars in the field of journalism studies. A growing body of research is considering journalism and entrepreneurship, specifically to understand meaning from trends and changes in industry but also examining the consequences for education. This developing interest in entrepreneurial journalism is clear from the response to the call for papers for this special issue of *Journalism Practice*. Following a rigorous selection process, involving a double-blind peer-review, nine articles were accepted for publication. As Guest Editor of this special issue, I would like to thank not just the contributors but also the many reviewers who have assisted with their insightful and helpful feedback on the submitted articles. The strong support of Editor Bob Franklin from the outset contributed greatly to the work on the special issue.

The impact of the embrace of entrepreneurialism *by* the world of journalism *on* the world of journalism is still unclear. The articles in this collection will hopefully contribute to a wider consideration of entrepreneurialism in the field of journalism, and should spur further research in this important area.

As a recent textbook in the area noted, entrepreneurial journalism "can mean a number of things, and for many journalism students the meaning can change by the day" (Kelly 2015, 94). Several contributors to this special issue address this definitional ambiguity. In their article, "Media Discourse About Entrepreneurial Journalism: Implications for Journalistic Capital", Tim P. Vos and Jane B. Singer examine the meaning of the term through a content analysis of trade publications in the United States from 2000 to 2014.

The textual and discursive construction of tensions that prioritise two elements, profit and individualism professionals' understanding of entrepreneurial journalism—vague in definition and generally positive in tone—gets to the core of why greater scholarly attention on this emerging concept is required. The implications of entrepreneurial journalism as understood in industry are very real for the aforementioned traditional normative conceptions of journalism.

These latter issues are addressed in the second article, "Ideology as Resource in Entrepreneurial Journalism: The French Online News Startup *Mediapart*", in which

Andrea Wagemans, Tamara Witschge and Mark Deuze show how journalism practice is moving—and in many respects, has already moved—beyond the traditional conceptualisations of the field. In a case study from France—but one with wider significance—we see the impact of the placement of startup culture in the field alongside the traditional enterprise producing media products for mass consumption media output. The study argues for a broader consideration of entrepreneurialism and innovation as a social process with value and knowledge creation being central to a collaborative social effort.

We see how securing financial viability for a new startup opens up issues about standards and values in journalism. Eugenia Siapera and Lambrini Papadopoulou's paper, "Entrepreneurialism or Cooperativism?: An Exploration of Cooperative Journalistic Enterprises", challenges those who approach the field of entrepreneurial journalism from a market-based perspective. The framework deals with tensions for journalism when priority is given to profit and individualism.

The fourth and fifth articles in this special issue deal with a specific funding model now available in the journalism field—crowdfunding; one of the new means of trying to making reportage a financially viable activity. The respective authors approach crowdfunding from different vantage points.

In their article, "Accountability and Transparency of Entrepreneurial Journalism: Unresolved Ethical Issues in Crowdfunded Journalism Projects", Colin Porlezza and Sergio Splendore raises key questions about conflicts of interest, accountability and transparency in an online system of audience-donated funds. Andrea Hunter, in her article, "'It's Like Having a

Second Full-time Job'—Crowdfunding, Journalism and Labour", questions the perceived empowerment generally associated with crowdfunding and puts a critical focus on the volume of work involved in this funding model.

The issues of effort and reward in the entrepreneurial journalism space are also among those identified by Dave Harte, Jerome Turner and Andy Williams in their article "Discourses of Enterprise in Hyperlocal Community News in the UK". As in several of the articles in this special issue, the precarious nature of very many journalistic start-up enterprises also emerges from this study of hyperlocal ventures in the United Kingdom.

Similar themes are identified by Rozane De Cock and Hedwig de Smaele in their paper "Freelancing in Flemish News Media and Entrepreneurial Skills as Pivotal Elements in Job Satisfaction: Perspectives of Masters or Servants?" If entrepreneurialism in journalism practice is to become a viable option for media workers then many of the conflicts identified—including the balance between time flexibility and an ability to make a viable living—will need to be resolved.

The final two articles investigate the role of the academy in dealing with entrepreneurial journalism both in the curriculum and in the classroom. In their article, "Towards a Broader Conception of Entrepreneurial Journalism Education: Starting with Everyday Practice", Kirsten Sparre and Helle Meibom Færgemann draw on work in Denmark to show the challenges in developing a strong entrepreneurial identity in journalism students. Related issues are addressed by Andreu Casero-Ripollés, Jessica Izquierdo-Castillo and Hugo Doménech-Fabregat in their article, "The Journalists of the Future Meet Entrepreneurial Journalism: Perceptions in the Classroom".

These studies of journalism students close a circle for this special issue, in that one of the conclusions to emerge is a vagueness and uncertainly about what is understood about the place of entrepreneurialism in the journalism field matched by a willingness by many to travel any new road to making journalism work, financially. In a way, the findings from the classroom are similar to the challenges for industry and scholars in more firmly coupling entrepreneurialism and journalism while dealing with the very many, and difficult, issues that arise from this association. Considering each of these nine articles alone—but also taking them collectively—adds greatly to our understating of entrepreneurial journalism, and raises awareness of the contribution and challenges which it offers for the professional practice of journalism.

REFERENCES

Chalaby, Jean K. 1998. *The Invention of Journalism*. London: Palgrave.

Jarvis, Jeff. 2012. "Foreword." In *Entrepreneurial Journalism. How to Build What's Next for News*, edited by Briggs Mark, xv–xviii. Thousand Oaks, CA: Sage.

Kelly, Sara. 2015. *The Entrepreneurial Journalist's Toolkit*. New York: Focal Press.

Legge, Maire Louise. 1998. Newspapers and Nationalism: Irish Provincial Press, 1850–92. Dublin: Four Courts.

MEDIA DISCOURSE ABOUT ENTREPRENEURIAL JOURNALISM
Implications for journalistic capital

Tim P. Vos and **Jane B. Singer**

Drawing on insights from field theory, this article examines journalists' textual and discursive construction of entrepreneurial journalism from 2000 to 2014. The goal is to understand how such discursive practices contribute to the articulation and legitimation of entrepreneurial journalism as a form of cultural capital as the field's economic imperatives change. The findings suggest that "entrepreneurial journalism" is a condensational term: it is defined broadly and loosely but generally in a positive way. Despite the potential for disruption to long-standing journalistic doxa, particularly normative stances related to the separation of editorial and commercial interests, much of the examined discourse seems to reflect a belief that entrepreneurialism is not only acceptable but even vital for survival in a digital age.

Introduction

In the wake of technological and economic upheaval that has cost thousands of journalists their jobs and shuttered some media enterprises altogether (King 2010; McChesney and Nichols 2010), growing numbers of observers have advocated entrepreneurialism as an alternative to legacy media work (Briggs 2012). Journalists now envision careers outside traditional newsrooms, either working for an entrepreneurial news company or starting one themselves (Picard 2015). While it is not always clear what *entrepreneurial journalism* means, it has nonetheless become an industry buzz term and a source of hope.

This exploratory study culls references from a broad range of industry publications and general news sites in the United States in order to examine the textual and discursive construction of entrepreneurial journalism by writers within the journalism field. Of special conceptual interest is discourse related to the tension between the field's economic and cultural capital, the latter particularly encapsulated by normative principles, which have consistently been important in journalists' consideration of industry innovation (Singer 2015).

On its face, the terminology of entrepreneurialism raises important issues. *Entrepreneur* magazine defines an entrepreneur as someone who "organizes, manages, and assumes the risks of a business or enterprise." Although twentieth-century journalism was a fairly stable social institution, the emergence and promotion of something labeled "entrepreneurial journalism" thus implies the need for risk and revitalization, inherently signaling instability. Moreover, the idea that journalists would strike out on their own to organize an innovative enterprise and assume the accompanying financial risks potentially collapses long-standing normative notions of a strict separation—indeed, a "wall"—

between journalism and business functions (Coddington 2015). In the past, publishers were the ones who took on an entrepreneurial role, while the journalists' role involved editorial judgment. Entrepreneurial journalism potentially conflates those roles. In doing so, it raises issues distinct from the notion of entrepreneurial companies, media or otherwise, and focuses on concerns at the level of the individual practitioner.

The conflation raises many questions about the complex and controversial relationship between journalistic practices and norms during periods of upheaval. Some have argued that digitization has left the principles of journalism unchanged (Craft and Davis 2013), but others propose that technological and economic transformation has occasioned a revisiting of the ethical frameworks that constitute journalism's cultural capital (Elliott 2008; Hanitzsch 2007; Singer 2010). In general, the ways in which changing practices do or do not affect normative principles are open to debate. As Schudson (2001, 150) has cautioned, an assumption that the former explains the latter "skips over a necessary step," since normative prescriptions can be, and often are, offered in contradiction to prevailing practices.

This article uses the framework of field theory to analyze professionals' discourse about entrepreneurial journalism in a way that raises the normative dimensions of the discourse to a plane of explicit consideration, potentially opening the concept to more systematic ethical theorizing. In addition, it provides insight into how changing institutional practices are related to that discourse.

The Journalistic Field

Bourdieu (2005, 36) has argued that despite inevitably heterodox ideas and practices among members of a social field, such as journalism, those members "accept a certain number of presuppositions that are constitutive of the very functioning of the field." He and others call these presuppositions "doxa." A kind of ideational and practical orthodoxy thus defines the broad contours of a field, so that a discussion of journalistic doxa encompasses a set of implicit concepts tacitly held by news workers (Schultz 2007). Yet although fields are characterized by this broad agreement on their own unique practices and outlooks, they also are arenas of struggle, with both individuals and organizations competing to valorize specific forms of capital that they possess (Benson 2006).

Bourdieu also outlines the tension between economic capital—within the journalism field, typically expressed in terms of advertising revenues, circulation, or audience ratings—and cultural capital, articulated in terms of skills, expertise, knowledge, and similar characteristics (Benson and Neveu 2005). However, Hanitzsch (2007) narrows the focus to three key types of institutional knowledge—institutional roles, epistemologies, and ethical orientations—as cultural capital constitutive of the journalistic field. This knowledge finds expression in normative discourse, which constructs certain practices, arrangements, and beliefs as proper and moral. For example, as indicated above, journalistic cultural capital has included the ethical admonition for news organizations to maintain a wall of separation between what US practitioners refer to as "church and state," their news and business functions.

Bourdieu reminds us that cultural capital is subject to change (Benson and Neveu 2005). While the received doxa of the past is an important source of inertia in the present, the field of journalism is continually subject to disruption by both exogenous and endogenous forces. Political and economic forces, for example, can and do challenge practices and beliefs (Baker 2002; Herman and Chomsky 2002); indeed, journalism has been described as "a contested practice embedded in larger political, economic, and cultural struggles" (Carlson 2009, 273). In particular, Bourdieu's field theory underscores the pull of economic capital, a pull that potentially affects the structure of journalism's cultural capital. Meanwhile, new entrants to the journalistic field can inject new beliefs as well as new practices (Elliott 2008; Singer 2007). Such forces—including the rise of entrepreneurialism as an acceptable type of journalistic practice—therefore have the potential to reshape the field's cultural capital.

A number of scholars, particularly in the United States and Britain, have actively explored connections between field theory and journalism. Benson, for example, has highlighted the emphasis of field theory on media change, including the impact created by new actors attempting to enter and make their mark in the field, as is the case here. "A rapid influx of new agents into the field can serve both as a force for transformation and for conservation," he writes. Nonetheless, "entry into the journalistic field requires acceptance of the basic rules of the game, which themselves are a powerful force of inertia" (Benson 1999, 468). Similarly, Couldry (2003, 673) points out that digitally enabled decentralization in the means of media production and distribution create a need to understand "how, in what ways, and to what extent the rules, categories, and capital" are changing for actors in journalistic and related fields.

Unlike doxa, cultural capital includes normative directives and thus must be explicitly, discursively expressed (Vos, Craft, and Ashley 2012). If changes in journalistic practice are to lead to a shift in cultural capital, that shift should be evident in the normative discourse of the journalistic field, which will cast some new practices and ideas as legitimate and some as illegitimate (Craft, Vos, and Wolfgang 2015). Moreover, whether emergent practices and ideas are defined as heterodox or as orthodox, relative to established cultural capital, is important in positioning the newcomers within the field (Waisbord 2013). For example, Hartley (2013) examined the struggle of online journalists to achieve legitimacy within a field whose doxa tend to position top-quality journalism as deep, investigative, informative, polished, and time-consuming to create.

Entrepreneurial Journalism[1]

Entrepreneurialism has been a hot topic in business schools for decades, since Drucker posited systematic innovation as integral to the management process (Maciariello 2015). Today, a range of academic journals, mostly within the management field, are devoted to the topic, as are innumerable books and extensive media coverage (Kuratko 2005). The connection of entrepreneurialism to journalism, however, is relatively new and not extensively explored or theorized in the journalism studies literature. As Compaine and Hoag (2012, 30) drily note, "Entrepreneurship of any sort is not a concept that has been closely identified with the media industry"—despite evidence that particularly in the United States, the industry as a whole actually has been more entrepreneurial in recent years than other service or manufacturing enterprises (Hoag 2008). This section summarizes some of what has been learned to date about entrepreneurial journalism, as a practice and as an area of curricular attention.

Entrepreneurial Journalists Today

In a wide-ranging literature review conducted in the mid-2000s, Hang and van Weezel (2005) identified two strands in a thin body of work, most of it published in the

2000s: entrepreneurship in the media and the media impact on entrepreneurship. Much of the research in the first category focused on film and music industries rather than journalistic enterprises. The second, consisting of fewer than a dozen relevant studies, included profiles of media entrepreneurs such as Rupert Murdoch, as well as challenges facing women entrepreneurs, in particular. In contrast, our work here focuses on discourse about the journalists engaged in work that can be considered entrepreneurial.

But over the past decade, as traditional media models have come under increasing pressure, attention to new journalistic approaches has accelerated. The voices urging journalists to understand news as a business have grown louder, with much of the rhetoric positioning such an understanding as necessary to survival (Coddington 2015). Although the tone of much of the published work has been relatively uncritical, two broad areas of concern can be identified, one economic and the other normative—much in line with Bourdieu's conceptualization of the tensions within the journalistic field itself.

Media economist Robert Picard has long been attuned to the financial side of entrepreneurial journalism, including business models, opportunities, challenges, and implications. In an early consideration of online business models, Picard (2000) stressed that the success of technological innovations hinged on the extent of overlap among the needs of competing interests: customers, content producers, and financiers. When those interests "converge or can be accommodated, the likelihood of success of a new application or technology increases," he wrote. Innovations "will succeed only if the market believes that they create value that is currently absent" and cannot be fulfilled by cheaper or simpler alternatives (61).

In a 2011 report for Open Society Foundations, Picard delved more deeply into the challenges facing media enterprises and those behind them. The fundamental problem, he said, is that traditional media content was created in "technical, economic, political and information environments that no longer exist." The industry challenge today is to ensure that it is providing a core value that consumers want and doing so in unique or distinctive ways appropriate to a digital network (Picard 2011, 8). According to Picard, existing business models are losing their effectiveness in this environment, but new ones have yet to prove sustainable over the long term.

A number of recent attempts to examine and categorize the efforts of entrepreneurial journalists have highlighted the challenges. While traditional journalism relies heavily on just two revenue sources—advertisers and media consumers—start-ups also must scramble to generate income from consulting, design work, syndication, event hosting, and whatever other opportunities present themselves (Sirkkunen and Cook 2012). Moreover, entrepreneurial enterprises inherently operate in highly uncertain circumstances, dependent on fickle users and investor whims; indeed, the elusiveness of sustainability suggests that "survival in itself must be recognised as a form of success" (Bruno and Nielsen 2012, 102).

The preconceptions of journalists-turned-entrepreneurs also can be a problem. In case studies of three US news start-ups that sought to replace community coverage lost because of newspaper shutdowns or cutbacks, Naldi and Picard (2012) found all three were characterized by what they called "formational myopia": unrealistic expectations about demand for their services and the economic value of their work. Each start-up tried to shift professional newspaper practices and norms to the new medium—a cost-intensive, hierarchical endeavor poorly suited to the online environment. All three sites failed to reach their goals of "providing broad coverage and community impact using significant numbers of professional journalists" (91).

The other general area of concern reflected in the literature has been normative. In particular, a growing emphasis on the perceived need for journalists to embrace economic imperatives can be seen as necessarily compromising the vaunted "wall" separating editorial and commercial considerations. More concretely and again in line with field theory, the widespread gutting of newsrooms in the late 2000s has served as "a concrete indicator of the power of the profession's business side and the degree to which it must be sated" (Coddington 2015, 78).

Media ethicist Stephen Ward has been among those alarmed by the prospect of journalists doubling as fund-raisers, predicting that issues of journalistic independence and conflicts of interest "will soon become the dominant theme in journalism ethics" (Ward 2009). Ward argues that "guidelines for protecting independence, responding to public skepticism, and managing conflicts of interest will have to be constructed." In response, Ward urged a combination of rigorous editorial oversight and disclosure of any potential conflicts in addressing "the looming ethical problems of an entrepreneurial age." Others have argued that conflicts between editorial mission and revenue are the biggest source of ethical concern for journalistic start-ups: "Money itself isn't tainted, but it comes with stipulations always" (Briggs 2010). A premium on transparency is commonly cited as a safeguard: "As important as having ethics is letting people know that you do" (Briggs 2012, 54).

Another normative concern relates to the extent to which entrepreneurial journalism diverges from the classic conception of journalism as a public service that enables an informed electorate to make sound civic choices—what Gans (2003) and others have called the journalist's view of democracy. Hanitzsch (2007, 375), for example, distinguishes a market orientation, associated with giving audiences what they want to know "at the expense of what they should know," from other cultural conceptualizations of journalism, including the independent watchdog that serves as a normative benchmark in much of Western society. Market-driven journalism (McManus 1994) addresses audiences not as engaged citizens but as clients and consumers, and the digital environment—home to most contemporary entrepreneurial journalism efforts—has long been recognized as an arena where journalistic practices are particularly vulnerable to market influence (Cohen 2002). Whether the pressures are exerted by foundations and donors, as in many nonprofit start-ups, or by commercial entities such as advertisers or sponsors, the rise of the content producer who doubles as revenue generator clearly suggests potential pitfalls.

Other research, however, has foregrounded the potential of entrepreneurial journalism to open up new opportunities for beleaguered professionals. For example, in their exploratory interviews with 30 US media entrepreneurs—defined as founders of an independent content business with a clear revenue model—Compaine and Hoag (2012, 43) identified three key findings: few barriers to entry, the critical role of technological innovation, and a somewhat surprising role of "big media" as a source of opportunity. In general, they noted an environment hospitable to media start-ups, as "technology and economics have conspired to undercut many of the barriers that had existed to would-be media entrepreneurs."

Entrepreneurial Journalists Tomorrow

Because new entrants to the field are potential disruptors of journalistic cultural capital and doxa, it is important to consider the role of journalism education in conceptualizing and legitimizing entrepreneurial journalism. A growing number of journalism schools and programs around the Western world are expanding their emphasis on entrepreneurialism (Breiner 2013; Schaich and Klein 2013) as a valuable, even necessary, skill for graduates entering a news ecosystem still enmeshed in a "culture of resistance" (Briggs 2012, 21). City University of New York (CUNY) was a pioneer in advocating curricular reconfiguration if not wholesale reinvention; CUNY launched its entrepreneurial journalism program in early 2011, emphasizing business opportunities, collaboration, technology, and creative practice (Claussen 2011). Since then, dozens of other j-schools also have incorporated entrepreneurialism in the curriculum, and several academics have published scholarly articles recounting the results. Virtually all of this work has positioned an entrepreneurial skills set—and mind set—as vital to the future of the journalistic field and thus a necessary curricular addition for entry-level practitioners.

Baines and Kennedy (2010, 97), for example, point out that the careers of future graduates are "increasingly likely to feature consecutive and concurrent periods of long-term employment, short-term contracts, self-employment, [and] working in temporary clusters on specific projects"; they urge educators to give journalism students "the opportunity to become entrepreneurial self-employed agents, who might compete with, as well as service, other media organisations." Their recommended strategies for empowering students to become "reliable analysts and brokers of information" include embedding enterprise in existing journalism programs; offering specialist support, such as incubator services to provide guidance on starting a business; and setting up knowledge exchanges, such as entrepreneurship workshops with business leaders (97).

A small-scale study by Ferrier (2013) of faculty members developing media entrepreneurship courses found that key objectives included introducing journalism students to business concepts and helping them identify opportunities for innovation. Classes typically involved the creation of products such as hyperlocal online news sites or regional niche hubs; students also commonly were taught to undertake market research, analyze potential competitors, and construct and deliver a pitch. Faculty members, including recent industry professionals, cited changes in the nature of media industry work—again, short-term contracts, self-employment, temporary group work on specific projects—among their prime motivation for creating such classes. "It's really important to empower students with the knowledge and skill sets to create their own jobs," one respondent explained (229).

Journalism think tanks such as the Poynter Institute also have highlighted the importance of entrepreneurial skills for students considering journalism careers, in addition to offering training and networking opportunities for more experienced journalists-turned-entrepreneurs (Wallace 2012). In its 2013 report on the state of journalism education, Poynter called unequivocally for innovation in the journalism curriculum, so that educators can "empower students to be open to the disruptions they'll inevitably face in their own careers" (Finberg 2013, 18)—essentially, to "train students for jobs that do not yet exist" (Culver 2013).

Similarly, UK university students taking part in a series of workshops were encouraged to "consider themselves not only within a framework of business and entrepreneurship but also as creative, imaginative individuals with a unique contribution to make to a sector that is in need of rejuvenation" (Hunter and Nel 2011, 15), as well as to recognize synergies between the seemingly disparate fields of business and creative industries. The authors conclude that students are, at least potentially, enterprising and adaptable, making them "ideally placed" to capitalize on industry shifts (22). More broadly, they advocate a pedagogical transition away from training students for employment in a specific industry and toward more general employability as creative communicators. In Australia, Quinn (2010) also has urged that journalism students be taught to be entrepreneurial: to learn how to run a small business, to understand audiences and audience research, and to be able to market themselves, among other attributes.

Entrepreneurial journalism curricula may be gaining traction but the evidence suggests some limitations. A recent survey of journalism program directors in the United States underscores the challenge of finding room in the curriculum to foster entrepreneurial skills. Blom and Davenport (2012) report that only 11 percent of j-school administrators include entrepreneurial journalism courses in their list of "seven most important core courses," behind 20 other topics that range from media law/ethics to feature writing. Similarly, the European Journalism Training Association commissioned a study to understand what qualifications were seen as important to prepare European students for a changing industry; it found that entrepreneurial journalism skills received low rankings from both practitioners and students, suggesting a preference for doing journalistic work "without interference from market forces or the public" (Drok 2013, 156). A smaller-scale study found that media education in Flanders was aimed primarily at preparing aspiring journalists "for a serial monomedia career" (Opgenhaffen, d'Haenens, and Corten 2013, 141).

Drawing on this body of theoretical and descriptive work, this article addresses the following research questions:

RQ1: How is "entrepreneurial journalism" being defined by journalists through discourse published in the trade and popular press?

RQ2: What is the tone of this discourse?

RQ3: What are the implications of this journalistic discourse for journalistic doxa and for the discursive construction of cultural capital within a changing journalistic field?

Study Design

This study has modest empirical goals, seeking simply to explore how various actors in the journalistic field are discursively constructing entrepreneurial journalism. What do they mean by the term, and what are the implications of those meanings? For this exploratory study, a traditional textual-discourse analysis (van Dijk 1980) is used to attend to the ways that practitioners talk about entrepreneurial journalism through their writing for both general and professional audiences.

Textual analysis of trade publications, reviews, and institutes fulfilled the goal of capturing and analyzing the discourse within the journalistic field. The point of textual analysis is to find out what interpretations will most plausibly be produced in a particular context. "By seeing the variety of ways in which it is possible to interpret reality, we also understand our own cultures better because we start to see the limitations and advantages of our own sense-making practices" (McKee 2003, 1). Hence, the goal is to gain a broad understanding, suitable as a basis for additional empirical study, of how journalists are making sense of entrepreneurial journalism and how they are negotiating its implications for the long-standing doxa of the field.

To address our interest in the field's discourse about entrepreneurial journalism, broadly defined, we searched for articles referencing the concept that were produced by journalists either for the general public or for fellow practitioners. The former included articles in newspapers and other general news outlets, while the latter included material from journalism trade journals, journalism reviews, and journalism institutes. For logistical reasons, we limited our sample to US publications and to those with accessible archives. Each of these outlets had to be referenced by another outlet in the sample to ensure that its output constituted discourse of the journalism field.

We scraped or searched for articles from each trade publication that referred to one or more of the keywords "entrepreneurial journalism," "entrepreneurial," and "entrepreneur," and to various iterations of these keywords. We limited the sample of trade press articles to those published between 2000 and 2014, a total of 175 articles. We also searched for news articles that mentioned "entrepreneurial journalism" using the Factiva database, which indexes articles from newspapers and selected other news sites. This yielded an additional 108 articles. However, a great many of the items indexed by Factiva either were press releases or were published in niche outlets whose journalists would be unlikely to accurately reflect a general practitioner perspective on entrepreneurial journalism. Ultimately, only 28 of the Factiva database articles fit our goals related to general industry discourse. Our sample, therefore, was a total of 203 trade press and general news articles that substantively referenced entrepreneurial journalism.

Our unit of analysis, however, is the discourse about entrepreneurial journalism. We ultimately analyzed the texts as discourse of the field; the speakers, writers, articles, and publications provide context for our analysis, but are not the focus. To underscore this focus, our findings do not always identify the speaker, writer, or publication by name. We are analyzing the *discourse of a field*. The articles were analyzed for the ways in which "entrepreneurial journalism" was defined, the tone of the depictions—for example, is entrepreneurialism a welcome arrival within the journalistic culture?—and the patterns and trends in those depictions, particularly those related to normative principles and practice. The discourse analysis thus pays special attention to the ways in which the legitimacy of entrepreneurial journalism is textually constructed and relevant themes emerge: What range of meanings is reflected in the industry discourse from which implications for the journalistic field might be derived? How might issues related to journalistic cultural practice be understood from this discourse?

Findings

Defining Entrepreneurial Journalism

While the term "entrepreneurial journalism" has clearly entered the industry discourse, there have been few attempts to explicitly describe or define what the term means. In the everyday journalistic discourse we examined, entrepreneurial journalism was presented as a familiar concept—which may or may not be the case for audiences either inside or outside the media industry—with a meaning malleable enough to describe a wide variety of practices and attitudes. Indeed, entrepreneurial journalism was as likely to be described in terms of an "entrepreneurial spirit" as it was a specific practice or set of practices.

In some respects, entrepreneurial journalism functions as a condensational term or symbol, described by Herbst (1993, 32) as a term that enables reference "to abstract, intricate ideas, and also to the profound emotions associated with those ideas." She says condensational terms or symbols are frequent in popular debate because speakers can tap a variety of meanings and thus appeal to a broader audience, as was true in our sampled articles. In other words, the broad and loose definition of entrepreneurial journalism is itself a discursive strategy that can elicit vaguely positive connotations while deflecting examination of the intricacies of the concept.

While the emotions may not be profound, some of the discourse does speak of entrepreneurial journalism in messianic or apocalyptic terms, with its evangelists using the term to reference a new and better kind of journalism that they see as desperately needed. These writers see entrepreneurialism as representing a fervent hope for the future in the midst of an uncertain present. For example, one media executive called it "the future of information dissemination," and a journalist-turned-educator said, "We're all very concerned about sustaining quality journalism, and we think the future of journalism is going to be entrepreneurial." A few, however, saw it as a profound threat to "Fourth Estate values" or even to traditional journalism's existence, such as the writer of an *Editor & Publisher* article (June 27, 2012) who warned that the role of entrepreneurial non-profits "should be to help increase the quality of journalism, but not at the expense of for-profit organizations."

Whether entrepreneurial journalism is supportive or disruptive of received journalistic capital is ultimately obscured by the vagueness of the concept in our sampled articles. Nonetheless, what emerges from this discourse about entrepreneurial journalism is a rough picture of what journalists seem to mean when they use the term. They describe it as an emerging field, a set of skills, a spirit, a drive, and a serious act. The entrepreneurial journalist is depicted as a founder, an innovator, a trailblazer, a business creator, and a freelancer; one 2014 article used the term "journopreneur." Entrepreneurial journalism start-ups and other enterprises are labeled as experimental, independent, young, and nimble.

All of these are primarily lexical or nominal definitions, which seek to stipulate the essential features of a thing—although the contours of what really is essential about "entrepreneurial journalism" appear blurred in journalistic discourse. Descriptions offered in our sample say little about what entrepreneurial journalists do that makes them entrepreneurial—or, for that matter, that makes them journalists. The articles sometimes offered their own definitions or descriptions. For example, a *New York Times* piece (September 20, 2010) stated: "Entrepreneurial journalism, broadly speaking, simply refers to pulling journalism, business and technology closer together." A *Broadcasting & Cable* profile of an entrepreneurial journalist (August 25, 2006) described him as "drawing on both his reportorial instincts and his business acumen." Yet such statements describing various characteristics of entrepreneurial journalism or journalists stop short of showing how the final amalgam—of journalism, business, and technology, or of reportorial instincts and business acumen—is produced.

Features of entrepreneurial journalism were also presented in the form of comparisons with and references to the financial difficulties and diminishing economic capital of the traditional media industry. The prevalence of CUNY professor and long-time media change advocate Jeff Jarvis—known for his pointed critiques of failed business models and mind sets in traditional news organizations—as a source could account in part for this positioning. But a comparative framework was implicit or explicit in other articles, as well. In a July 9, 2012 item about j-school curriculum changes, for example, Poynter analyst Rick Edmonds tells *Crain's New York Business* that "the traditional progression of working your way up from a small newspaper to a bigger one isn't what it once was."

Another kind of definition is a stipulative definition, typically offered for a relatively new phenomenon, which tends to be explained in terms of things already known. Entrepreneurial journalism is indeed relatively new, and this stipulative approach was apparent in a number of articles. In particular, articles about journalism education were apt to provide a definition connected to known terms, as faculty sources were given space to outline what their classes covered. In addition to what Jarvis termed in a April 19, 2009 interview with the *Washington Post* "the eternal verities of journalism," definitions typically included multi-media capabilities and some sense of the workings of business, though these were outlined vaguely if at all. In general, it would appear to be quite difficult for readers, listeners, or viewers to grasp what "entrepreneurial journalism" entailed if they did not already believe they knew.

A third kind of definition is illustrative, given meaning through the use of concrete or abstract examples. Some articles in our sample relied on concrete examples of such disparate news start-ups as the San Francisco Bay Citizen, an investigative journalism site; Sahara Reporters, a watchdog enterprise started up by a Nigerian living in New York; and Faster Times, a general-interest publication built on the output of freelancers. *Entertainment Newsweekly* profiled Sportspress Northwest (December 17, 2010), which was described as "featuring veterans from traditional journalism as well as citizen journalism" with "the right business model, intellectual capital, advertisers, sponsors and fans to sustain entrepreneurial journalism in the digital arena." *Folio* ran numerous stories profiling entrepreneurs who started new magazines and offered advice to others wishing to create their own enterprises. Other examples offered more abstract definitions, for instance defining entrepreneurial journalism as non-profits and "hyperlocal journalism," generally online but sometimes including print publications or digital production studios.

What the diverse definitions have in common is an emphasis on innovation and crafting new business strategies, including targeting niche audiences. Journalistic or reportorial work—the traditional bedrock of the journalism field's cultural capital, as suggested above—is not ignored but is seldom given extensive attention, especially in trade publication discourse. The emphasis of trade publications on business applications and strategies is perhaps understandable, given their audience of industry insiders. However, the portrayals in the popular press are much the same. For example, entrepreneurial journalists are described in one account as journalists who master the "tools of the business side to achieve professional independence." An exception to the general lack of emphasis on journalistic practice is the widespread reference to multimedia skills, though again, such skills have commonly been positioned as heterodox (Hartley 2013). References are also sometimes made to project reporting. For example, one self-described entrepreneurial journalist explained a multi-faceted project to retrace John Steinbeck's travels in *Travels with Charley* and to write about the trip for his local newspaper.

The lack of an explicit, lexical definition is obviously not a strategic choice by any single entity. However, the lack of an agreed-upon definition can be used strategically by practitioners, with normative implications. For example, a new enterprise that transgresses accepted normative standards can simply be excluded from an illustrative definition of entrepreneurial journalism—or more explicitly held up as a counter-example of something that is "not journalism," as was true of a trade press article about a start-up involved in short-selling stocks, described further below. This strategy allows advocates of entrepreneurial journalism to cast the practice in consistently positive terms.

Tone of Discourse

Almost all of the articles in our sample, particularly in the popular press, were broadly supportive of entrepreneurial journalism, typically highlighting its potential to offset economic damage to the troubled media industry and quoting sources advocating its benefits. Among the articles overtly supportive of entrepreneurial journalism, several focused primarily or exclusively on journalism education and curricular innovation, and others also referenced university programs. Curricular changes typically were given a positive frame by sources and/or the writer as benefiting both students and the industry, providing the skills and knowledge "desperately needed" in the digital age.

Indeed, the discourse in much of our sample seemed to thrust journalism educators into a leadership role in shaping how entrepreneurial journalism is conceived. For example, in a January 29, 2012 article in the *Memphis Commercial-Appeal*, the writer lauds entrepreneurial professors for "taking the lead in their institutions of learning" to "better equip our students to have the tools, resources and know-how to participate in a job market that currently is quite harsh, and actually looks completely different today for those graduating than when they entered school." A May 10, 2010 *Boston Globe* article titled "Me, Inc.," by a University of Massachusetts journalism professor, quotes another professor who says that students with entrepreneurial skills "gain a sense of mastery, self-control, that when a problem occurs, instead of being a victim, you say, how can I turn that problem into a solution?" Similarly, a columnist writing in the *Christian Science Monitor* in March 12, 2009 says:

> Answers for the future will not necessarily come from those whose ideas were moulded in the past. Young journalism students who have grown up with new media are not afraid to imagine something different and find ways to make it work.

Some articles were neutral, such as a *New York Times* report on the potential merger of two California news websites and a transcribed National Public Radio "Talk of the Nation" program in which participants debated the value of objectivity, the future of news, and aspects of entrepreneurial journalism, with opposing views offered in rough equilibrium. Other articles were presented in neutral journalistic style but leaned toward support in their use of sources, quotes, and examples.

Articles taking a critical tone were scarce. A 2014 article in *Columbia Journalism Review* raised criticisms, but only to dispute them. Among the sampled articles from the popular press, only one offered substantial criticism of entrepreneurial journalism. In a May 16, 2010 *New York Times Magazine* piece titled "Putting a Price on Words," Andrew Rice focused on the economics of news start-ups, particularly the difficulty of placing a value on content in the information-rich online environment. In doing so, he touched on a normative issue, the potential for editorial independence to be compromised by commercial pressures: "One thing many of these new strategies have in common is a willingness to transgress time-honored barriers—for instance, by blurring the division between reporting and advertising." However, he then went on to quote a source who expressed the hope that attitudes are shifting and "we're breaking down the silliness of how church and state was historically implemented."

Implications for the Ethics and Practice of Journalism

In this study we found that, with a few exceptions, practitioners do not frame entrepreneurial journalism as a particularly controversial subject. This may be in part because entrepreneurial journalism is construed as something of a necessity. "I believe most entrepreneurial journalists when they say they're sincerely interested in both preserving the traditional values of this profession and acknowledging the new ways people find and consume news," wrote Ann Friedman in a July 31, 2014 *Columbia Journalism Review* piece. "I have to, because there's no going back." And as an *Advertising Age* writer put it, "changes in the media landscape forced some variation of 'entrepreneur' or 'business development' onto the modern journalist's job description" (February 27, 2011). Such naturalizing discourse discourages considering new developments as problematic. Hence, the implications of entrepreneurial journalism, ethical or otherwise, are seldom a matter of open debate in the published discourse.

A handful of articles in our sample did raise ethical concerns. These centered on implications of the funding structure for entrepreneurial journalism. A 2010 *American Journalism Review* article was a notable example. It described an investigative business magazine start-up whose proprietors were allegedly engaged in short-selling stocks and otherwise profiting from the information the magazine provided. Yet the issue was framed as a problem created by a set of ethically challenged individuals in a small subset of the field, and thus not truly reflective of flaws or potential flaws in entrepreneurial journalism overall. Although the behavior was egregious, it also was presented as isolated.

A number of other articles raised more general concerns about the ability of journalists engaged in starting a business to adequately separate their commercial and editorial roles. For example, journalism ethics professor, administrator, and sometime media critic Ed Wasserman pointed out that news start-ups may be "hasty, reckless, slaves to mob sentiment and their funders' wishes. They're too impatient to verify and have only the vaguest commitment to public service." And given the experimental nature of many entrepreneurial journalism efforts, entrepreneurial journalists will sometimes be put in unfamiliar situations —situations that raise ethical issues. Wasserman, in a 2011 column about conflicts of interest published in the *Charleston Gazette* (August 21, 2011), noted that "The solutions that these mainly shoestring operations have devised aren't always optimal," adding, "but then neither are the ways that rich monopoly news outfits have done business." He ultimately lauded local entrepreneurial news outlets for taking ethics seriously.

The world of freelance entrepreneurial journalism comes with its own set of ethical issues. At an entrepreneurial start-up spearheaded by *Forbes*, for example, writers were described as "paid based on what kind of traffic and web interaction they attract," suggesting issues related to autonomous news judgment. Rice's *New York Times Magazine* article, cited above, also highlighted the way that contributors are paid (or not) for their efforts: not infrequently based on the popularity of their work as indicated by online usage data. "There is, of course, nothing wrong with giving readers what they secretly want every once in a while," Rice wrote. "The problem arises when you start producing articles solely for the id of the search engines." Yet none of the discourse about entrepreneurial journalism directly addressed a fundamental definitional issue: conflation of two roles and functions that have normatively been distinct, those of publisher and of editor. We explore this gap further in the final section.

Conclusions

In this article, we sought to address three research questions. The first dealt with the ways in which the journalistic field is defining a new term, "entrepreneurial journalism," through discourse in the trade and popular press. We found that definitions are elusive; many can aptly be categorized as what Herbst (1993) calls "condensational," vague enough to result in a variety of constructed meanings. Indeed, the term was rarely defined explicitly, as journalists relied extensively on a listing of characteristics or comparisons to traditional journalistic practice or forms. An unexpected number of articles in our sample focused on or drew on journalism educators, who were accorded the role of establishing a definition of "entrepreneurial journalism" through their references to material covered in their classes on the subject, an emphasis also reflected in the academic literature. In a few limited cases, our sample revealed attempts to define specific start-ups as "not journalism," typically on ethical grounds drawing on traditional concepts of journalistic cultural capital.

Our second research question considered the tone of the journalistic discourse. Given well-documented cultural resistance to fundamental change, we expected much of the discourse to be critical. Indeed, Bourdieu (2005) has posited that journalistic doxa is a form of inertia in the field (Benson and Neveu 2005). Most of the discourse we analyzed came from established actors in the journalistic field, such as writers at industry trade journals, people we would have predicted to be skeptical of heterodoxy. Yet we found the overall tone to be broadly supportive of entrepreneurial journalism, however it was defined. Most of the sampled articles in both the trade and popular press highlighted successful start-ups and, more broadly, the need for innovative approaches to the journalistic enterprise. Whether this approach to coverage is mere rhetoric driven by widely used sources who champion entrepreneurialism, or reflects practitioners' own response to a field rocked by economic crisis and newsroom cutbacks, is a matter that should be addressed by additional research incorporating journalists' own views and voices.

Our third research question turned to implications for the industry of the attitudes represented in these reports about entrepreneurial journalism, particularly in relation to normative conceptions of journalistic practice, culture, and field. We did find some questions raised about the ability of entrepreneurial journalists to adequately safeguard their editorial independence, given the necessity of finding and obtaining financial support for news start-ups. Yet such articles were rare, and the few we found focused on specific examples, such as the business site described above. In general, despite the potential for significant disruption to long-standing journalistic doxa, our sample suggests a field somewhat surprisingly open to embracing what is undeniably a quite different form of the journalistic enterprise. Indeed, many of the sampled articles seemed to reflect the belief that entrepreneurialism was not only acceptable but even vital for "survival" in a digital age. Although the relatively narrow normative issue of editorial independence was raised in a few articles in our sample, broader issues related to the journalist's role in democratic society were virtually ignored.

Moreover, we failed to find any recognition of what we see as a clear implication of such a change: that the impetus for entrepreneurialism is shifting from the publisher to the editor. Most entrepreneurial journalists have newsroom backgrounds or journalistic training at the university level; few spent any time sitting in the publisher's leather chair before venturing out on their own. Indeed, the definitional approaches highlighted above commonly emphasize a need to gain at least basic business acumen that journalists do not typically possess. Yet the broader implications of this conflating of roles—journalist with business leader, publisher with content producer—do not seem to be reflected in the discourse to date. Those implications affect not only journalistic culture but also the wider society, given the declining role of many traditional media outlets as the internet continues to fragment their audiences and sap their revenues. Journalistic norms are vital to journalism's cultural capital, providing a source of stability in the face of economic and political forces (Benson and Neveu 2005). Conflating the poles of cultural and economic capital would collapse a long-standing polarization generally seen as constitutive of the journalism field (Bourdieu 2005; Hanitzsch 2007).

This is not to argue that entrepreneurial journalism represents the collapse of the journalistic field; rather, it is to say that this conflating of two previously distinct roles would represent a reconstitution of a norm of the field. Norms are subject to change. It is because they can change that they must regularly be discursively maintained if they are to retain their moral authority (Schudson 2001). Likewise, it stands to reason that if norms are to change, they must be discursively reconstructed. However, field theory has little to say about changing norms, other than to point to how new entrants to a field can be a disruptive force. This study identifies at least one way that a field's norms might be reconstructed—it suggests that if a heterodox practice is expressed with a condensational term, it diffuses the ethical or normative considerations that might otherwise be discursively highlighted. This conclusion is speculative, but it merits further examination.

This exploratory study, of course, has a number of limitations that suggest opportunities for future empirical work. It sought to gather wide-ranging data, and the sample was therefore designed to be as inclusive as possible; a closer examination of particular outlets, for example those seen as agenda-setters for others in the industry, could yield a more focused picture of the discourse surrounding entrepreneurial journalism. Our study also was limited to discourse in US outlets, but entrepreneurialism is a hot topic in other nations as well. In addition, our study dilutes the voices of journalists themselves, limited as it is to analysis of the artefacts they produce. Understanding the "why" of this coverage, and of practitioners' conceptions about entrepreneurial journalism in general, is crucial as this form of journalistic enterprise becomes increasingly prevalent, as we predict it will.

DISCLOSURE STATEMENT

No potential conflict of interest was reported by the authors.

FUNDING

No external funding was received in support of this work.

NOTE

1. Parts of the literature cited in this paper also have informed the publications by Singer (2016a, 2016b).

REFERENCES

Baines, David, and Clara Kennedy. 2010. "An Education for Independence? Should Entrepreneurial Skills Be an Essential Part of the Journalist's Toolbox?" *Journalism Practice* 4 (1): 97–113.

Baker, C. Edwin. 2002. *Media, Markets, and Democracy*. New York: Cambridge University Press.

Benson, Rodney. 1999. "Field Theory in Comparative Context: A New Paradigm for Media Studies." *Theory and Society* 28 (3): 463–498.

Benson, Rodney. 2006. "New Media as a 'Journalistic Field': What Bourdieu Adds to New Institutionalism, and Vice Versa." *Political Communication* 23 (2): 187–202.

Benson, Rodney, and Erik Neveu. 2005. "Introduction: Field Theory as a Work in Progress." In *Bourdieu and the Journalistic Field*, edited by Rodney Benson and Erik Neveu, 1–25. Malden, MA: Polity.

Blom, Robin, and Lucinda D. Davenport. 2012. "Searching for the Core of Journalism Education: Program Directors Disagree on Curriculum Priorities." *Journalism & Mass Communication Educator* 67 (1): 70–86.

Bourdieu, Pierre. 2005. "The Political Field, the Social Science Field, and the Journalistic Field." In *Bourdieu and the Journalistic Field*, edited by Rodney Benson and Erik Neveu, 29–47. Malden, MA: Polity.

Breiner, James. 2013. "How J-Schools Are Helping Students Develop Entrepreneurial Journalism Skills." Poynter.org, 17 May. http://www.poynter.org/latest-news/top-stories/213701/how-j-schools-are-helping-students-develop-entrepreneurial-journalism-skills/.

Briggs, Mark. 2010. "Ethics Lessons for News Entrepreneurs." Journalism 2.0, 14 July. http://www.journalism20.com/blog/2010/07/14/ethics-lessons-for-news-entrepreneurs/.

Briggs, Mark. 2012. *Entrepreneurial Journalism: How To Build What's Next for News*. Washington, DC: CQ Press.

Bruno, Nicola, and Rasmus Kleis Nielsen. 2012. *Survival is success: Journalistic Online Start-ups in Western Europe*. Oxford: Reuters Institute for the Study of Journalism. http://reutersinstitute.politics.ox.ac.uk/publication/survival-success.

Carlson, Matt. 2009. "Media Criticism as Competitive Discourse: Defining Reportage of the Abu Ghraib Scandal." *Journal of Communication Inquiry* 33 (3): 258–277.

Claussen, Dane S. 2011. "CUNY's Entrepreneurial Journalism: Partially Old Wine in a New Bottle, and Not Quite Thirst-Quenching, but Still a Good Drink." *Journalism & Mass Communication Educator* 66 (1): 3–6.

Coddington, Mark. 2015. "The Wall Becomes a Curtain: Revisiting Journalism's News-Business Boundary." In *Boundaries of Journalism: Professionalism, Practices and Participation*, edited by Matt Carlson and Seth C. Lewis, 67–82. New York: Routledge.

Cohen, Elisia L. 2002. "Online Journalism as Market-Driven Journalism." *Journal of Broadcasting & Electronic Media* 46 (4): 532–548.

Compaine, Ben, and Anne Hoag. 2012. "Factors Supporting and Hindering New Entry in Media Markets: A Study of Media Entrepreneurs." *International Journal on Media Management* 14 (1): 27–49.

Couldry, Nick. 2003. "Media Meta-capital: Extending the Range of Bourdieu's Field Theory." *Theory and Society* 32 (5/6): 643–677.

Craft, Stephanie, and Charles N. Davis. 2013. *Principles of American Journalism: An Introduction*. New York: Routledge.

Craft, Stephanie, Tim P. Vos, and J. David Wolfgang. 2015. "Reader Comments as Press Criticism: Implications for the Journalistic Field." *Journalism* . doi:10.1177/1464884915579332.

Culver, Katy. 2013, "How Journalism Educators Can 'Train Students for Jobs That May Not Yet Exist.'" Poynter.org, 30 August. http://www.poynter.org/how-tos/journalism-education/184308/how-journalism-educators-can-teach-students-to-be-more-entrepreneurial/.

van Dijk, Teun A. 1980. *Text and Context: Explorations in the Semantics and Pragmatics of Discourse* (1st paperback edition). New York: Longman.

Drok, Nico. 2013. "Beacons of Reliability: European Journalism Students and Professionals on Future Qualifications for Journalists." *Journalism Practice* 7 (2): 145–162.

Elliott, Deni. 2008. "Essential Shared Values and 21st Century Journalism." In *The Handbook of Mass Media Ethics*, edited by Lee Wilkins and Clifford G. Christians, 28–39. New York: Routledge.

Ferrier, Michelle Barrett. 2013. "Media Entrepreneurship: Curriculum Development and Faculty Perceptions of What Students Should Know." *Journalism & Mass Communication Educator* 68 (3): 222–241.

Finberg, Howard I. 2013. *State of Journalism Education 2013*. Poynter. http://www.newsu.org/course_files/StateOfJournalismEducation2013.pdf.

Gans, Herbert J. 2003. *Democracy and the News*. New York: Oxford University Press.

Hang, Min, and Aldo van Weezel. 2005. "Media and Entrepreneurship: A Survey of the Literature Relating Both Concepts." 18th Scandinavian Academy of Management Meeting, Aarhus School of Business, Denmark, pp. 18–20.

Hanitzsch, Thomas. 2007. "Deconstructing Journalism Culture: Toward a Universal Theory." *Communication Theory* 17 (4): 367–385.

Hartley, Jannie Møller. 2013. "The Online Journalist between Ideals and Audiences: Towards a (More) Audience-Driven and Source-Detached Journalism?" *Journalism Practice* 7 (5): 572–587.

Herbst, Susan. 1993. *Numbered Voices: How Opinion Polling Has Shaped American Politics*. Chicago: University of Chicago Press.

Herman, Edward S., and Noam Chomsky. 2002. *Manufacturing Consent: The Political Economy of the Mass Media*. New York: Pantheon Books.

Hoag, Anne. 2008. "Measuring Media Entrepreneurship." *International Journal on Media Management* 10 (2): 74–80.

Hunter, Anna, and François P. Nel. 2011. "Equipping the Entrepreneurial Journalist: An Exercise in Creative Enterprise." *Journalism & Mass Communication Educator* 66 (1): 9–24.

King, Elliot. 2010. *Free for All: The Internet's Transformation of Journalism*. Evanston, IL: Northwestern University Press.

Kuratko, Donald F. 2005. "The Emergence of Entrepreneurship Education: Development, Trends and Challenges." *Entrepreneurship: Theory and Practice* 29 (5): 577–598.

Maciariello, Joseph A. 2015. "Foreword to the Routledge Classics Edition." In *Innovation and Entrepreneurship*, edited by Peter Drucker, (Routledge Classics Edition; first published by Butterworth-Heinemann, 1985), ix–xviii. New York: Routledge.

McChesney, Robert W., and John Nichols. 2010. *Death and Life of American Journalism: The Media Revolution That Will Begin the World Again*. Philadelphia: Nation Books.

McKee, Alan. 2003. *Textual Analysis: A Beginner's Guide*. Thousand Oaks, CA: Sage Publications.

McManus, John H. 1994. *Market-driven Journalism: Let the Citizen Beware?*. Thousand Oaks, CA: Sage.

Naldi, Lucia, and Robert G. Picard. 2012. "'Let's Start an Online News Site': Opportunities, Resources, Strategy, and Formational Myopia in Startups." *Journal of Media Business Studies* 9 (4): 69–97.

Opgenhaffen, Michael, Leen d'Haenens, and Maarten Corten. 2013. "Journalistic Tools of the Trade in Flanders: Is There a Fit between Journalism Education and Professional Practice?" *Journalism Practice* 7 (2): 127–144.

Picard, Robert G. 2000. "Changing Business Models of Online Content Services: Their Implications for Multimedia and Other Content Producers." *International Journal on Media Management* 2 (2): 60–68.

Picard, Robert G. 2011. "Mapping Digital Media: Digitization and Media Business Models." Open Society Foundations. http://www.opensocietyfoundations.org/sites/ default/files/digitization-media-business-models-20110721.pdf.

Picard, Robert G. 2015. "Journalists' Perceptions of the Future of Journalistic Work." Report for the Reuters Institute for the Study of Journalism. http://www.opensocietyfoundations.org/sites/default/files/digitization-media-business-models-20110721.pdf.

Quinn. Stephen. 2010. "Opportunities for Journalism Education in an Online Entrepreneurial World." *Asia Pacific Media Educator* 20: 69–80.

Schaich, Maria Jose Vázquez, and Jeffrey S. Klein. 2013. "Entrepreneurial Journalism Education: Where Are We Now?." *Observatorio* 7 (4): 185–211.

Schudson, Michael. 2001. "The Objectivity Norm in American Journalism." *Journalism* 2 (2): 149–170.

Schultz, Ida. 2007. "The Journalistic Gut Feeling: Journalistic Doxa, News Habitus and Orthodox News Values." *Journalism Practice* 1 (2): 190–207.

Singer, Jane B. 2007. "Contested Autonomy: Professional and Popular Claims on Journalistic Norms." *Journalism Studies* 8 (1): 79–95.

Singer, Jane B. 2010. "Norms and the Network: Journalistic Ethics in a Shared Media Space." In *Journalism Ethics: A Philosophical Approach*, edited by Christopher Meyers, 117–129. New York: Oxford University Press.

Singer, Jane B. 2015. "Out of Bounds: Professional Norms as Boundary Markers." In *Boundaries of Journalism: Professionalism, Practices and Participation*, edited by Matt Carlson and Seth C. Lewis, 21–36. New York: Routledge.

Singer, Jane B. 2016a. "The Journalist as Entrepreneur." In *Rethinking Journalism Vol. II: The Societal Role and Relevance of Journalism in a Digital Age*, edited by Chris Peters and Marcel Broersma. Abingdon, UK: Taylor & Francis. Forthcoming.

Singer, Jane B. 2016b. "Journalism as an Entrepreneurial Enterprise: Normative Boundaries, Economic Imperatives, and Journalistic Roles." In *Remaking the News*, edited by C. W. Anderson and Pablo J. Boczkowski. Cambridge, MA: MIT Press. Forthcoming.

Sirkkunen, Esa, and Clare Cook. 2012. *Chasing Sustainability on the Net*. Tampere, Finland: Tampere Research Centre for Journalism, Media and Communication. http://www.submojour.net/.

Vos, Tim P., Stephanie Craft, and Seth Ashley. 2012. "New Media, Old Criticism: Bloggers' Press Criticism and the Journalistic Field." *Journalism* 13 (7): 848–866.

Waisbord, Silvio R. 2013. *Reinventing Professionalism: Journalism and News in Global Perspective*. Malden, MA: Polity.

Wallace, Wendy. 2012. "The Need for Entrepreneurship in Journalism." *Journal of Business and Entrepreneurship* 23 (winter): 112–114.

Ward, Stephen J. A. 2009. "Journalism in the Entrepreneurial Age." Center for Journalism Ethics, School of Journalism and Mass Communication, University of Wisconsin-Madison, 15 September. https://ethics.journalism.wisc.edu/2009/09/15/journalism-in-the-entrepreneurial-age.

IDEOLOGY AS RESOURCE IN ENTREPRENEURIAL JOURNALISM
The French online news startup *Mediapart*

Andrea Wagemans, Tamara Witschge, and **Mark Deuze**

The emergence of a startup culture in the field of journalism is global: since the early years of the twenty-first century, new independent journalism companies have formed around the world. Although setting up one's own journalistic practice is not particularly novel in the news industry, the last couple of years have witnessed exponential growth in the startup space. In this context we chose to look more closely at one of the more successful recent online news startups: the French site Mediapart. *We were interested in the factors involved in creating and running a journalism startup, and how the professionals involved give meaning to what they do in the fast-changing journalism field. We found that, although one of the main unique selling points of the journalism professed at* Mediapart *is that it challenges and provides an alternative to mainstream French press, at the heart of it is a strong traditional journalism ideology. While* Mediapart *has in many ways challenged and inspired the ways in which other French news organizations operate, it does not challenge our understanding of journalism, but rather reinforces a traditional and homogenous definition.*

Introduction

The emergence of a startup culture in the field of journalism is global: since the early years of the twenty-first century, new independent (and generally small-scale and online-only) journalism companies have formed around the world (for Europe, see Bruno and Kleis Nielsen 2012; for Australia, see Simons 2013; for some US cases, see Schaffer 2010; Coates Nee 2014). In the context of self-damaging business models (for print and broadcast), audiences migrating to the digital space, and an organizational context rife with atypical working conditions (International Labour Organization 2006), ongoing managerial overhauls, and declining editorial budgets, both newcomers and senior reporters choose, or see a necessity, to strike out on their own. Although setting up one's own journalistic practice—either within or outside of legacy news organizations—is not particularly new in the news industry, in recent years there has been exponential growth in the startup space.

The current shift in focus to entrepreneurial journalism has not only taken place within the industry. Researchers and educators have matched this attention with scholarly work and curricular innovation, which further urges journalists to take on entrepreneurialism as a core element in their identity (for a critical take, see Anderson 2014). Courses and degrees in entrepreneurial journalism have been developed in countries as varied as the United States, the United Kingdom, Canada, France, Colombia, Mexico, and the Netherlands

(Vázquez Schaich and Klein 2013; Mensing and Ryfe 2013). Emphasizing individual traits, skills, attitude, and mindset, such curricular interventions envisage the future of journalism in the form of journalists who (alone or in collaboration) are able to monetize content in innovative ways, connect to publics in interactive new formats, grasp opportunities, and respond to (and shape) its environment (Briggs 2012).

While the future of journalism is increasingly sought in both journalism practice and education in this entrepreneurial form of journalism, we have to recognize the startup space as profoundly precarious. Many, if not most companies fail to make it past good intentions. Financing is scarce, competition fierce, and costs can be high. Stress levels among workers in the media industry are high, among those more or less securely employed just as much as among independents (Ertel et al. 2005; Reinardy 2011). Diversification and cross-subsidizing editorial practice seem key to survival; the extent to which this contributes to a potential compromising of journalistic standards and values remains to be seen. What is clear is that journalism practice currently moves beyond traditional conceptualizations of the field as consisting of neatly organized core industries producing media products for mass consumption. The ways of practicing journalism include a wide (and widening) range of editorial, redactional, and curational settings taking place in all kinds of organizational contexts.

To understand the ways in which these new startups impact on the field and wider understanding of journalism, we need rich, in-depth descriptions of cases of these new forms of journalism, the new types of business models, and ways of practicing and perceiving journalism. To contribute to our understanding of the challenges and opportunities of new forms of journalism, we provide in-depth insight into one of the more successful online news startups: the French site *Mediapart*. It is one of the few news startups that have managed to develop a sustainable business model for their online journalism, whereas most other similar "pure players" in the field seem to struggle to establish or hold on to what tends to be a mix of different sources of revenue (if any; see Sirkkunen and Cook 2012).

The business model of *Mediapart*, that completely rejects the selling of advertising space to pay its bills, was unique when it was launched in 2007 and there was a good deal of initial skepticism about its chances of success. Alain Minc, who was president of *Le Monde*'s supervisory board at the time, said that based on his experience in the media business he was sure that the *Mediapart* model would never work. In an interview with radio station France Info on October 10, 2008 he stated: "the model chosen by Edwy Plenel is an absurd one. The online press cannot work except when it is free. A paid online press cannot work."[1]

By succeeding, *Mediapart* not only challenges these industry preconceptions, but also scholarly ones: existing theories about business models in journalism suggest that newspapers always depend on cross-subsidies (whether from advertising or public funding) to some extent. According to Kaye and Quinn (2010), the revenues from selling content were never high enough to cover the expenses, and Briggs (2012, 15) adds "the most damaging misconception that still pervades the newspaper industry today is the belief that consumers used to pay for their news." He claims readers have never actually paid for content and this is not going to be common in the digital age either, even though media have been exploring the options for charging content online.

Mediapart is an interesting case to investigate not only because of its unique and successful business model. We see that the subscription model is becoming more common, though its longer-term success is not as clear in each of these cases as it is in the case of *Mediapart*—see, for instance, *De Correspondent* in the Netherlands, *Krautreporter* in Germany, or *The Atavist Magazine* in the United States. What makes *Mediapart* a particularly interesting case is that outsiders describe it as a unique case, while the company regards itself as a laboratory, as a *nouvelle presse* project that is exploring the digital age and might serve as an example for other journalism startups. By investigating *Mediapart* closely, we gain insight into both its uniqueness and the extent to which this forms a laboratory for other cases.

A Unique Laboratory for New Forms of Journalism

Mediapart was founded in 2007 by Edwy Plenel (former editor-in-chief at *Le Monde*), François Bonnet (*Libération, Le Monde*), Laurent Mauduit (*Libération, Le Monde*), Gérard Desportes (*Libération*), and Marie-Hélène Smiejan. These senior journalists wanted to create an independent online newspaper focused on investigative journalism and reinvent a business model for journalism based completely on paid subscriptions.

What sets *Mediapart* apart from other online-only platforms is first that it bills itself as an online *newspaper* publishing three daily editions (rather than continuous updates). The stories that are included in these editions are selected and prioritized on the basis of relevance, and not just the time of publication. The same story is sometimes republished in multiple editions. In addition to these newspaper-like articles, *Mediapart* also offers its subscribers video content in the form of Web documentaries, self-produced talk shows (*Mediapart Live, Objections, Contre-courant*), and a weekly video column of comedian Didier Porte. Second, an important part of the website is dedicated to what they call *Le Club*, the interactive platform where people can comment on articles, publish their own blogs, and engage in discussions with other people, experts, and journalists. *Mediapart* journalists also use this part of the website to publish stories that interest them personally. Third, *Mediapart* organizes events like offline debates, festivals, and rallies that further and extend the discussions held on the platform, such as an event to support Greece or the battle against corruption. Fourth, part of the newspaper and *Le Club* are also available in an English and Spanish edition. All in all, it becomes clear that *Mediapart* is a company with a diversified, multi-media strategy. In this article, we will discuss the ways in which these elements come together in a successful new type of news organization.

Key for this article focusing on the entrepreneurial aspects of new journalism is that *Mediapart* aims to be an independent medium that does not rely on advertisers for its business model. Full stories are accessible through a paid subscription at the relatively low price of €9 a month, while the homepage and *Le Club* can be accessed for free. As such, there are a number of aspects that set *Mediapart* apart from other digital media startups. In France, at the time, it was unique in the sense that it was a news medium that did not rely in any way on selling advertisement space. It was the only news site in France that did not, and still does not, have advertisements. Offline, there was already *Le Canard Enchainé* and in the audiovisual domain there was also website *@rret sur images*. In the meantime, online media like *Contexte* (in 2013) and *Brief.me* (in 2014) were created that also denounce advertising.

Internationally, the idea of a paywall was still a rare policy in the media industry when *Mediapart* adopted this strategy. The *Wall Street Journal* had successfully installed the first online paywall in 1997, but was alone in that policy. According to *The Conversation*, the paywall debate only took off in 2009, two years after *Mediapart* was created.[2] *The New York Times* introduced a paywall in 2011, *The Times* (London) in 2012, but this is all considerably later than the French startup. Moreover, in many of these cases we are dealing with metered paywalls. In the case of *Mediapart* all content except the homepage (with short introductions to the articles) was behind a paywall from the outset. In France too, this is a relatively unique feature, as is also remarked in research conducted in 2010 that examined 24 online media in France (Couve and Kayser-Bril 2010). The researchers concluded that the "freemium" model was by far the most used model, making special mention of the distinctiveness of *Mediapart*'s model.

Given these specific characteristics of the news platform, the following research question drove the research presented here: what are the factors involved in creating and running *Mediapart*, and how do the news professionals involved give meaning to what they do in their working environment? We deliberately chose a descriptive general question, since the space of news startups is relatively under-researched, and existing work tends to define survival and success more or less exclusively in business terms (Sirkkunen and Cook 2012; Naldi and Picard 2012; Küng 2015, 91ff).

The analysis presented here is based on interviews with the founders and a document analysis of the business plan, the annual budgets, the mission statement, and the *Mediapart Live* edition covering this subject (interviews and analysis conducted in 2014 and 2015). Together they offer insight into the creation of *Mediapart*, the events leading up to it, the choices made, and the difficulties faced. The analysis of business-related documents, like *Mediapart*'s budget, business plan, and mission statement, offered insight into the business creation, the steps taken, the objectives, and the choices made. This was also covered in the manifesto *Combat pour une presse libre* (in 2008) and the revised manifesto *Le droit de savoir* (in 2013), both written by co-founder and president Edwy Plenel. Semi-structured interviews with Plenel and two other co-founders further enriched this data with anecdotes, hesitations, challenges, and successes while creating and running *Mediapart*, while semi-structured interviews with journalists working at *Mediapart* and founders of other French startups gave insight in the day-to-day routines at *Mediapart*, how *Mediapart* differs from established media organizations, how the journalists give meaning to working in this new type of media organization, how this relates to their professional objectives and in what ways it affected French journalism.

The people we interviewed at *Mediapart* itself were: Edwy Plenel (founder and president), Christophe Gueugneau (editor-in-chief), Laurent Mauduit (co-founder and economics editor), Pierre Puchot (international editor), Stéphane Alliès (political editor), Lucie Delaporte (education editor), and François Bonnet (editorial director). The founders of other French startups we interviewed were: Nicolas George (pigiste [Freelance] for *i>Télé*, *RTL*, and *Le Routard*), Jean-Christophe Boulanger (founder and president of *Contexte*), and Laurent Mauriac (founder of *Rue89* and *Brief.me*).

The 10 interviews were conducted between November 2014 and January 2015. Each interview lasted for about an hour (two were conducted over the phone, two in a cafe, one at the home of the interviewee, the other five in offices of the interviewees). As entrepreneurial journalism is still a relatively new field of study, we employed a grounded theory approach to code and analyze the results. The number of people we interviewed is limited, and the interview data only begin to explore the experiences, motivations, and emotions of the journalists involved. However, the variety of perspectives does provide a diverse account of *Mediapart* as a journalism startup and the role it plays in French journalism. Furthermore, the analysis of the data clearly identified shared experiences, allowing us to venture beyond the case of *Mediapart* and reflect on wider practices of entrepreneurial journalism.

In this article, we will start by contextualizing our research of this case by situating it in our understanding of entrepreneurial journalism. We address the importance of a broad definition of resources in examining entrepreneurship and the need to consider the role that ideology plays in creative enterprises such as startups in journalism. We will then apply these concepts, resources, and ideology to the specific case of *Mediapart* and show the way that ideology becomes one of the most important ways to point out (and sell) the uniqueness of the organization. We critically interrogate the ways in which *Mediapart* argues it is different from traditional organizations, and reflect on the limits of the challenge that this entrepreneurial project provides to the understanding of journalism.

Setting Up a New News Organization

The direct event leading up to the creation of *Mediapart* was the acquisition of *Le Monde* by the investment group Lagardère in 2005 and the resulting departure of then editor-in-chief Edwy Plenel. He explains how he warned about the consequences of the acquisition, but during the general assembly only 36 percent of the journalists voted against the proposition and so *Le Monde* was purchased by the investment group. Plenel left the newspaper on October 30, 2005—remembering the exact date when talking about it in the interview.

Laurent Mauduit resigned as assistant editor-in-chief, but continued to undertake investigative journalism for *Le Monde* for another year. The direct event causing him to resign was the censoring of part of his investigative story on then president of *Le Monde*'s supervisory board Alain Minc. According to François Bonnet, it is a French peculiarity that all media are owned by companies whose main occupation is not information, but arms, telecom, concrete, or something else. These relationships between business owners, investors, government, and the media fueled the founders' wish to create an independent medium.

There was some momentum in 2007. First, key personnel were available—Plenel, Mauduit, and other journalists who had exited *Le Monde*. Second, with his settlement payment from the newspaper, Plenel was in a position to invest in the *Mediapart* project. The founders were experienced and renowned journalists who wanted to create an independent medium, by which they mainly refer to economic independence. An online venture was less expensive than setting up a print medium, allowed for interaction with readers, and gave them a first mover's advantage in 2007, as *Mediapart* was one of the first online media to succeed with a business model that completely eliminated advertisement sales as a source of revenue.

But although the founders had extensive journalistic experience, none had set up or run a business previously. As Laurent Mauduit recounts, this influenced their business decisions. For example, the initial team comprised 25 journalists, one technician, and one administrative employee. The founders saw themselves creating a newspaper and to do that they needed journalists. They were barely aware that creating an online business also requires a general manager, financial manager, marketing department, and a technical support team. When the website crashed because the first scoop increased traffic, they had to hire more technical staff. It took three years before they hired Estelle Coulon who manages online marketing and who has expanded the marketing team. As Laurent Mauduit recounts:

> We were crazy, crazy, crazy, it was madness. Madness because we said we are doing journalism, so we need journalists, but we didn't understand that we were creating a business, so we also needed a general director in charge of financial matters, a marketing specialist, etcetera.

The founders deliberately chose a business model and medium that were new to them, but that allowed for independent journalism, interaction with readers, and required less financial capital to create than a print medium. Despite their lack of business experience—and the way this biased their choices towards the journalism rather than the business side of the enterprise—they managed to successfully create and run this journalism startup. They benefited from the variety of resources they possessed as renowned journalists, as they could more easily access capital, manage their creative employees, and become visible.

Despite the absence of a marketing department, *Mediapart* became known and visible quickly, as becomes clear from the number of mentions in French media.[3] The interviews conducted for this research (with people both within and outside of *Mediapart*) suggest this can be in part explained by the charisma and symbolic capital of founder and president Edwy Plenel. Already a public figure before starting *Mediapart*, he describes his own role as president of *Mediapart* as being the spokesperson of the business. Stéphane Alliès explains how personification is something typically French and can be identified with all the big printed press institutions. According to other startup founders, it was a deliberate choice made by the founders to construct the newspaper around the personality of Edwy Plenel with his big moustache and reputation. It is a choice that was not without risk, because Plenel is a divisive personality, loved by some but hated by others. To gauge his role amidst the other features that helped make this case a successful case, we need to identify the features that help us understand entrepreneurship.

Understanding Entrepreneurial Journalism

To understand the way in which journalism startups function, in this case *Mediapart*, we need to look at the broader context of startups. For the purposes of this research, a startup is considered to be a small or medium-sized enterprise (SME) with less than 250 employees (Powell and Ennis 2007, 376). For the *journalism* part of entrepreneurial journalism, we can further define it as a startup organization that identifies with journalism as it has historically been practiced, is not affiliated with existing media, and mainly operates online, while innovating journalism in some way (Bruno and Kleis Nielsen 2012, 3–4), for example, by producing a different kind of journalistic content or by creating a new viable business model. *Mediapart* claims to do both. In its 2014 annual report, Edwy Plenel writes:

> In its six years of existence, Mediapart has become known for its original, new and exclusive information. But what is not sufficiently known yet is that this digital newspaper without equivalent is also an economic exception in the French press.

The term "entrepreneurial journalism" has attracted considerable attention, both in the industry and in academia. It marries two parts long seen as needing to be separate, even at times in one individual, the entrepreneurial journalist: the business side of the enterprise and the journalistic side of the enterprise. Those two sides interact and influence the success of the startup. This combination often leads to tension, particularly in the case of companies and organizations within the broader field of the creative industries, of which the news industry is part.

Creative industries are "those activities which have their origin in individual creativity, skill and talent and which have a potential for wealth and job creation through the generation and exploitation of intellectual property" (Townley, Beech, and McKinlay 2009, 939). Creative industries face specific managerial challenges as the nature of their products is symbolic, experiential, and of non-utilitarian value (ibid). Because of those unpredictable aspects, creative businesses employ strategies to manage risk, and risk determines both aspects of the enterprise—whether that enterprise is the portfolio career of an individual entrepreneur or a large company. Creativity and commercial acumen thus both stand in equal service of managing risk and uncertainty in the production of culture and cultural work (Bilton 2007), particularly in the field of journalism (Naldi and Picard 2012).

For the news organization—whether that is a large-scale legacy organization, a collaboration of a few people, or constituted by one individual entrepreneur—one of the main challenges is how to balance the public service that journalism seeks or professes to provide and the economic interests (Picard 2005). Both of these aspects are important to consider when understanding entrepreneurial journalism: whereas studies in entrepreneurship tend to focus on the economic aspects, to understand the "journalism" part of the equation, we also need to consider the specific nature of the journalistic profession and its position in societies. Here we will consider more in detail two concepts that help our analysis, resources and professional ideology, as well as the relationships between them.

Resources

Crucial to understanding startups is to note that resources include, but are not limited to, the financial capital available to those setting up a journalistic organization. It also refers to different types of capital needed to create and run a business, as suggested by Naldi and Picard (2012). Capital is a useful concept when analyzing business formation in the news industry, because it allows us to distinguish between different types of resources, the relationships between those different forms of resources, and how possessing one type of resource makes it easier to acquire other types of resource. The role that resources play in business formation is especially interesting for the creation of *Mediapart*, because its founders had worked at and managed renowned French newspapers before establishing their own venture. This suggests they may have had better access to initial financial capital, a useful social network, and a reputation that gave them an advantage over young entrepreneurs in the same situation. Naldi and Picard (2012, 69–97) identify limited access to capital as one of the main reasons why startup enterprises ultimately fail, and though the existence of resources can never entirely explain the success of an organization, it can help us understand *Mediapart*'s endurance.

Resources entail social, economic, and symbolic capital. Social capital refers to the network that business founders can make use of, such as ties with journalists, sources, the business community, and community organizations (Naldi and Picard 2012). Johannisson (1988, 83) ascribes crucial importance to social capital when he states "the key to entrepreneurial success is found in the ability to develop and maintain a personal network. The personal network is the vehicle by which the established entrepreneur exchanges information with and acquires resources from the environment." Also, founders have a head start when they do not have to build up this network, but can make use of the network they already have as capital is cumulative. It allows the entrepreneur to attract economic capital, which includes the initial financial capital the founders have at their disposal, their monetary income, and personal assets. Economic capital can also be accessed through a strong personal network. It is important to note that, contrary to the idea that anyone can now be a journalist by starting their own business, launching a digital medium still requires significant investment (Tessier 2007, 40; Curran and Witschge 2010). So even though the online production and distribution costs are much lower than those of a printed medium, economic capital is a financial precondition for creating a business (though not necessarily sufficient for making it run successfully).

Social and symbolic capital play a role in both attracting economic capital and running a startup as Johannisson (1988, 87) states, the "entrepreneur's organization is basically an extension of his personality, whether formally represented by his employees or by a personal network." Johannisson places great emphasis on the role of the entrepreneur and his personal traits in the ability to maintain a social network. These personal traits can be understood as what Townley, Beech, and McKinlay (2009, 944) call symbolic capital: "the legitimacy or respect proffered according to terms valued within the field; prestige reflecting knowledge of, and recognition within, the field." These can be acquired, for example, through prior entrepreneurial and business experience, prior experience in related industries or prior experience in other industries. Charisma is also a form of symbolic capital. Furthermore, intellectual capital (creative ideas) and cultural capital (particular knowledge and skills, the ownership of cultural goods, recognized authority or expertise) play an important role as personal traits allowing one to build and maintain a personal network.

Social capital and symbolic capital play an important role in addressing the managerial challenges faced while running a creative business like *Mediapart*. The central point made in theories about the specifics of managing creative business is that the goals and vision of creative businesses are the temporary outcomes of perpetual discussion between the managers and the employees (Powell and Dodd 2007; Townley, Beech, and McKinlay 2009). In the case of *Mediapart*, the founders' reputations and prior experience indicate a profound knowledge of how journalism works, providing them with some leverage over their journalists in these discussions, as we will discuss in more detail below.

Ideology

The managerial challenges faced by creative businesses like those in journalism can be softened significantly if the professional goals of creative employees of the organization relate to the organizational goals of the business. It is the tension between managing resources and upholding values that is central in analyzing entrepreneurial journalism. Many of these challenges come to the fore at the level of everyday practices: how do they manifest in the work and in the self-understanding of the professional? We therefore also looked at how journalists experience working at *Mediapart* and the extent to which the practices at *Mediapart* align with its employees' professional values.

One of the main critiques of entrepreneurial journalism is that it could exacerbate the trend in the field of journalism that suggests that professional values are increasingly set aside to meet more commercial goals in the face of declining revenues (Van Zoonen

1998; Witschge and Nygren 2009). The case of *Mediapart* is particularly interesting as certain market considerations—for example, expressed in seeking advertising revenues—are not a part of *Mediapart*'s business model. At the same time, there are commercial interests at hand: *Mediapart* relies on people subscribing. The question then is if, and in what ways, commercial decisions affect journalistic decisions.

When considering the balance between commercial interests and professional values —such as editorial independence and autonomy—that make up the occupational ideology of journalism (Deuze 2005), it is important to look beyond individual factors surrounding the journalism startup and consider the political and societal context of business formation that may either frustrate or spur business development. What is important to recognize is that, in the case of journalism, looking at economic motives and resources will not provide the whole picture.

As Naldi and Picard (2012, 69–97) explain, one of the main reasons for starting a new journalism business is the job destruction at existing media companies, the discontent with existing journalism, and the demise of legacy media institutions (notably newspapers). Journalism startups in France as well as in other countries are therefore more often than not framing themselves as a counterforce, renewing journalism with independent investigations (Küng 2015). As Sirkkunen and Cook (2012, 52) note: "several sites pride themselves on independent quality journalism that rejects the status quo—even one might say cashing in on a counter-culture that stands for independent, investigative journalism."

The Relevance of Resources

When we consider both aspects of entrepreneurship in the case of *Mediapart*, resources and ideology, we firstly see the unique set of resources available to *Mediapart*. In the above introduction of how *Mediapart* was established, we discussed the set of actors who were involved and the type of capital they brought into the organization. The case of *Mediapart* illustrates how both economic capital and social capital are crucial in meeting the requirements for creating a startup. A network of friends and acquaintances who were willing to invest some money and the availability of the founder's personal financial assets allowed them to raise the initial capital needed to launch the online newspaper.

However, our case also shows how, in a way, they had to start all over despite their financial assets, extensive social networks, and reputations. They did struggle financially during the first three years, as their symbolic capital did not help them in convincing investors that *Mediapart* would be a viable business decision. Thus they were mostly reliant on their own capital and the goodwill of their friends and acquaintances. When *Mediapart* was launched, it had collected €2,939,000 in initial capital. The personal investments of the founders constituted €1,325,000. Next to that there were two bigger investors, namely Doxa and Ecofinance (each about €500,000, totaling €1,110,000). Third, the Société des Amis de Mediapart, consisting of about 40 friends, acquaintances, and other sympathizers that each invested between €5,000 and €50,000, contributed a total amount of €504,000.[4]

This combination of investors is key to understanding how *Mediapart* was able to launch. Given that the motivation of the founders was primarily located in its ideology, not in a business model, "regular" investors were difficult to attract. General director Marie-Hélène Smiejan, who handles the financial side of the business, explained:

> We were not at all beginners, we had professional, editorial and management experience, so we went to see potential partners. They all told us no. It was either the press never makes any money, so it will always lose money. Or it was, but what exactly is your project, it's to earn a lot of money? But no. No, it's that the newspaper exists, develops, takes its readers into account, yes, well, but our goal is to make money … It's risky, an independent newspaper, because why would you want us to invest in it?

So the founders were forced to rely on their own resources and decided to invest in the project themselves. A beneficial side-effect of this decision was that it gave other small investors more confidence in the project. If the founders were willing to invest in it themselves, maybe it was a project worth investing in. In addition, the small investors—the Société des Amis—invested more out of support for *Mediapart*'s cause than for economic reasons.

Although creating and running an online medium is less expensive than creating a print medium, the venture still required approximately €5 million in investment in its first three years in operation. The choice of a paywall model (*modèle payant*) was especially risky, as it requires content to attract subscribers and thus needs a large team of journalists from the start to create this content. In 2010, the costs were €3.5 million, 70 percent of which was staff costs for 33 employees, of whom 25 were journalists (Couve and Kayser-Bril 2010). Of the initial team of 25 journalists, 19 were promised the same salary as the job they had to leave in order to join *Mediapart* and a three-year contract. This helped convince journalists who were hesitant to join *Mediapart* from the outset. François Bonnet recounts how there were not many applications, because people considered it a crazy project. However, for their business model to work they needed journalists with knowledge and expertise concerning investigative stories about politics, economics, education, and the police; and who were also willing to work differently from how they were used to at printed media. They found these journalists with a lot of symbolic capital by asking specific colleagues (*"par des reseaux professionelles de chacun"*) in their networks. This in turn attracted young journalists like Pierre Puchot, Lucie Delaporte, and Stéphane Alliès who were interested in working with these well-known senior journalists.

The venture grew from 25 people, mostly journalists, to an organization of more than 50 people, consisting of four elements:

- The editorial section with about 35 journalists, which is located in Paris and managed by co-founder François Bonnet as the editorial director.
- The technical department, with about 10 staffers, which is located in Paris and managed by Etienne Samsom.
- The marketing department, with about 4 staffers, which is located in Paris and managed by Estelle Coulon.
- Subscribers relations, which is located in Poitiers and managed by Marine Santain.

As this French startup was a relatively new type of organization, those involved faced legislative challenges, notably when it came to taxation policy. Until February 2014 the French government clearly distinguished between the printed press, on the one hand, and websites, on the other, for VAT purposes. The printed press enjoyed a reduced rate of 2.1 percent, while websites had to pay the normal rate of 19.6 percent. After the new press syndicate SPIIL lobbied for equal VAT rates for all media, including online newspapers, the government eventually equalized the rate. Now all media organizations pay 2.1

TABLE 1
Mediapart's revenues and profit per year (in euros)

Year	Revenues	Net profits
2009	1,331,000	−2,133,000
2010	2,819,000	−1,355,700
2011	5,026,500	572,300
2012	5,968,500	702,900
2013	6,843,700	903,600
2014	8,761,800	1,484,253

Source: http://www.societe.com/societe/societe-editrice-de-mediapart-500631932.html.

percent. In the end *Mediapart* managed to become a successful organization, both in terms of profitability (the entrepreneurial aspect of it) and in terms of their self-classification as a journalistic success (which is discussed in the next section). After an initial loss, the organization reached financial equilibrium in 2010 and has been increasingly profitable in subsequent years (see Table 1).

Ideology as Resource

Being a new organization brought challenges and many resources were needed to address the challenges. But *Mediapart* became increasingly popular, in particular after what has become known as the Bettencourt affair. The organization grew to more than 10,000 subscribers in their first six months,[5] then gradually doubled, and after the huge scoop about the Bettencourt affair in July 2010, the subscription numbers increased from 26,000 to 42,000.[6] There was steady growth in 2011,[7] in 2012,[8] and in 2013, taking the number of subscribers to the 100,000 mark.

It is clear that the Bettencourt affair was very important in the growth of the number of subscribers. This involved the publication of secretly taped phone calls which implicated former UMP treasurer and then Minister of Employment Éric Woerth with having received €50,000 from L'Oréal billionaire Liliane Bettencourt through his wife, who was working for the 92-year-old Bettencourt at the time.[9] *Le Monde* had passed on the recordings of telephone conversations with Bettencourt, as had *Le Nouvel Observateur*. Management at *Mediapart*, however, decided to go with the story. Between publication of the Bettencourt story in June 2010 and the end of the year 2010, the number of subscribers almost doubled (26,000 to 46,870). In their annual report of 2011, they wrote: "after two years of steady growth in terms of audience and subscriptions, the Bettencourt affair allowed *Mediapart* to pass a tipping point."

The tapes' controversy not only allowed them to break a big investigative story, it also strengthened their claim that the existing media in France were not doing their job correctly. By refusing to publish the information about corruption offered to them, *Le Monde* and *Le Nouvel Observateur* supported *Mediapart*'s argument that they were keeping important information from their readers for the wrong reasons. As such, *Mediapart* is a clear example of a new entrepreneurial project challenging the status quo in the field of journalism, and ideology seems to be one of their strongest assets.

In its manifesto, *Mediapart* states that France is in need of a new press and *Mediapart* is this project. They refer to their belief that existing media are not doing investigative journalism and are no longer independent, which limits them in performing their democratic duty to inform the public. *Mediapart* claims to be reinventing journalism in France. Borne out of a joint enterprise of journalists and Web specialists, the startup says it aims to respond to three crises: democratic, economic, and moral. The economic crisis refers to the lack of a viable business model as readers are leaving, advertisement revenues are falling, and debts are increasing. This is a crisis because a financially unstable press is a weak press ("*une presse fragile est une presse faible*"), according to Plenel.

Interestingly, through addressing this economic "crisis," *Mediapart* aims to address the moral crisis they identify in journalism. This crisis for them is connected to the economic crisis: as they see it, the fragility of newspapers causes a destabilization of journalistic values, morals, and professional culture when the economic dependence of newspapers on advertisers, corporations, or government limit them in their editorial choices. Which brings them to the final crisis, the democratic crisis, by which they mean the presidential system in France which, they argue, allows one powerful person to dictate the journalistic agenda. Through these evaluations of the press in France, Edwy Plenel argues that *Mediapart* might serve as an example for other journalism businesses in France and internationally both in the way they have organized their business model and in the way they do journalism.

Challenging the Status Quo

This strong ideological stance, which can be identified as a return to "traditional" journalistic values while challenging traditional media organizations, provides interesting insights into both how this entrepreneurial project perceives (and sells) itself, as well as how it considers other media businesses. By talking about what sets it apart, those involved provide an interesting dichotomy distinguishing themselves from others. Each concept used to describe *Mediapart* has a counterpart that describes the traditional press in France for them. These distinctions were made, both at the level of the organization (Table 2), and at the level of the journalism they produce (Table 3).

Towards a New Organization of Journalism?

Tables 2 and 3 show how *Mediapart* not only challenges the conceptualization of journalism in France, but also reinvents the way that a journalistic organization can be organized. In its self-conceptualization we can find many negations of the traditional press in France. Compared to the printed media the founders had managed before, *Mediapart* is a much smaller, more flexible organization and less hierarchical. The editors-in-chief state that they can primarily focus on journalistic work, because the combination of doing journalism online and relying on a business model that primarily gets its revenues from paid subscriptions eliminates the need to please advertisers, eliminates the production and distribution costs, and eliminates the need for a 200–300-person team.

The journalists also feel they are much less preoccupied with organizational issues like time, length, and revenues, which allows them to focus more fully on producing what they consider good journalism. Most of the *Mediapart* journalists had worked at other renowned media before joining the new startup, and a number had even left comfortable jobs for it. They reference the value of contact with readers, both virtually and in reality, the liberty that they experience and the time and space they get to produce their

TABLE 2
Differences in organizational features between *Mediapart* and traditional press according to people working at *Mediapart*

Organization features	*Mediapart*	French press
Income model	Subscriptions	Advertisement/investors
Business model: profitability	Profitable	Losing money/sold off to investors
Ownership	Independent	Owned by corporations
Production costs involved	Less expensive	Expensive
Type of organization: overhead	Slim	Heavy
Income flow	Stable	Unstable
Organization size	Small	Large
Type of organization	Horizontal	Hierarchic
Establishment of news agenda	Free choice by journalists	Appointed by editors
Organization of news beats and journalist work	Together, working with different colleagues in multiple domains	Divided, each journalist working on own news beat
Age of employees	Young and old people	Mostly old people
Culture	Dynamic	Established

TABLE 3
Differences in journalism produced between *Mediapart* and traditional press according to people working at *Mediapart*

Organization features	*Mediapart*	French press
Journalism model	Anglo-Saxon	French
Agenda set by	Investigation	Other media and the political agenda
Produced for	The public	The audience
Amount of articles	Few	Many
Type of questioning	Pugnacious	Polite/lazy
Differentiation	Unique identity	Homogenization
Aim of output	Quality	Quantity
Rhythm of publishing	Distinct editions	Continuous stream of articles
Editorial decision making	Selective, exclusive	Copy–paste culture
Affinity	Close to the public	Close to those in power
Sourcing of stories	Original sources	"Usual suspects"
Length of output	Long	Short
Depth of output	Profound	Superficial
Output on site ordered by	Most important	Most recent

work. Moreover, they state they are not limited by the institutional agenda as journalists at traditional media often are, but instead are completely free to choose their own subjects as opposed to media where they worked previously. There they were much more tied to the news of the day and to orders from the editor-in-chief. At *Mediapart*, the initiative is with the journalists. The journalists describe how they felt limited at their former employers. They were not practicing what they believed journalism should be. They were guided by external factors. More generally, they feel free to practice what they regard as good journalism. Lucie Delaporte states that she is completely free to choose her own subjects, as long as it is a story that is different from that which other media do.

However, it is important to note that, although there may be significant differences in practice, a lot of this pertains to discourse. For instance, the idea that *Mediapart* is a horizontally, democratically organized company is to a large extent more in discourse than in practice. In reality there are two chiefs, Edwy Plenel and François Bonnet, and there are others who perform "management" roles, though they are not necessarily named as such. Christophe Gueugneau, for instance, who is editor-in-chief together with Sophie Dufau, explained that his responsibilities are those of an editor-in-chief, but his title is journalist. Together they form the part of the organizational structure that is referred to as *le central* and falls under editorial director François Bonnet.

Equally, the *Mediapart* founders employ a strong type of public service discourse (Witschge and Nygren 2009; Sirkkunen and Cook 2012), referring to "the citizens' right to know" and "for democracy," which is not always equally performed in practice. It presents itself as a unique medium that is an "economic exception," "unequalled," with "original, new and exclusive content." However, the journalists do not seem to agree with the founders about the larger goal of *Mediapart*. They are skeptical about the extent to which *Mediapart* is able to fulfill a civic responsibility. The people they are seeking to convince are the people who are interested in this already, says Christophe Gueugneau. According to the journalists, *Mediapart*'s goal is therefore not to reinvent journalism, but to simply do journalism as it has been ideologically supposed to be done. As such, it becomes clear that challenging the status quo by reverting to traditional values (such as truth-telling in the context of complete editorial autonomy and independence) becomes one of the most important resources available to *Mediapart*.

Indeed, what *Mediapart* produces—investigative journalism—is not new content wise. What they did do successfully is to repackage it in different formats, like videos and podcasts, and the online environment allows for more interaction. But here too, we see that the practice does not always live up to the ideal: journalists admitted that interaction with users was mainly useful in the starting phase of the new medium, when the readership resembled more of a community. As the startup grows, the relevant comments and suggestions from readers are usually only those sent to the journalists in an e-mail or private message, not those on the site. Indeed, like other organizations, *Mediapart* also upholds a clear distinction between content produced by readers and content produced by journalists, emphasizing the fact that these are two different things. As such, the status of the contributions of citizens remains up for negotiation (for a typology of the types of interactivity in online news spaces, see Peters and Witschge 2014).

Mediapart's focus on what sets the venture apart is both a burden and a blessing in the daily work of the journalists. Journalists at *Mediapart* explain that they could be perceived as arrogant, because they are telling other journalists that they are not producing "proper" journalism. Lucie Delaporte, education editor, describes how education editors working at other media do not do investigative journalism in the education field, because that is not what is expected of them. At *Mediapart*, her argument goes, there is space for such investigations. Sources too, would notice such differences. Stéphane Alliès, political editor, describes that sources experience greater liberty at explaining their statements, because they know there is room for longer quotes in *Mediapart*'s articles.

What becomes clear is that billing the new entrepreneurial project as reinventing journalism is a clever technique to gain visibility and it has been useful in attracting readers and funding. The public service nature of the message has clearly spoken to ideological motivations of people to support the new business venture. It has proved effective in capitalizing on the founders' social capital. This does not mean that the newcomer has not instigated some real changes in the field. They did provide impetus for investigative journalism, which is relatively uncommon in France (Kuhn 2013), driving legacy media like *Le Monde, Le Nouvel Observateur*, and *Le Point* to invest in their own investigative units. *Le Monde* even rehired Fabrice Lhomme from *Mediapart* after he broke the Bettencourt story.

Mediapart also developed an online marketing strategy that legacy media adopted, and it changed the playing field for online journalism in France when it comes to rules and regulations, allowing them to compete more equally with legacy media. As another startup founder explained, *Mediapart* has been very innovative when it comes to marketing despite their lack of a marketing department during the first three years in existence. The most inventive is the €1 trial period, which *Le Monde* and other large newspapers also adopted. This suggests journalism startups can be an innovative factor in the journalism field that do not only change the ways in which their journalists work, but also the ways in which existing media work.

Conclusion

The case of *Mediapart* provides useful insights into the new ways in which journalism is produced, distributed, and conceptualized. One of the main findings offered here is how the new entrepreneurial news organization aims to challenge the status quo in journalism, both in terms of its organization and in terms of its ideology. At the same time, the ideology that is professed fits with the traditional conceptualization of journalism (Deuze 2005). All the journalists working at *Mediapart* describe how they wanted to work there because the practices at their previous employers did not match their view of journalism. The startup does not so much change the professional identity of the journalists, but seems to offer a place where they can work according to their own perceived professional identity. Put differently, the professional identity precedes the startup and the startup offers an environment within which the journalists can express this professional identity in their work. Both the founders and journalists of *Mediapart* argue that they feel liberated from organizational issues and unconstrained by space or time. This implies that journalists are treated more like "pure" professionals (adhering to a strict definition of reportorial autonomy) at *Mediapart* than they were at traditional media outlets.

There is an interesting paradox here: the organization professes (and is experienced as such) to provide complete liberty and autonomy of the journalists while at the same time there is a strong and homogenous work ethic and conceptualization of journalism. Although it is less hierarchical than traditional news organizations, *Mediapart* is not as democratically organized as the founders portray, nor do we find truly alternative understandings and practices of journalism. The symbolic capital that can be found in some of the key players in the organization allowed the organization (with strong-minded employees) to be managed effectively. This is mainly because the journalists working in the organization trust the decisions made by the two main leaders, François Bonnet and Edwy Plenel, even when they do not always agree with them. A shared set of values and ways of working was in part produced through the selection and hiring process, creating a group of like-minded staff, and an environment where people (want to) work together. In doing so, the inner workings of the startup do not differ from the relatively homogeneous working environments and examples of group-think in legacy newsrooms.

More generally, it seems like journalism startups in France are looking more at the Anglo-Saxon journalistic culture than French tradition in constructing their businesses (Reese 2001). This is to say that they are inspired by American businesses that already exist, and they propagate a fact-based, objectivity-driven kind of journalism. Together with their discourse of civic responsibility and the feeling of being almost completely autonomous as journalists, their references to journalism are distinctly ideological—that is, inspired by ideal-typical values (Deuze 2005). For all the freedom experienced in the organization in determining what news to investigate and report on, the journalists still expressed the need to address the biggest events of every day as one of the main challenges. As such, it seems that *Mediapart*, which in many ways, both financially and journalistically, is innovative, still follows traditional ideological values that have governed journalism for a long time (in this case immediacy). With a passionate return to traditional journalistic ideological values as their unique selling point within the particular French context, we may wonder whether—and if so how—entrepreneurial ventures, while challenging the status quo, in fact challenge conceptualizations of journalism. On the other hand, the journalistic innovation in the case of *Mediapart*—combining collaboration with an expert audience with an innovative business form, and an entrepreneurial organization of work—suggests that a return and confirmation of an ideal-typical core of journalism does not necessarily stand in the way of new forms of journalism developing and flourishing. Ideology can be a resource for innovation as much as it works as a moat to hold off invaders.

DISCLOSURE STATEMENT

No potential conflict of interest was reported by the authors.

NOTES

1. All quotes translated from French by the authors.
2. See http://theconversation.com/newspapers-ongoing-search-for-subscription-revenue-from-paywalls-to-micropayments-40726.
3. Source: Wagemans (2014, appendix B), analysis of French media using a LexisNexis database search with the keyword *Mediapart*, which went from 25 in the first month of existence, to 537 in 2008 and 592 in 2009, to 2626 in 2010 (a rise that is mainly due to the Bettencourt affair, see below).
4. For all figures, see http://www.mediapart.fr/journal/france/090308/comment-mediapart-a-construit-son-independance.
5. Source: http://www.cguittard.com/article-22849100.html.
6. Source: http://www.journaliste-entrepreneur.com/2010/11/mediapart-le-pari-de-l%E2%80%99enquete-et-de-l%E2%80%99abonnement/.
7. Source: *Mediapart* annual report.
8. Source: http://www.frenchweb.fr/le-succes-de-mediapart-en-chiffres-et-en-images/104113.
9. See, for instance, http://www.theguardian.com/media/2010/jul/12/bettencourt-tapes-mediapart.

REFERENCES

Anderson, C. W. 2014. "The Sociology of the Professions and the Problem of Journalism Education." *Radical Teacher,* 99 (Spring): 62–68.

Bilton, Chris. 2007. *Management and Creativity: From Creative Industries to Creative Management.* Malden: Blackwell.

Briggs, Mark. 2012. *Entrepreneurial Journalism: How to Build What's Next for News.* London: CQ Press.

Bruno, Nicola, and Rasmus Kleis Nielsen. 2012. *Survival is Success: Journalistic Online Start-ups in Western Europe.* Oxford: Reuters Institute for the Study of Journalism.

Coates Nee, R. 2014. "Social Responsibility Theory and the Digital Nonprofits: Should the Government aid Online News Startups?" *Journalism* 15 (3): 326–343.

Couve, Phillipe, Nicolas Kayser-Bril. 2010. "Médias: Nouveaux Modèles Economique & Questions de Déontologie. http://www.journaliste-entrepreneur.com/wp-content/uploads/2010/11/medias_nouveaux_modeles_PhCouve.pdf

Curran, James, and Tamara Witschge. 2010. "Liberal Dreams and the Internet." In *New Media, Old News: Journalism and Democracy in the Digital Age,* edited by N. Fenton, 102–118. London: Sage.

Deuze, Mark. 2005. "What is Journalism? Professional Identity and Ideology of Journalists Reconsidered." *Journalism: Theory Practice & Criticism* 6 (4): 443–465.

Ertel, Michael, Eberhard Pech, Peter Ullsperger, Olaf Von dem Knesebeck, and Johannes Siegrist. 2005. "Adverse Psychosocial Working Conditions and Subjective Health in Freelance Media Workers." *Work & Stress* 19 (3): 293–299.

International Labour Organization. 2006. "The Changing Nature of Work: A Global Survey and Case Study of Atypical Work in the Media Industry.".Research Report. http://www.ifj.org/pdfs/ILOReport070606.pdf.

Johannisson, Bengt. 1988. "Business Formation—A Network Approach." *Scandinavian Journal of Management* 4 (3): 83–99.

Kaye, Jeff, and Stephen Quinn. 2010. *Funding Journalism in the Digital age.* New York: Peter Lang.

Kuhn, Raymond. 2013. "The Media and the Executive in France: An Unequal Power Relationship." *European Journal of Communication* 28 (2): 122–135.

Küng, Lucy. 2015. *Innovators in Digital News.* London: I.B. Tauris.

Mensing, Donica H., and David M. Ryfe. 2013. "Blueprint for Change: From the Teaching Hospital to the Entrepreneurial Model of Journalism Education." *#ISOJ The Official Research Journal of the International Symposium on Online Journalism* 2 (2): 144–161.

Naldi, Lucia, and Robert G. Picard. 2012. "'Let's Start an Online News Site': Opportunities, Resources, Strategy, and Formational Myopia in Startups." *Journal of Media Business Studies* 4: 47–59.

Peters, Chris, and Tamara Witschge. 2014. "From Grand Narratives of Democracy to Small Expectations of Participation." *Journalism Practice* 9 (1): 19–34.

Picard, Robert G. 2005. "Money, Media and the Public Interest." In *The Press,* edited by Geneva Overholser and Kathleen Hall Jamieson, 337–350. Oxford: Oxford University Press.

Powell, Shaun, and Chris Dodd. 2007. "Managing Vision and the Brand Within the Creative Industries." *Corporate Communications: An International Journal* 12 (4): 394–413.

Powell, Shaun, and Sean Ennis. 2007. "Organisational Marketing in the Creative Industries." *Qualitative Market Research: An International Journal* 10 (4): 375–389.

Reese, Stephen D. 2001. "Understanding the Global Journalist: A Hierarchy-of-influences Approach." *Journalism Studies* 2 (2): 173–187.

Reinardy, Scott. 2011. "Newspaper Journalism in Crisis: Burnout on the Rise, Eroding Young Journalists' Career Commitment." *Journalism* 12 (1): 33–50.

Schaffer, Jan. 2010. "New Voices: What Works." *J-Lab: The Institute for Interactive Journalism*. http://www.kcnn.org/WhatWorks/introduction/.

Simons, Margaret. 2013. *What's Next in Journalism?* Brunswick: Scribe.

Sirkkunen, Esa, and Clare Cook. 2012. *Chasing Sustainability on the Net: International Research on 69 Journalistic Pure Players and Their Business Models*. Tampere: University of Tampere.

Tessier, Marc. 2007. "La presse au défi du numérique." *Rapport au ministre de la Culture et de la communication*, Paris, février.

Townley, Barbara, Nic Beech, and Alan McKinlay. 2009. "Managing in the Creative Industries: Managing the Motley Crew." *Human Relations* 62 (7): 939–962.

Vázquez Schaich, Maria Jose, and Jeffrey S. Klein. 2013. "Entrepreneurial Journalism Education: Where Are We Now?" *Observatorio (OBS*)* 7 (4): 185–211.

Wagemans, Andrea. 2014. "*Beyond Journalism – Charging for Online Journalism is not Such a Ridiculous Idea After all*." Unpublished MA thesis, University of Amsterdam, Amsterdam, The Netherlands.

Witschge, Tamara, and Gunnar Nygren. 2009. "Journalism: A Profession Under Pressure?" *Journal of Media Business Studies* 6 (1): 37–59.

Zoonen, Liesbet van. 1998. "A Professional, Unreliable, Heroic Marionette (M/F Structure, Agency and Subjectivity in Contemporary Journalisms." *European Journal of Cultural Studies* 1 (1): 123–143.

ENTREPRENEURIALISM OR COOPERATIVISM?
An exploration of cooperative journalistic enterprises

Eugenia Siapera and **Lambrini Papadopoulou**

This article understands entrepreneurial journalism as part of broader socio-economic developments associated with cognitive capitalism. Entrepreneurialism represents an attempt to accumulate profit from social and collaborative processes of knowledge creation. However, knowledge and information creation are collaborative processes that build on previous accumulated knowledge and rely on openness and exchange. The tensions within cognitive capitalism emerge from the collaborative nature of knowledge production and the problems associated with attempts to enclose this for profit. In terms of journalism, added tensions involve its public mission and social role that are antithetical to both profit and individualism. Cooperative enterprises can contribute to a reconciliation of such tensions because they operate for social benefit, and because they rely on cooperation and collaboration. This article examined journalistic cooperatives in Greece and found that they have organic bonds with the society they serve, and success is measured in terms of the benefit they produce rather than profit; they innovate in their cooperative decision making and in the forming and maintenance of social relationships; and they re-establish lost trust and community standing. In this manner they may form a credible alternative to profit-driven entrepreneurial journalism.

Introduction

Entrepreneurial journalism has become a buzzword in the disrupted media field. The considerable currency that the notion of entrepreneurialism has acquired can be attributed to both the efforts of digital gurus such as Jeff Jarvis and to the pressing need for journalistic renewal and viable business models. Entrepreneurialism, with its emphasis on the business aspects of journalism as well as on technological innovation, is touted as giving journalism a sustainable future. In this narrative, as legacy news organizations are dying, journalists can create their own ventures and save themselves and journalism, through a combination of journalistic and business know-how. The role of journalists in Jarvis's vision of entrepreneurial journalism is clear: "journalists must become entrepreneurs ... They need to sense and serve the market" (Jarvis 2009a).

Putting forward entrepreneurial journalism as a panacea for a distressed profession has not been without its critics. Pein (2014) argues that entrepreneurialism is not about journalism but about sales. Placing all the emphasis on the market, technology and profit-driven strategies leaves little room for journalistic values. In part, the dilemma is emerging because of the incompatibility between journalistic values, such as public service, and the commercial imperatives that underlie entrepreneurial journalism. As Pein (2014) put it, "the individualistic mythology of entrepreneurship, with its emphasis on big exits and one-time windfalls, is in irreconcilable conflict with the public-spirited mission of journalism".

Addressing these concerns, Jarvis argues in favour of a pragmatism that requires a shift towards entrepreneurialism as a replacement for the fading business model of journalism. It is no longer a question of whether journalism is compromised but a question of survival. From this point of view, most discussions on entrepreneurial journalism revolve around new ways of capturing value, with "value" being understood as revenue and profit. However, this does not address the fundamental question of the social role and values of journalism, and the extent to which profit and business values are inimical to these. After all, why would we want journalism to survive if it no longer serves a social purpose?

Consequently, the question for journalistic ventures is, can they have innovation, creativity and social value while also surviving? The answer to this question may be found in a new breed of journalistic ventures that seeks to elude the dilemma of traditional journalistic roles versus entrepreneurialism, by subverting both. These are cooperative ventures that seek to replace profit with reinvestment and the role of journalism as mediator between politicians and publics with being an organic part of society. Two key questions arise from these cooperative journalistic ventures. First, can cooperatives offer a way to reconcile entrepreneurial dynamism and the quest for innovation with the public mission and social role of journalism? Second, can journalists be entrepreneurs without compromising their journalistic ethos and identity?

This article addresses these questions through an analysis of cooperative journalistic enterprises in Greece. Through a series of ethnographic observations and in-depth interviews with journalists participating in these initiatives, we examine the extent to which cooperatives constitute a viable reconciliation between entrepreneurialism and journalism.

These developments in journalism have to be linked to broader developments in society and in the ways it is organized. The theoretical part of this article contextualizes both journalism and entrepreneurialism as part of cognitive capitalism, and proposes that the emphasis on entrepreneurialism be linked to this shift. This discussion is based on Castells' (2001) ideas on entrepreneurial culture and Moulier-Boutang's (2012) work on cognitive capitalism. Our discussion leads to a consideration of cooperative models of knowledge production and exchange, with a specific consideration of cooperative journalism. This is followed by an empirically informed discussion of cooperative journalistic enterprises in the context of Greece.

Entrepreneurialism, Cognitive Capitalism and Journalism

We begin this section with a discussion of entrepreneurialism, arguing that it gives rise to a new set of tensions that prioritize two elements, profit and individualism. We then contextualize entrepreneurialism in the broader context of cognitive capitalism, and we end by proposing cooperative journalism as a potential alternative.

Manuel Castells (2001) discusses the culture of entrepreneurialism as constitutive of internet culture more broadly. For Castells, the internet "galaxy" is comprised of four distinct cultures: the techno-meritocratic culture, the hacker culture, the virtual communitarian culture and the entrepreneurial culture. Castells argues that these cultures operate in layers, building on each other, so that the "entrepreneurial culture works on top of the hacker culture, and on the communitarian culture, to diffuse Internet practices in all domains of society by way of money-making" (37). The techno-meritocratic culture is characterized by the ethos of scientific discovery, openness and cooperation, while the hacker culture builds upon this ethos by constructing its own values and rules for exchange and collaboration; the communitarian culture adds a social dimension through socializing this ethos of openness and cooperation. Entrepreneurialism comes on top of all these layers, providing the impetus for these cultures to spread because of the profit or money-making opportunities involved. The commercial uses of the internet are based "on forms and processes invented by the communal culture, the hackers and the technological elites" (55). From this point of view, it is clear that entrepreneurialism operates parasitically in relation to the other three cultures.

Following Castells, entrepreneurialism proper is not the invention of ideas but the process of making money out of ideas—as he puts it: "The realization of the potential of transforming mind power into money-making, became the cornerstone of the entrepreneurial culture in Silicon Valley and of the Internet industry at large" (Castells 2001, 56). Entrepreneurialism does not rely on capital for generating profit but on the ability of the human mind to generate "bankable" ideas. The upshot of this is that within the entrepreneurial culture, the amount of money to be made and the speed at which it is made become the benchmarks for success (56).

For Castells, the entrepreneurial process works on the basis of entrepreneurs managing to sell the future to venture capitalists. The first step is to build on their technological know-how in order to create products, services or processes they believe will appeal to others. The second step is to convince the financial world that their ideas are worthy of investing in, while at the same time trying to sell directly to the end users. Innovation, technological know-how, business acumen and profit go together in what comes close to a win–win scenario. Castells appears to admire the dynamism of entrepreneurialism, arguing that it combines innovative design and research excellence with a conscious orientation to the financial market as the ultimate arbiter of success. In the end, however, entrepreneurialism is "a culture of money" (Castells 2001, 58) but this money is created out of ideas, relying on "the power of the mind" (60). This money is then used as a reward for the entrepreneur, who is characterized by attributes such as looking for immediate gratification, lack of civic engagement, and an impoverished personal and social life; Castells quotes a study by Koch and Miller (2001), according to which socialization with co-workers in Silicon Valley is 22 per cent lower than in the rest of the United States. Individualism is, therefore, at the centre of entrepreneurialism.

While theorists from other disciplines complicate this view, pointing to elements such as deregulation and the fall of managerialism (Harvey 1989), as well as entrepreneurial capital—referring to the broader social environment and knowledge that contributes to the creation of successful enterprises (Audretsch 2007), as factors for the rise of entrepreneurialism, this more complicated picture is lost when entrepreneurialism is applied to journalism.

The main exponent of entrepreneurial journalism is Jeff Jarvis, and for him the focus and emphasis is squarely on technology, money and individualism. Jarvis argues that journalism is no longer about getting a job in a legacy news institution but about innovating and developing new approaches to the news, primarily through new technologies. These new ideas can then attract investors, thereby generating profits for journalism. This is crucial, as for Jarvis journalism will not be sustainable unless it can attract capital; as he puts it, "I wish that the capital that has gone into not-for-profit news ventures in cities across the country had gone instead into creating for-profit enterprises: so we can prove the market, so we can learn how to make news sustainable" (Jarvis 2009a).

Sustainability is equated with profit in Jarvis's view. Entrepreneurial journalism in this model, which has clear parallels with Castell's theorizing, begins with a new idea about the news, mostly new in terms of a combination of technology and journalism, and then turns to seek investment in order to make it happen. Sustainability comes from investment, and from recouping this investment, i.e. from profit. Success for entrepreneurial journalism is defined exclusively in monetary and market terms, and entrepreneurial journalists are themselves solely motivated by money and profit. Moreover, innovation is expected to come from single individual brilliant minds who will "disrupt", leading to some kind of creative destruction. Jarvis (2009a, 2009b) is both against news institutions, which he refers to as "dinosaurs", and against public funding, which he sees as "skewing the market" (2009b) and making journalism dependent on governments. The only future for journalism is the market, in its mainstream, profit-making version, whereby journalism is a product that is sold for profit.

However, both the quest for profit as the main motivator and individualism are at odds with the social functions of journalism, and with the professional identities of journalists. In the classic *Four Theories of the Press* (Siebert 1956), none of the theories—authoritarian, libertarian, communist and social responsibility—refers to money-making. In the libertarian conception, the press operates in a free-market environment, but even here money is seen as a "hygiene" factor rather than a motivator (Herzberg 1964), i.e. it is present for the maintenance of journalism rather than as motivation for better journalism. Moreover, the individualism at the heart of entrepreneurialism seems antithetical to the main function of journalism as serving the public interest—regardless of how one defines this public interest. While Jarvis may be looking at money or profit only as a means for sustaining journalism, his emphasis on the immediate transformation of ideas into monetary capital points to a prioritization of money and moreover of "quick" money acquired through investment capital—this is seen as the only criterion for success.[1] Entrepreneurialism is not about the idea so much as it is about the "capture", the potential for monetization in the idea. Furthermore, it does not consider the social labour that has given rise to the idea in the first place.

The emphasis on money and profit, and on individualism, as the main motivators and sources of innovation, has been criticized by work that focuses on the social creation of value and knowledge. Indeed, as Castells argued, entrepreneurial culture rests on techno-meritocracy, hacking and communitarianism. None of these relies on money and none of these relies on single individuals, yet all three of them are vital for the creation of knowledge upon which entrepreneurialism subsequently capitalizes. Jarvis, however, seems to have replaced the focus on knowledge and value creation with a quest for profit and a focus on the bottom-line.

In *Cognitive Capitalism*, Yann Moulier-Boutang (2012) argues that capitalism has entered a new phase, characterized by the accumulation of immaterial capital, the dissemination of new knowledge and the driving role of the knowledge economy. For Moulier-

Boutang, the main source of growth within cognitive capitalism is the production of new knowledge, as knowledge and science form the precondition for innovation. Growth depends on the capture of the "interactive cognitive processes of social cooperation and of tacit knowledge" (51). However, knowledge and its production rely not on individuals, but on cooperation and social exchange. "The production of new knowledge", argues Moulier-Boutang, "can only be done on the basis of an accumulation of knowledge that is not reduced to technical material means" (55). In other words, knowledge resides not only in books or archives but in social relationships and "on the mobilization of collective brain activity" (56). In this emphasis on cooperation, Moulier-Boutang is following Benkler (2006), whose *The Wealth of Networks* shows how co-operation through networks and peer-to-peer exchanges can form a viable alternative organization in contrast to both hierarchical and market-based models. Benkler (2006) further argues that an emphasis on money, profit and personal gain are neither necessary nor sufficient motivational factors for social production.

Taking into account the social nature of the production of all knowledge, alongside the public function of journalism, it is clear that an entrepreneurial model that myopically focuses on monetization and the individual innovator is inadequate and problematic, and may end up backfiring. To make this point clearer, we can use one of Moulier-Boutang's metaphors: for Moulier-Boutang (2012, 117), previous forms of capitalism have managed to capture the productive labour of worker-bees when they make honey, but cognitive capitalism hasn't yet managed to find ways of capturing the value of their efforts at "pollination", this creative encounter that generates something else. Entrepreneurialism seeks to do precisely this: to capture this value, but without realizing that this is part of broader social and cultural processes of cooperation and exchange in the production of knowledge and information. Moreover, in attempting to capture value at this level, it may end up imposing new enclosures which are inimical to this mode of production.

Indeed this is very clearly played out in journalism, where we can see the tensions involved, when on the one hand there are the representatives of the old order of "industrial journalism", such as Rupert Murdoch's News Corporation, who want to impose paywalls, enclosing journalism, while on the other the new gurus such as Jarvis who want to capture the outcome of pollination, but without taking into account the collaborative and synergistic processes that feed into it. Wark (2015), speaking more generally about the ruling class, argues that they are now "forking" or dividing: "one [is] still dependent on extracting surplus labor power and selling commodities; one dependent instead on asymmetries of information and commanding the processes of social creation themselves". While perhaps the mutation of the ruling class in Wark's quote may be better applied to a comparison between News Corporation and new digital corporations such as Google and Facebook, entrepreneurial journalism can be positioned as part of this, insofar as it seeks to reproduce it at a smaller scale, drawing inspiration precisely from Google, Apple and the Silicon Valley model. These tensions both at the level of retaining journalistic values and profit maximization, as well as within cognitive capitalism itself, may help to account for the very large number of failures in journalistic "start-ups".[2]

Could a different way of producing journalism, one that relies firmly on its social character and on cooperation, help to overcome some of these tensions? This is the question explored in the remainder of this article, initially in conceptual and then empirical terms.

Cooperative Journalism: Journalism as Part of the Commons

The public character and functions of journalism suggest that viewing it as any other kind of commodity may not be appropriate. Some of the tensions explored previously stem from precisely the failure to consider the specificity of journalism and reversing its relationship with money. To recap, even in the liberal conception of journalism, which relies on the position of journalism in a free, *laissez-faire* market, money is seen as a means to an end, which is free and independent journalism, rather than as an end in itself. Yet, in the dominant version of entrepreneurial journalism as expressed by Jarvis, money has become an end in itself and a criterion for journalistic success. We propose here that journalism may be re-conceptualized as part of the Commons. While the Commons is difficult to define and subject to contention, we follow Bollier (2014; Bollier and Helfrich 2012) here in understanding the Commons as referring to a self-organized system which allows communities to manage resources with minimal or no reliance on the market or the state; the Commons can further refer to a sector of the economy that generates value in ways that are often taken for granted and to the wealth in both material (e.g. the oceans, rivers and forests) and immaterial (e.g. knowledge, cultural works and so on) terms that people have inherited and must pass on to future generations either intact or enhanced. Cooperative enterprises that run for-benefit as opposed to for-profit can be part of the Commons, because they participate in market exchange but they do not subscribe to the market model of profit and capital accumulation, while they also operate outside the state, insofar as receiving minimal to no public funds.

Cooperative enterprises have experienced a renaissance in recent years, in part because of the post-2008 economic crisis and in part because of a shift in culture and mentality. According to Kostakis and Bauwens (2014), neoliberal economics has integrated the market-state into a single entity, considering only competition, individualism and private property as drivers of growth and innovation. Frustration with this lack of consideration of any positive human traits may have contributed to the re-emergence of new economic forms based on equity, including the cooperative economy, the social economy and the solidarity economy (Kostakis and Bauwens 2014). While the differences between these new forms are not very clear, they all share an emphasis on the creation of use value and serving the community, pooling in common resources and operating for benefit rather than for profit.

Following from this, cooperative journalism can be seen as operating in the social domain but outside the market and the state, relying on the social for survival but without enclosing it for profit. In fact, Boyle (2012) has argued that cooperative ownership and management of the media has a distinct set of advantages because they can be financially resilient, invest in the community, and offer accountability and trust. Cooperatives can be owned by journalists, by readers or by another combination, including technical support staff, distributors, advertisers—anyone who has a stake in the process. All participants in the cooperative are compensated and have a share in the income generated. This allows for a truly collaborative news production process, in which all participants are equal. Moreover, cooperatives have a different management style based upon the mutual needs and abilities of their members, and in which responsibility for production, management and finances is shared by all.

The International Cooperative Alliance (ICA) defines cooperative enterprises as: "autonomous association(s) of persons united voluntarily to meet their common economic, social and cultural needs and aspirations, through a jointly owned and democratically controlled enterprise" (ICA, n.d.). Cooperatives are held together by six core values and seven guiding principles, all revolving around ideas of equality, democracy and community. Specifically, cooperatives are underpinned by "the values of self-help, self-responsibility, democracy, equality, equity and solidarity"; these values are operationalized through seven principles: voluntary and open membership; democratic member control; member economic participation; autonomy and independence; education, training and information; cooperation among cooperatives; and concern for community (ICA, n.d.).

Studies have found that historically cooperatives are more resilient in times of crisis, typically performing better than their non-cooperative counterparts (Birchall and Ketilson 2009). For example, cooperative financial institutions, banks and credit unions performed better than shareholder-owned banks in the financial crisis of 2008, requiring less if any public funding for bailouts, while on the whole they enjoy higher survival rates in crises, both for start-ups and for established cooperatives (Birchall and Ketilson 2009). One of the reasons that cooperatives are more resilient is that they can function on lower incomes and minimal rates of profit. While an investor may never invest in an idea that brings benefit to a community but little return on investment, community members, or journalists and readers, may well invest with a view to reaping the benefit. The question of trust and accountability is crucial, especially in a context where the trust and credibility of mainstream news media is continuously under question (Leveson 2012). While people tend to trust more public service news outlets such as the BBC (United Kingdom), NPR (United States) or RTÉ (Ireland) (see Pew Research Center 2014; Reuters Institute 2015), it is evident that they may also invest their trust on cooperative news producers that are independent of both private and state interests. Moreover, in encountering the perennial problem of how to get online readers to pay for free content, cooperatives are better placed again because, from the point of view of readers, they are more likely to part with their money when they know it is not going to a rich and impersonal corporation (Boyle 2012).

While these are the main operating premises of cooperative journalism, we lack empirical detail as to how they work in practice. Moreover, if cooperative journalism is to be pegged as an alternative to entrepreneurial journalism, then we must also examine the extent to which cooperatives actually innovate and the forms this innovation takes. The next section provides an empirical sketch of journalistic cooperatives in a given national context, that of Greece.

Methodology

The focus on Greece is important, as it constitutes a very specific context, full of tensions and unrest, a veritable playground for the kind of "creative destruction" imposed by neoliberalism and austerity politics, and in which both the market and the state are in deep crisis (Lapavitsas 2010; Katrougalos 2012). This context invites increased risk taking and social experimentation, possibly contributing to the development of new solutions to old problems. It is also a context in which journalism becomes uniquely important in—and necessary for—society to continue to function. Finally, notwithstanding its particularities in terms of the media and journalistic landscape (Papathanassopoulos 2001; Hallin and Mancini 2004; Siapera, Papadopoulou, and Archontakis 2015), the Greek context can constitute an important lesson in financial survival and resilience for the media sector.

In this study, we have adopted a mixed ethnographic model in order to study the emerging sector of cooperative journalism. In looking for such initiatives, our work was made more difficult by the fact that there are no formal and published attempts to map and classify journalistic and media cooperatives in Greece. According to one of our interviewees, Angeliki Boubouka, there are seven social cooperative enterprises ("Koinsep"[3]) connected to the media, and 26 more cooperative news outlets that operate under different legal statuses but which are based on cooperative principles and are connected to the social economy.[4]

The article is based on an in-depth analysis of four cooperative journalistic ventures in Greece, including one print and online (*Efimerida Syntakton*—Efsyn), two online media (Alterthess and The Cricket) and one FM and Web radio station (Flash FM), and on a secondary analysis of materials across the other cooperatives, with an emphasis on those with a clear journalistic character. Efsyn and Flash are cooperative reincarnations of previous commercial media, while Alterthess and The Cricket represent efforts of the younger generation of journalists. The research relies on material collected through in-depth interviews with seven journalists (head editors and reporters) of these initiatives as well as on material from informal discussions with other workers from different departments (such as accountants, marketing and sales people, and so on).

The interviewees were all directly involved in setting up and running these cooperatives, and were all highly educated. In terms of gender, three were women and four were men. The interviews typically lasted for over an hour, with themes covering the role and function of journalism in society, and especially in the context of the crisis in Greece, the difference between the operation of cooperative ventures as opposed to for profit outlets, the relations between the various parts of the organizations, questions of finance, sustainability and trust, the news values and aesthetics underpinning these projects, and the relationship with readers. These themes were then used to guide the analysis.

Informal discussions in contrast had no formal structure and were held with other workers in the cooperatives; the discussions asked more personal questions about the specific trajectories of some workers in these cooperatives, clarifications about specific aspects, for example, about balancing the books, finding additional revenue sources, working shifts or distribution issues, and so on. These discussions were meant to add detail and nuance to the research, but also to clarify and get an insight into day-to-day practical matters. These informal discussions were part of a broader ethnographic approach, which was used in order to get a firsthand experience of the relationships, the hierarchies and the various procedures followed.

The ethnographic observations took place in the spring and summer of 2015, with one of the authors (Papadopoulou) visiting the premises of Efsyn, Flash FM and Alterthess; notes were kept on the physical structure of the newsrooms, the ways in which workers addressed each other and the general work climate. The Cricket does not have a formal newsroom. It should be noted that the spring and summer of 2015 were notable for the ongoing negotiations between the Syriza government and the European Commission, European Central Bank and International Monetary Fund institutions, the declaration of a controversial referendum and the eventual U-turn of the left-wing Syriza government on its fiscal policies. In this context, journalists were extremely busy covering these unfolding events. In general, the methodology was adjusted to the experimental nature of the ventures, adapting and adjusting to the circumstances surrounding the cooperatives.

The analysis was guided firstly by the theoretical questions discussed above concerning the tensions involved between journalism as a public service, its quest for economic survival, and the need to be dynamic and innovative. Secondly, the analysis was guided by the empirical material, with some issues and themes emerging as more central than others.

Journalistic Cooperatives in Action

This section discusses cooperative enterprises in Greece, starting with the impetus for their formation, their founding principles, their structure and organization, the values that guide their operation, the professional identities of the journalists working there, the kind of journalism they practice, and their views of and relationships with readers. All these are closely interlinked and mutually determining. In concluding this section, we discuss where we locate the innovation aspect of cooperatives, the role of technology and the possibilities for the future.

Impetus—Why Cooperatives?

All our interviewees told a story of deep and deepening crisis both in the news media sector and more broadly in society. The media in Greece have been hit very hard by the economic crisis that has also been added to the ongoing crisis in the media sector in general (Siapera et al. 2015). Lay-offs, deteriorating working conditions and wage cuts have contributed to low morale and a tendency to exit the profession. Moreover, the field has undergone a tremendous loss of symbolic capital, evidenced in the historic low levels of trust—15 and 23 per cent for television and print media, respectively, compared to European Union averages of 48 and 41 per cent (Eurobarometer 2013). Journalists spoke of a disconnect between mainstream media and Greek society, evidenced in both the loss of trust and in falling newspaper circulations and closure of titles.

It is against this context that cooperatives have emerged as a response to a multilayered need. The need for journalists to express themselves, to express a portion of society which stood on the sidelines, to inform citizens who have lost confidence in traditional media, to find a means to survive and to provide a creative response to the crisis. Laid-off journalists gave up hope of ever finding a new job, while a younger generation of journalists never even broke into the profession despite qualifications to degree level in journalism.

Parallel to their need to make a living, these journalists experienced a very pressing personal need to express themselves freely, outside the confines of mainstream media, in which the working conditions were oppressive, with strict hierarchies and limited opportunities to pursue their own interests. Disconnect between mainstream media and Greek society is interpreted by our respondents as denoting a need to address and fill in this gap, through providing trustworthy and credible news and though giving a voice to these parts of society that are typically ignored. Finally, the continued frustration experienced in the context of crisis, the multiple dead ends and spiral of depression led to the need to develop more creative responses independently of the mainstream media, which are seen as part of the crisis. It is in the combination of all these elements that we can locate the impetus for the creation of cooperatives.

In Flash FM and Web radio, unpaid workers took over the station and its equipment from the bankrupt previous commercial enterprise. Efsyn emerged out of a collective of laid-off journalists following the high-profile bankruptcy and closure of one of the historical Greek newspapers, *Eleftherotypia*. The Cricket and Alterthess emerged out of the need of a group of mostly younger journalists—all in precarious employment or unemployed—to find an outlet for their creativity and a means by which they can operate professionally as journalists. Need is therefore at the starting point of these cooperatives, and in this manner their emergence has been more organic and less forced than in typical entrepreneurial start-ups. The following quotes illustrate this dynamic:

> We began with the ambition to do something that we really like, to write something we really like, to capture what we are going through, what the Greek society is going through, to have a very particular aesthetic … so that we all do exactly what we want to do. (The Cricket)

> We have experienced the multifaceted consequences of the crisis in Greece, especially in the field of the press and we took the initiative to intervene decisively in the course of events. (PressPublica)

> We are interested in a news collective that gives voice and expression to all those excluded from the mainstream media. (Alterthess)

Structure and Finances—How Do Cooperatives Work?

As mentioned previously, the broader legal and regulatory context of journalistic cooperatives in Greece is not very clear. Cooperatives cannot be categorized in a rigid manner because they are live experiments. Therefore they cannot be defined by a single ownership structure; for example, in Efsyn workers are the majority shareholders, but they have offered shares to their readers. Some, for example The Cricket and PressPublica, have a formal status as a social cooperative company [Koinsep] with a legally binding remit for serving the public and collective interest. Others may have a different legal status, for example as private capital companies ("IKE") in which this capital can be offered in kind. All these outlets, however, operate on the basis of equity and parity between their members. In terms of internal organization, the two main elements identified include a horizontal structure and a democratic style of decision making. In terms of income and revenue there are mixed models, but with emphasis on the long term, independence and longevity of the cooperative.

Revenue generation is a crucial question but all our respondents were adamant that they "are not in this for the money". Some are working without pay while others work as freelancers elsewhere while still contributing to the coop, considering this work as their investment for the future. Advertising is still a main source of revenue. Some have decided not to accept advertisements from some fields, for example banking, as this may compromise them. Others, for example Efsyn, have decided to prioritize their economic survival and accept advertisements from across the board, only to find that some companies do not want to advertise with them because of their critical stance. The kind of advertising that seems to work is local advertising or similar, socially based firms, such as cooperative supermarkets, restaurants and craft shops, all of which participate in a new social economy, consciously supporting one another—this is the case in Alterthess.

Other sources include collaboration with other media—for example, Alterthess offers media services to Sto Kokkino, a radio station owned by the political party Syriza. Some ask for donations or contributions from their readers, while others also rely on public subsidies, donations from charitable institutions or bid for European Union grants—all of these on a non-exclusive basis, as it is important for them not to rely on a single source of income because this would generate dependency and compromise their independence. They have avoided bank loans and all operate with very low budgets. Because they rely on their members they have no other staffing costs. As an Efsyn informant put it: "We have borne any losses ourselves. The debts are for us, the partners, and it has been our choice not to mortgage the project to banks, lenders or traders". Any profits obtained are reinvested in the project itself, thus creating conditions for further growth. Moreover, this independence is seen as contributing to re-establishing trust and credibility which then become trading tools. "This alone can trade better than having anchors in the market" one of our Flash informants told us, referring to this independence and its association with more credibility.

All have modest expectations and some have been reasonably successful given the current economic climate in Greece. For example, Alterthess has managed to pay salaries to four people, while Efsyn is comprised of 140 partners and has managed to become second in terms of circulation in the three years of its existence.

For all our respondents, there was no question of "fast money" or "quick exits" as in the entrepreneurial model. They consider that they have invested more than money: energy, time, effort and hope, and they do not expect to recoup these immediately or to transform them into money or capital. Here, the central notion of cognitive capitalism that equates ideas and cognitive labour with money is undermined, as respondents are looking for returns in the long term, over time, and not only or necessarily in monetary returns. As we see below, this investment in time has also found an outlet in the kind of journalism they practice and in their relationships with readers. As one respondent expressed it, "this kind of medium needs time, persistence and hard work" (Alterthess).

So far as the internal organization of cooperatives is concerned, the main decision-making process is taken in assembly meetings, where members meet as peers. This is how one of our respondents described the process: "At the meetings we are all equal. We propose a theme and through discussions and different opinions sometimes this topic completely changes compared to the original proposal" (The Cricket). In others, there is a rotating process, where all participate in decision making but they rotate in terms of the duties and responsibilities they have. In Efsyn, a voting process determines the chief editor, section editor, and so forth. One interesting development is that this flattening of hierarchies exists beyond professional boundaries, so that all those contributing have an equal status. This includes, for example, photographers, graphic and Web designers, technicians and financial staff. While this may make the everyday operation somewhat less flexible, our respondents consider this kind of decision-making process as fundamental to the cooperative.

Values and Identities: What Distinguishes Cooperative Journalists?

Most self-descriptions of cooperatives refer to traditional journalistic values of fairness, accuracy, pluralism and transparency. However, based on the declining rates of trust and falling circulations, they argue that mainstream media in Greece have failed to adhere to the basic journalistic values and that therefore they are the only ones that function properly as journalistic institutions. Moreover, they differ in two important and related respects: they prioritize the public interest and they do not compete with other journalists or news outlets; rather they network and collaborate. This collaboration, however, is limited to those who operate in the same or similar terms, as they would otherwise consider the use of their material by others, for example commercial media, as exploitative.

This is clear in the Creative Commons licensing used by most of the cooperatives, but also in some of the collaborations between them, such as the one between Alterthess and Sto Kokkino, in sharing each other's articles through their social media accounts, and in the case of Flash, hosting the Web radio. Another aspect is that some of these cooperatives, for example The Cricket, act as umbrella organizations offering the possibility for freelancers to do commercial jobs for third parties and paying their VAT through the VAT registration of the cooperative. This offers a kind of social benefit offered to other journalists, especially those in precarious positions, and it differs from the typical competition that exists among journalists—as for example that described by Tuchman (1978).

Cooperativism and self-management are at the heart of these media and the identities of their workers, who take pride in being pioneers in this field and are often critical of their mainstream counterparts.

> We concluded that our greatest weapon is our identity as a radio station owned by its workers. (Flash)

> We are *sui generis* … and to an extent this may have to do with the self-perception of most journalists, their limits, the way in which they operate … they want a boss, not interested in taking it upon themselves. (Efsyn)

The realization that they can take their fate in their own hands has been liberating and empowering. In parallel, cooperative journalists have an organic connection with their medium which, on the one hand, involves stronger feelings of loyalty, and on the other, as they put it, makes them feel that they "grow with it": "it's like a living thing, an organism, our child, it grows, it evolves and we evolve with it" (Efsyn). There is, on the one hand, an identification with the medium and, on the other, a realization that this is something that has emerged through the collaboration, bringing together people with the sum being more than the parts. "Osmosis" is the word used by our Efsyn informants and it has clear resonance with Moulier-Boutang's notion of pollination discussed previously. Furthermore, metaphors such as "our child", an organism, a "living thing", point to the biopolitical turn within cognitive capitalism which sees workers producing not only commodities but social and affective relationships (Lazzarato 1996; for journalism, see Siapera and Iliadi 2015). Instead of reproducing exploitative relations of wage labour and capital accumulation or profit, these journalists produce a new set of social relationships both among themselves and between themselves and their readers, as we shall see shortly. In these terms, they consider themselves as part of a broader social movement towards more just forms of social organization, and as such their professional identities are interlinked with their social and political identities, especially in the context of the protracted crisis in Greece. These shifts or additions in values and identities are also clear in the journalistic practices and contents of these outlets, as discussed below.

Journalistic Practices: What is Covered and How?

The freedom over what they choose to write, the motivation to provide an outlet for the voiceless or those marginalized and ignored by the mainstream, points to changes in journalistic practices and themes. The first main change observed is the investment of time and the extent to which certain themes are covered. Rather than the ephemeral and occasionally superficial treatment of news topics in the commercial media, cooperative journalists take pride in focusing on certain issues considered important, and following them up continuously and with dedication. In addition, they balance a tension between what is of direct concern to citizens and what they themselves want to write about. Given that such cooperatives constitute important outlets for the self-expression of journalists, they pursue topics that interest them in particular. However, they also need to take into account what interests the public and what they may need. This tension is dissolved by cooperative journalists assuming a position within society and "sensing its pulse"—as mentioned earlier, the starting point of these outlets was need, both the need of journalists to work and the need of the public to be informed. Instead of following a "populist" route, they seek to stay true to the principles and values that they initially set alongside their need for personal and creative expression. Commitment, authenticity and staying true to their values, as well as responding to social needs, underpin their journalistic practices, the topics they cover and the angle they cover them from, which is always from the point of view of social benefit.

Some examples may illustrate these points. Efsyn's journalistic remit is to include as many voices as possible in their paper and site, constituting a pluralistic news platform for all opinions; "sometimes even reactionary ones", as one Efsyn interviewee told us. However, they agreed from the start that they would consider Golden Dawn—the extreme nationalistic and fascist political party in Greece—as a criminal organization rather than a political party, notwithstanding the fact that they had about 17 elected Members of Parliament. They never offered a platform to any of them or any of their supporters, even when other Greek media interviewed them, or published lifestyle photos of them to generate more readers and shares. In another instance, another Efsyn interviewee commented:

> We generally write about everything, gold, banks, refineries etc. [NB all very controversial topics in Greece, involving scandals and corruption]. This has a cost, our advertising fell, some cut us off completely, but we are never going to change our journalism for money.

In another example, Alterthess has been persistently reporting on a controversial goldmine in Skouries in northern Greece at a time when no Greek medium would touch the story because one of its shareholders is a media oligarch. Other controversial topics covered from a social benefit perspective include immigration and the refugee crisis—for example, an Alterthess interviewee was one of the first journalists to go to the Greek border with Macedonia because she was texted by a refugee support activist in order to cover the humanitarian emergency. Finally, they are all very committed to issues of labour rights and regularly report on cases of irregular employment, unpaid workers, strikes, and so forth.

Readers

Serving the public interest and working for social benefit would be pointless if readers, the public or society are not somehow involved in the process. Throughout this study, the presence of the public was very keenly felt. Rather than absent or in the background, readers were frequently very directly involved, their input highly appreciated and taken into account. The point of investing time and effort in pursuing some kinds of topics, especially those that deal with questions of social justice, have meant that a central aspect for cooperative journalism is to build and sustain social relationships. The purpose of journalistic practices such as those discussed in this article, staying true to their values and prioritizing social benefit have, as a goal and an outcome, the building and maintenance of social bonds and the assumption of a position as social advocate and mediator. What is striking is not so much the emphasis on social relationships, as this is something that is gaining currency in discussions of, for example, "reciprocal journalism" (Lewis, Holton, and Coddington 2014); instead it is that these relationships are not a means to an end (the commercial success of the medium) but as an end in themselves. This is why authenticity and sticking to values are considered so important by our interviewees. Spending or rather investing time in speaking and in dialogue with people, following up on previous reports and showing care for the community are all crucial.

These relationships are built on the basis of establishing trust and through being part of the society itself rather than a separate class or professional caste looking from above or outside. The following excerpt clearly confirms this point:

> We never planned to adjust our contents to the readers' preferences. In the course however we discovered [NB through social media analytics] that they like what we like to write about. (The Cricket)

So for The Cricket, topics such as immigration and the "other" which they consciously focused on turned out to be the ones most read and shared. This points to the organic relationship and bonds they have built with their readers. In another example, Alterthess was approached for help by a victim of homophobic violence precisely because of their reputation as a socially committed news outlet which would not exploit this story in sensationalist terms. Out Alterthess informant told us that she helped the victim find a lawyer and submit a relevant police report. In this respect, Alterthess is fulfilling an important social role.

Their status as cooperatives directly contributes to this social standing. For example, our interviewees in Efsyn showed us the results of market research conducted in June 2014, where 93 per cent of their readers knew about their cooperative status, and 87 per cent considered it as a distinct advantage. In these terms, the perception that these media work for social benefit and not for private profit has been pivotal in establishing credibility and trust, thereby contributing to the building and maintenance of social bonds.

Innovation and Success

As we outlined previously, discussions of entrepreneurialism focus on innovation as the level of technology and consider success in terms of "fast money" and return on investment. Instead, where cooperatives locate innovation is at the level of social relationships, and consider success in terms of social benefit and survival. While technology is important for these cooperatives, they prioritize and invest in the kinds of relationships built with one another and with their readers. While entrepreneurial start-ups tend to revolve around a key feature of a single innovator-journalist who will build everything on their own, cooperatives make the most out of their cooperation and collaboration with others, including programmers, Web designers but also management and marketing people. Innovation is a social process that emerges in the bringing together of several social sources, including readers and publics, and in forming a lasting social bond. To use the terminology of innovation studies, cooperative journalism disrupts the existing model of journalism as commodity and reimagines it as a collaborative effort for social benefit. From this point of view, it is an entirely successful model of journalism.

In short, our analysis showed that these cooperative enterprises are concerned with innovation at the level of organizing the newsroom and the division of labour between their members, which revolves around a peer-to-peer rather than a hierarchical model; at the level of financing, where they combine several modes of revenue generation, preventing dependence on one source of income; and at the level of news values embedded in their work, which revolve around servicing the needs of society rather addressing politicians or other journalists. Finally, although all have invested time and effort in thinking their digital presence, they consider technological innovation as rather peripheral to what they are doing and important only to the extent that it allows them to reach all parts of society. These lead to the conclusion that the success of cooperative journalistic ventures hinges on the kind of journalism they produce and its position in the social domain rather than on technological innovation and monetary gain. While as Bruno and Nielsen (2012) have shown, survival is success for journalistic start-ups, our study further showed that in the context of Greece, social contribution, the building of trust and the re-articulation of journalism as a social process are considered equally fundamental.

Conclusions: Are Cooperatives the Future?

This article sought to contextualize entrepreneurial journalism in broader discussions of societal shifts associated with the increasing importance of knowledge production and innovation. Such discussions show the one-sided version of entrepreneurialism interpreted as market success measured in capital returns and instigated by a single individual entrepreneur omits the broader picture of innovation as a social process, and value and knowledge creation as a collaborative social effort. Moreover, the equation of success with money and the emphasis on the market are in a state of tension with the public mission of journalism and its social orientation—journalism is not only for customers but for every citizen.

Focusing on cooperative journalistic enterprises in Greece, we have sought to outline another model for journalism that prioritizes social benefit rather than profit and which repositions journalism as an organic part of society rather than as a cut-off professional caste. Specifically, we found that cooperatives are founded on need, social, economic and creative; that they operate as flat hierarchies; that they value and prioritize collaboration; that they consider and reframe journalism as a social process of building and sustaining relationships; that they are organically linked with society; and that success is first of all social success, the production of social benefit and the servicing of the needs that gave rise to the cooperative.

Can this be a model for journalism more broadly? The complexities of socio-political and economic organization preclude an easy answer to this question. For thinkers such as Bauwens and Kostakis (2014; Kostakis and Bauwens 2014), it is time that we transition to a new model of social organization based on peer-to-peer exchange and collaboration which relies on a form of open cooperativism. They, therefore, see the future of society as relying on the expansion of the for-benefit model across all areas of production. Regardless of whether one agrees with this, the shift towards cognitive capitalism and the tensions it involves points to the need to generate new models of organizing and value creation. These tensions and complexities further point to the inadequacy of simplistic ideas of individual entrepreneurship and technological solutionism as providing answers. A cooperative model is firmly oriented towards social benefit, relies on, and reinvests in, society, thereby adding more value to journalism. From this point of view, cooperative journalism constitutes an attractive future for a journalism that wishes to re-establish its social role and its position in the Commons.

DISCLOSURE STATEMENT

No potential conflict of interest was reported by the authors.

NOTES

1. In his class in 2009, Jarvis had his students come up with an idea, an "app, Web site, blogging tool, etc.—and convince the jury (a group of media types, like *The New York Times's* Brian Stelter and David Carr, along with startup founders have made appearances on it) to award you grant money from a pool of about $50,000" (Abad-Santos 2011).
2. Henry Blodget of the *Business Insider* (2013) estimates a success rate of 3–5 per cent among all start-ups.
3. Social cooperative enterprises (Koinseps) are required by law to return up to 35 per cent of any profits as productivity bonuses for workers, whereas the majority of profits (at least 60 per cent) must be allocated to investment and job creation. The remaining 5 per cent remains as a reserve.
4. The seven social cooperative enterprises are: Ekdoseis ton synadelfon, https://ekdoseisynadelfwn.wordpress.com/; Margot Filmhouse, http://www.margotfilmhouse.com; City of Errors, http://cityoferrors.com; FreeThoughtGroup, http://synek.gr; The Cricket, http://thecricket.gr; Hackademy, hackademy.gr; RedOnAir, http://redonair.com; and PressPublica, http://www.presspublica.gr/. The 26 ones with a different legal status include: chimeres.info/, Chimeres, Web radio; www.lacooperativa.gr/, La cooperativa, Web radio; www.toradiofono.gr/, To radiofono, Web radio; www.dromografos.org/, Dromografos, an alternative news collective; www.radiobubble.gr/, Radiobubble, Web radio; 360pedia.gr/, 360 Pedia, educational news; www.shedia.gr/, *Schedia*, magazine produced and sold by homeless persons; omniatv.com/, OmniaTV, collaborative news platform; enfo.gr/radio, Enfo Radio, Web radio; efsyn.gr, *Efimerida Syntakton*, editors' newspaper and news site; http://www.doc4life.net/, Doc4life, cooperative photographic agency; http://96radiofm.blogspot.gr/, Flash 96 FM, Web and FM radio; http://www.ertopen.com/, Ert Open, news site; http://www.metadeftero.gr/, MetaDeutero, Web radio; http://www.chronosmag.eu/, *Chronos*, online magazine; http://www.pints.gr/, *Pints*, online magazine; http://www.humbazine.gr/, *Humba*, sports magazine; http://www.microvia.gr/, Microvia, news site; http://www.empneusi.gr/, Empneusi, FM and Web radio; http://www.okeanews.fr/, Okea News, news site in French; http://maga.gr/, *Maga*, e-magazine and Web radio; http://www.trollradio.gr/, Troll Radio, Web radio; http://multikulti.gr/, Multikulti.gr, multicultural news site; idreamteam.gr, iDREAMteam, sports news site; www.musicsociety.gr, Music Society WebradiON, Web radio; fractalart.gr, *Fractal*, online magazine.

REFERENCES

Abad-Santos, Alexander. 2011. What It's Like to Learn Journalism from Jeff Jarvis. *The Wire*, September 27. http://www.thewire.com/business/2011/09/what-its-learn-journalism-jeff-jarvis/42176/.

Audretsch, David B. 2007. "Entrepreneurship Capital and Economic Growth." *Oxford Review of Economic Policy* 23 (1): 63–78.

Bauwens, Michel, and Vassilis Kostakis. (2014) From the Communism of Capital to Capital for the Commons: Towards an Open Co-operativism." *Triple-C: Communication, Capitalism & Critique*, 12(1). http://www.triple-c.at/index.php/tripleC/article/view/561.

Benkler, Yochai. 2006. *The Wealth of Networks*. New Haven, MA: Yale University Press.

Birchall, J., and L. H. Ketilson. (2009), *Resilience of the Cooperative Business Model in Times of Crisis: International Labor Organization*. Sustainable Enterprise Programme. http://www.ilo.org/wcmsp5/groups/public/—ed_emp/—emp_ent/documents/publication/wcms_108416.pdf.

Bloget, Henry. 2013. "Dear Entrepreneurs: Here's How Bad Your Odds Of Success Are." *Business Insider*, May 28. http://www.businessinsider.com/startup-odds-of-success-2013–5?IR=T.

Bollier, David. 2014. "The Commons as a Template for Transformation." *Great Transition Initiative*. http://www.greattransition.org/publication/the-commons-as-a-template-for-transformation.

Bollier, David, and Silke Helfrich, eds. 2012. *The Wealth of the Commons*. Amherst, MA: Levellers Press.

Boyle, Dave. 2012. *Good News: A Co-operative Solution to the Media Crisis*. Cooperatives UK. http://www.uk.coop/sites/storage/public/downloads/good_news_-_fresh_ideas_2.pdf.

Bruno, Nicola, and Rasmus Klein Nielsen. 2012. *Survival is Success: Journalistic Online Start-ups in Western Europe. RISJ Challenges*. Oxford, UK: Reuters Institute for the Study of Journalism, University of Oxford.

Castells, Manuel. 2001. *The Internet Galaxy: Reflections on the Internet, Business and Society*. Oxford: Oxford University Press.

Eurobarometer. 2013. "Media Use in the European Union, 80, CEC." http://ec.europa.eu/public_opinion/archives/eb/eb80/eb80_media_en.pdf.

Hallin, Dan C., and Paolo Mancini. (2004). *Comparing Media Systems: Three Models of Media and Politics*. Cambridge: Cambridge University Press.

Harvey, David. 1989. "From Managerialism to Entrepreneurialism: The Transformation in Urban Governance in Late Capitalism." *Geografiska Annaler. Series B. Human Geography* 71 (1): 3–17.

Herzberg, Frederick. 1964. "The Motivation-Hygiene Concept and Problems of Manpower." *Personnel Administrator* 27 (1): 3–7.

ICA (International Cooperative Alliance). n.d. "What is a Co-op." http://ica.coop/en/what-co-operative.

Jarvis, Jeff. 2009a. "The Future of News is Entrepreneurial." *Buzzmachine*, November 1. http://buzzmachine.com/2009/11/01/the-future-of-journalism-is-entrepreneurial/.

Jarvis, Jeff. 2009b. "The Future for Journalism Will Always Embrace Change." *The Guardian*, November 2. http://www.theguardian.com/media/pda/2009/nov/02/journalism-in-crisis-debate.

Katrougalos, Georgios. 2012. *The Crisis and its Solution*. Athens: Livani. [in Greek].

Koch, James L. and Ross Miller. 2001. *Community: A Comparison of the Silicon Valley-Peninsula Region with the National Social Capital Benchmark Results*. Santa Clara, CA: Report prepared for the Center for Science, Technology, and Society at Santa Clara University.

Kostakis, Vassilis, and Michel Bauwens. 2014. *Network Society and Future Scenarios for a Collaborative Economy*. Basingstoke, UK: Palgrave Macmillan.

Lapavitsas, Costas. 2010. "The Greek Crisis—Politics, Economics, Ethics: A Debate held at the Birkbeck Institute for the Humanities, Birkbeck College, University of London, 5 May 2010." *Journal of Modern Greek Studies* 28 (2): 293–310.

Lazzarato, Maurizio. 1996. "Immaterial Labour." In *Radical Thought in Italy: A Potential Politics*, edited by M. Hardt and P. Virno, 133–47. Minneapolis: University of Minnesota Press.

Leveson, Brian. 2012. *An Inquiry into the Culture, Practices and Ethics of the Press*. London: HMSO.

Lewis, Seth C., Avery E. Holton, and Mark Coddington. 2014. "Reciprocal Journalism: A Concept of Mutual Exchange Between Journalists and Audiences." *Journalism Practice* 8 (2): 229–241.

Moulier-Boutang, Yann. 2012. *Cognitive Capitalism*. Cambridge: Polity Press.

Papathanassopoulos, Stylianos. 2001. "Media Commercialization and Journalism in Greece." *European Journal of Communication* 16 (4): 505–521.

Pein, Cory. 2014. "Amway Journalism." *The Baffler*, July 28. http://www.thebaffler.com/blog/amway-journalism/.

Pew Research Center. 2014. "Political Polarization and Media Habits, report." http://www.journalism.org/files/2014/10/Political-Polarization-and-Media-Habits-FINAL-REPORT-7-27-15.pdf.

Reuters Institute. 2015. "Digital News Report." https://reutersinstitute.politics.ox.ac.uk/sites/default/files/Reuters%20Institute%20Digital%20News%20Report%202015_Full%20Report.pdf.

Siapera, Eugenia, and Ioanna Iliadi. 2015. "Twitter, Journalism and Affective Labour." *Sur le journalisme About journalism Sobre jornalismo* 4 (1): 76–89.

Siapera, Eugenia, Lambrini Papadopoulou, and Fragiskos Archontakis. 2015. "Post-Crisis Journalism: Critique and Renewal in Greek journalism." *Journalism Studies* 16 (3): 449–465.

Siebert, Fred S. 1956. *Four Theories of the Press: The Authoritarian, Libertarian, Social Responsibility, and Soviet Communist Concepts of What the Press Should be and do*. Chicago: University of Illinois Press.

Tuchman, Gaye. 1978. *Making News: A Study in the Construction of Reality*. New York: The Free Press.

Wark, McKenzie. 2015. "Cognitive Capitalism." *Public Seminar*, February 19. http://www.publicseminar.org/2015/02/cog-cap/.

ACCOUNTABILITY AND TRANSPARENCY OF ENTREPRENEURIAL JOURNALISM

Unresolved ethical issues in crowdfunded journalism projects

Colin Porlezza and **Sergio Splendore**

*Crowdfunding is a new business model in which journalists rely—and depend—on (micro-) payments by a large number of supporters to finance their reporting. In this form of entrepreneurial journalism the roles of publisher, fundraiser and journalist often overlap. This raises questions about conflicts of interest, accountability and transparency. The article presents the results of selected case studies in four different European countries—Germany (*Krautreporter*), Italy (*Occhidellaguerra*), the United Kingdom (*Contributoria*) and the Netherlands (*De Correspondent*)—as well as one US example (Kickstarter). The study used a two-step methodological approach: first a content analysis of the websites and the Twitter accounts with regard to practices of media accountability, transparency and user participation was undertaken. The aim was to investigate how far ethical challenges in crowdfunded entrepreneurial journalism are accounted for. Second, we present findings from semi-structured interviews with journalists from each crowdfunding. The study provides evidence about the ethical issues in this area, particularly in relation to production transparency and responsiveness. The study also shows that in some cases of crowdfunding (platforms), accountability is outsourced and implemented only through the audience participation.*

Introduction

The journalistic ecosystem is under pressure and many news organizations are faced with budget cuts, forcing newsrooms to operate with fewer resources (Kaye and Quinn 2010). In responding to issues such as increased complexity, instability and continuous cuts (see, e.g., Curran 2011; McChesney and Nichols 2010; McChesney and Pickard 2011), media organizations have tried to focus on managerial qualities and innovation. Andersson and Wiik (2013, 706) observed that, "manoeuvring in the new, constantly changing business environment of news production gives rise to new demands for business competence within organizations" (see also Gade 2008).

Entrepreneurial skills and personal branding for journalists are increasingly viewed as vital in traditional news organizations but, particularly, for independent and small (online) media outlets. Storey, Salaman, and Platman's (2005) study on staff outsourcing in the media industry, whereby employees become freelance workers, confirmed that the growing entrepreneurialism of journalism may be seen as a consequence of the increased managerial discourse. This trend is reinforced by the growing offer of entrepreneurial journalism classes in journalism schools around the world with the objective of teaching students skills to become independent agents (see Bakker 2014; Claussen 2011; Hunter and Nel 2011; Paniagua Rojano, Gómez Aguilar, and González Cortés 2014).

Entrepreneurial journalism in the form of new digital journalistic start-ups focuses on several success stories but its future remains uncertain (Bruno and Kleis Nielsen 2012). Challenges such as commercial sustainability, positioning within a given media market and the continuity of quality content remain issues decisive for survival. Moreover, entrepreneurial journalism has to deal with another challenge, one that touches the ethical core of journalism: are journalists in start-ups able to distinguish between their different and overlapping roles of publisher, fundraiser and journalist? The boundary—the so-called "Chinese Wall" (Porlezza 2013)—that separates the editorial and commercial interests is crumbling, as individual journalists or small teams in journalistic start-ups wear constantly different hats, making the question about journalistic autonomy crucial.

This article examines issues of journalistic independence and conflicts of interest in the case of crowdfunding, a business model where journalists solicit (small) funds from supporters to finance their journalistic projects (Carvajal, García-Avilés, and González 2012). In these cases, journalists depend on contributions from their backers, thereby putting these backers into a situation of power. This reality raises specific ethical issues with regard to the journalistic responsibility, the editorial autonomy, as well as accountability and transparency of crowdfunded journalism. What kind of media accountability practices are implemented in selected online start-ups? What measures exist in order to assure that funds are used correctly and in a transparent way? Is the public able to participate and is there an ongoing dialogue between the audience and the media professionals?

Based on interviews with journalists that launched successful crowdfunded journalism projects and platforms in four European countries, Germany (*Krautreporter*), Italy (*Occhidellaguerra*), the Netherlands (*De Correspondent*), and the United Kingdom (*Contributoria*), as well as in the United States (Kickstarter), this article investigates the ethical challenges in crowdfunded entrepreneurial journalism. In this study, we apply a theoretical model that describes online media accountability as a three-step process in reference to different phases and aspects of production: actor transparency, production transparency and responsiveness (Domingo and Heikkilä 2012). By shedding light on the application of normative principles to entrepreneurial and crowdfunded journalism, we extend existing research as we focus on potentially dysfunctional aspects of a particular business model, providing evidence of specific ethical challenges particularly in terms of (production) transparency, the implementation of ethical codes and the responsibility towards the supporters.

Crowdfunded Journalism, Accountability and Transparency

In the current media ecosystem, with different forms of journalism and new ways of content production, the issues around appropriate normative principles become even more significant when it comes to new practices such as entrepreneurial journalism. Journalism start-ups are usually built on small teams that handle all activities related to a news organization: from content creation to advertising, from marketing to business administration. There is no institutionalized "separation of Church and State" (see Porlezza 2013), where editorial activities are detached from those concerning the business since team members cover overlapping roles. These journalistic ventures raise new ethical challenges in terms of autonomy and independence. Not surprisingly, media ethicists like Stephen J. Ward (2009) state that conflicts of interest "will soon become the dominant theme in journalism ethics" and that the changes in the media industry, "requires not just a reform of media ethics, it requires radical reform" (Ward 2015, 75f).

Arising from traditional industry disruption and shrinking advertising income, journalism start-ups require alternative financial support. Crowdfunding as a possible business option, however, not only changes the "funding institution" but also raises new ethical issues. Jian and Usher (2014, 155) define crowdfunded journalism as "a novel business model in which journalists rely on micropayments from ordinary people to finance their reporting". Entrepreneurial journalists fill the role of manager and journalist, which raises questions about potential conflicts of interest. The ethical concerns are magnified because potential publics help to realize a project, which suggests that "[i]n crowdfunded journalism, consumers' financial contributions directly affect which stories actually get written" (157).

There are not only issues with regard to overlapping roles but also with reference to the norms of autonomy and independence, in particular, independence from the audience. According to Singer, the dilemma between autonomy and customer-orientation is becoming increasingly relevant:

> The extent to which a start-up's audience-as-customer must be catered to in order to survive financially, balanced against the value of autonomous editorial judgment and the journalist's traditional norm of public service broadly defined, is another topic ripe for exploration from a normative perspective. (Singer 2015, 31)

The traditional norm of public service is also challenged as journalists engaging in crowdfunding campaigns have to renegotiate their roles and self-identity, taking responsibility for—as Aitamurto (2011, 437) notes—"the whole journalistic process, including marketing the pitch and convincing the community about the importance of the story topic". This can result in a delicate balancing act between shaping the crowdfunding campaign to please potential donors and the journalist's own idea of a relevant story. Hunter (2015, 283) analysed these conflicting norms of journalistic autonomy and responsibility towards the funders, concluding that even if many journalists see themselves as providing a public service, "it is a subtle, but important shift from thinking *about* your audience, to thinking *about pleasing* your audience".

Given these conflicts, journalists must declare from the outset what kind of relationship they want to establish with the funders—"including input into story design and development, and outline this in their initial pitch" (Hunter 2015, 284). This declaration is essential, as in a process of "co-creation" it is difficult to equalize between the expectations of journalists and publics (Aitamurto 2013).

It is important to examine the motivations of all parties involved in a crowdfunding campaign. Most published articles in the field of crowdfunding in journalism focused on the motivations of journalists to engage or donors to support a crowdfunding campaign.[1] Aitamurto (2011) analysed the impact of crowdfunding on journalism through a case study of the platform spot.us, focusing on the different requirements for journalists when it comes to fundraising and on donors' motives. She concluded that "donors wanted to participate in a good cause, and they donated to the common good, hoping to make a difference in society" (442). On the other hand, Jian and Usher (2014, 165) found out that "donors to crowdfunded journalism seem to have a taste for specific news topics that are of immediate utility to them in daily living". These results are confirmed by Jian and Shin's (2015) research, in which they looked at motivations behind donors' contributions, concluding that, above all, fun and the "f/f-effect" (family and friends) are most likely to be significant motivations behind contributions.

Based on Aitamurto's (2011) findings, it seems that donors are not particularly interested in the development of a story, given that the community members usually are not returning to the Web page in order to take a look at the advancement of the story or even the finished report. This means, as Aitamurto states, that the public "donates for a cause, and not for mere journalism" (442). The lack of interest in the outcome of a campaign might also indicate that donors are not excessively interested in what the journalists are actually doing with the money they receive—which is not a big incentive for crowdfunded projects to invest in any form of accountability instruments.

Studies from fields such as fan studies indicate (Benecchi 2015; Booth 2015) that there are transparency issues with regard to crowdfunding. Gutiérrez (2013, 102) noted in a recent case study of the *Veronica Mars* movie, based on the successful television show, that film studios used these platforms in order to get their projects funded—without making it transparent who stood behind these campaigns. Briggs (2012, 54) emphasized the importance of letting people know what you do right from the beginning: "As a journalism entrepreneur, it's crucial to be open about the goals and standards of your site".

In journalism, transparency can be understood as *openness*, as the disclosure of a certain kind of information, which would otherwise remain hidden (Karlsson 2010; Kovach and Rosenstiel 2007). Phillips (2010) makes the case for transparency as the new objectivity, in order to help protect public reporting, while Karlsson (2011) sees in the norm of transparency and the interactive potential of digital journalism the opportunity to restore a new journalistic authority.

The concept of accountability refers to journalists taking responsibility for their decisions, actions, consequences and, ultimately, also the quality of their performances. However, accountability not only includes the awareness of the journalists' responsibility, it also relates to what McQuail (2003) calls answerability, or else the voluntary readiness of news organizations to accept criticism and to enter into a dialogue with the public about their news production. There are different instruments of accountability that can be implemented in the Web, and they can be understood as a process (Domingo and Heikkilä 2012). Such instruments include codes of ethics, journalists' profiles, a collaborative news production, but also social media that allow a broader audience participation—and eventually, to reconnect with a declining readership, particularly in a networked digital environment (Loosen and Schmidt 2012).

Methodology

Given the comparative approach, and the diversity of the case studies analysed in this article, our research has opted for integrating three different research methods. First, a content analysis of the websites was undertaken. For each website we investigated two specific aspects: (1) What kind of media accountability instruments are present? and (2) How are commercial and editorial interests kept separate? A preliminary content analysis was accomplished before we commenced semi-structured interviews. The content analysis was replicated at the end of the interviews. The results presented and discussed in this paper are grounded on this second stage of the analysis, given the fact that during the collection of the interviews two websites (*Krautreporter* and *Contributoria*) applied substantial changes in terms of function and layout. The template used for the content analysis recorded the presence/absence of several transparency and accountability instruments (subdivided in three different categories: actor transparency, production transparency and responsiveness).

Secondly, semi-structured interviews with each editor of the newsroom responsible for the respective website were conducted from March 2014 to February 2015. Two semi-structured interviews (Legard, Keegan, and Ward 2003) were conducted face to face (Laura Lesevre from *Occhidellaguerra.it*; Matt McAlister from *Contributoria.com*). Two other interviews (Sebastien Esser from *Krautreporter.de*; Maurits Marteijn from *Decorrespondent.nl*) were conducted online via Skype (Hanna 2012). Each interview was recorded. As key actors in the five selected organizations were interviewed—and since the analysis is based on case studies—we opted to be transparent about the names of the interviewed representatives. On average, the interviews lasted 60 minutes. Due to their interviews policy it was not possible arrange an interview with a representative of Kickstarter (Justin Kazmark).[2] In this particular case, the question focused on manifest practices of transparency and accountability on their website only.

The interviews focused on the following four main topics:

1. Website launch and crowdfunding as new business model.
2. Process of newsmaking (from proposal selection to articles' distribution).
3. Relation between the organization/journalists and their contributors.
4. Accountability and transparency of the entrepreneurial start-ups.

Thirdly, from 15 September 2014 to 31 March 2015 we also collected the 200 most recent tweets produced by each of the Twitter accounts of the four European start-ups, @occhidiguerra, @krautreporter, @decorrespondent and @contributoria (given the broader achievement of Kickstarter we have excluded the US website from this analysis). The tweets, which were codified manually, were analysed on the basis of the interaction with and the involvement offered to followers.

Our analysis is thus to be understood as a textual analysis that investigates the prevalent communicative registers used (broad or narrow casting; aimed to build a community of participants or users/consumers). The aim of this analysis is twofold: (1) verifying whether the interviewees' statements and the social media presentations of their organization correspond; and (2) identifying rhetoric strategies to encourage fundraising as well as distribution of the produced items. This mixed-methods approach is used to answer the following research question:

RQ1: What are the ethical implications in terms of accountability and transparency with regard to crowdfunding journalism platforms and start-ups?

Details of the five websites in our sample are given in Table 1.

Results

Journalistic Principles and Mission Statements

Each website—with the exception of *Occhidellaguerra* and Kickstarter—presents a mission statement that outlines its ideals, the organizational structure as well as the ideology behind the start-up. *De Correspondent* calls it a "manifesto" while *Krautreporter* has a set

TABLE 1
The five websites in our sample

	De Correspondent	***Contributoria***	***Krautreporter***	***Occhidellaguerra***	**Kickstarter**
Founded	2013	2014	2014	2014	2009
Country	The Netherlands	United Kingdom	Germany	Italy	USA
Founders	Rob Wijnberg (editor-in-chief), Harald Dunnink Sebastian Kersten (both of Momkai), Ernst-Jan Pfauth (publisher)	Matt McAlister, Sarah Hartley, Dan Catt	Sebastian Esser (publisher), Philipp Schwörbel (CEO), Alexander von Streit (editor-in-chief)	Andrea Pontini	Perry Chen, Yancey Strickler, Charles Adler
Type of platform	Journalism-specific, online media outlet	Journalism-specific network and platform specialized in collaboration and commissioning	Journalism-specific online media outlet	Journalism-specific online media outlet	General crowdfunding platform
Partnerships	Momkai (digital creative agency), The Groene Amsterdammer (ended in March 2014)	A division of Guardian Media Group	–	*Il Giornale*	–
Contextual information	Raised over €1 million from over 15,000 donors in just 8 days after launching the crowdfunding campaign. Today about 24,000 subscribers	*Contributoria* folded in September 2015	Founded in 2013 as the first journalism-specific crowdfunding platform in Germany. After a relaunch, the site became an online media outlet. About 18,000 subscribers	Raised over €80,000	In 2014 Kickstarter introduced a standalone category with regard to journalism-related projects

of "principles". *Contributoria*, on the other hand, has adopted 10 "community guidelines" that are more specifically focused on the interaction between the users rather than the overall mission of the platform. Kickstarter does not have a mission statement, instead opting for a stricter policy with specific terms of use (also present on *Contributoria*), where the kind of dysfunctional behaviour to be avoided is defined ("This section is a list of things you probably already know you shouldn't do—lie, break laws, abuse people, steal data, hack other people's computers, and so on. Please behave yourself. Don't do this stuff."), and what Kickstarter is not responsible for.

Moreover, in the Kickstarter Basics, the crowdfunding platform outlines its guidelines with regard to accountability, while additional FAQs help to provide backers and creators with necessary answers when it comes to crowdfunding. There are no specific guidelines for journalism-related projects. On the Web page of *Occhidellaguerra* there is no specific mission statement. On the other hand, the online counterpart of *Il Giornale*, that works closely together with the crowdfunding start-up, has a specific code of ethics that is also binding for all its partners, thus also for *Occhidellaguerra.* Yet, the code of ethics presents neither guidelines with regard to crowdfunding, nor tackles any ethical concerns with regard to digital journalism and the relationship between journalists and the audience, except for the general rule to establish a "solid relationship inspired by the general values of fairness, honesty, efficiency and professionalism".[3]

The mission statements of the two crowdfunded projects in Germany and the Netherlands have several points in common (Table 2), which is not surprising, since the journalists behind *Krautreporter* were influenced by the Dutch success story.[4] Neither start-up relies on advertising. They are not devoted to the coverage of daily events, offering background reporting instead. Both stand for certain principles and ideas of how journalism should operate. In the words of *De Correspondent*:

> De Correspondent prioritizes relevance over recentness; looks for alternative ways of doing journalism; ... and takes the ways in which news media shape our perceptions of events into account in its own reporting. (*De Correspondent* Web page[5])

These ideas of journalism—and the principles the start-ups are committed to—are crucial for analysis of accountability and transparency in a specific media outlet. The ideals define the way journalists perceive their professional role, how they deal with the public, and how they understand their commercial activity. Ultimately, such statements —as Ward (2009) affirms—help to protect independence and respond to public scepticism. The Dutch Web page describes its *raison d'être* as follows:

> De Correspondent does not pretend to constitute a substitute for existing, "old" or "mainstream" media; rather, it intends to supplement those media, filling a gap in the current news landscape by looking beyond, above and behind the daily news grind. (*De Correspondent* Web page)

This approach is also confirmed by one of the interviews with a journalist from *De Correspondent*:

> One of our slogans is from news to new. So, the idea behind that is if you offer readers background articles about the news, they would get a better understanding of the world they are living in. One of things that Rob [Rob Wijnberg, editor-in-chief and

TABLE 2
Core principles in the mission statements as outlined by *De Correspondent, Krautreporter* and *Contributoria*

De Correspondent	*Krautreporter*	*Contributoria*
Daily, but going beyond "today's latest"	Every day the stories behind the news	We welcome debate and dissent, but personal attacks (on authors, other users or any individual), persistent trolling and mindless abuse will not be tolerated
From "news" to "new"	Boundless curiosity	We acknowledge criticism of published material, but we will not allow persistent misrepresentation of our community and our members to be published on our website
Ideals over ideology	Together we are Krautreporter	We understand that people often feel strongly about issues debated on the site, but we will consider removing any content that others might find extremely offensive or threatening
Themes and connections	Firsthand information	We reserve the right to redirect or curtail conversations which descend into flame-wars based on ingrained partisanship or generalizations.
Journalism before profit	Authors with attitude	We will not tolerate racism, sexism, homophobia or other forms of hate-speech, or contributions that could be interpreted as such
From Readers to Participants	Personal	We will remove any content that may put us in legal jeopardy
Partners, not advertisers	No advertising	We will remove any posts that are obviously commercial or otherwise spam-like
Like-minded people, not target audiences	A journalistic experiment	Keep it relevant
Ambitious in ideals, modest in claims	Transparency	Be aware that you may be misunderstood, so try to be clear about what you are saying
Fully digital	Made for the internet	The platform is ours, but the conversation belongs to everybody

> founder of the *De Correspondent*] said is that if you only notice the news around you, you don't necessarily learn more about the world. That was one of the most important idea behind *De Correspondent*. (Maurits Marteijn, *De Correspondent*)

> *Krautreporter* is in permanent beta. We are always looking for new journalistic expressions. We understand journalism not as a product, but as a process. (Sebastian Esser, *Krautreporter*)

The German counterpart focuses on the innovative side of the journalistic approach as well, but their idea of journalism is broader because they understand journalism as a process. *Krautreporter* organizes events, workshops and meetings between supporters and authors. Although there are differences when it comes to the start-ups' ideas about journalism, the main discourse focuses on the importance of re-thinking journalism and supporting its independence. In this respect, both *Occhidellaguerra* and *Contributoria* are exemplary cases. That they stress their independence might also be due to the fact that they are the only two journalism projects related to bigger companies such as *Il Giornale* or the Guardian Media Group.

> [*Occhidellaguerra*] has been founded by *IlGiornale.it* to back a journalism without filters and intermediations. (Laura Lesevre, *Occhidellaguerra*)

> Contributoria is an independent journalism community, a place where journalists and writers collaborate on all aspects of the writing process, including commissioning, editing and publication. Our aim is to ensure that the Contributoria platform is a useful place for writers to work. We want to improve the methods for producing quality journalism in the world and to provide financial support for independent voices. (*Contributoria* Web page)

Business and Autonomy

Crowdfunded journalism has been regarded as a competitive arena in which articles are funded based on pure market success (see Aitamurto 2011). In our analysis, this is only partially true. The dynamics in financing entire start-ups or single articles appear to be more complex, given that the market success model applies only to *Contributoria* and Kickstarter. Then again, the two platforms are different with regard to their orientation as the former has a clear journalistic commitment, with the latter being a crowdfunding platform for all different kinds of projects that go beyond journalism. Journalism is actually the category with the second-lowest number of successfully funded projects.[6]

At *Occhidellaguerra* proposals are decided by the newsroom of *Il Giornale.it*. Once the newsroom has decided the stories (rarely more than two), they publish them on the Web page and try to get them funded. The success of each story strongly depends on the relation between the parent company and legacy media *Il Giornale*, *Occhidellaguerra* and its readers. The criteria used to decide what kind of story to launch on the crowdfunding platform are not entirely journalistic. They depend on reflections based on the cost of foreign correspondents as well as the expected success among the audience of *Il Giornale*. In this regard, *Occhidellaguerra* combines different criteria that transcend journalistic interests.

> A foreign correspondent of a newspaper costs only in terms of insurance €1000 each day, to which you have to add also the cost of security. If you add the costs of living this means €5000 per week, still sustainable for a newspaper like ours, but in other places this means, together with the insurance and security €50,000. At this point it is best to rely on freelancers who have different constraints and requests. Thus we opted for crowdfunding. (Laura Lesevre, *Occhidellaguerra*)

In the case of the Dutch and German start-ups, the funding is almost entirely based on the trust between the organization and its future readers. Commercial aspects were in both cases less important, since the crowdfunding campaign was used to fund the entire start-up and not a single story. Obviously, the funds obtained through the crowdfunding campaign determined the commercial success, but once the start-up businesses were formed, news selection was exclusively based on journalistic selection criteria. This conduct is also supported by the fact that the two journalism start-ups do not have advertising on their Web pages in order to prevent any dependencies or influence from advertisers:

> There are no paid ads on *Krautreporter*. Members support *Krautreporter* with €5 a month. This is why *Krautreporter* is completely dependent on its members—and on no one else. (Sebastian Esser, *Krautreporter*)

> To prevent becoming "advertiser-oriented", *De Correspondent* has the subscription fees paid by readers—currently €60 a year—as its main source of income. *De Correspondent* is open to entering into partnerships with third parties, like universities or research institutes, but these partners will have no stake in the profitability of *De Correspondent*, and *De Correspondent* will be fully transparent about the nature and terms of such partnerships. (Maurits Marteijn, *De Correspondent*)

Although being a platform for crowdfunding rather than a crowdfunded journalism project like *De Correspondent* or *Krautreporter*, one of *Contributoria*'s community guidelines focus equally on commercial or spam-like posts:

> Our aim is that this site should provide a space for people to interact with our content and each other, and we actively discourage commercial entities passing themselves off as individuals, in order to post advertising material or links. (*Contributoria* Web page)

Overall, all organizations in the sample share similar commercial goals in terms of financing journalistic items, whether they are start-ups or articles. Some also try to join traditional business models and crowdfunding. With *Occhidellaguerra*, for instance, journalists can earn money by selling their features to other media. At the same time, the start-up tries to enlarge the commercial activities, selling reportages as a sort of wire agency. In this way they generate additional income and are also able to finance the parent company. Kickstarter as a platform claims not to be responsible for any of the projects and simply retains a certain percentage of the funding.

Accountability and Transparency

The organizations included in this study each adopt different strategies with regard to accountability and transparency. The two journalistic start-ups *De Correspondent* and *Krautreporter* mention transparency in their manifesto/principles.

> De Correspondent … is transparent about its journalistic choices and dilemmas; values thorough fact-checking; and takes the ways in which news media shape our perceptions of events into account in its own reporting. (*De Correspondent* Web page)

> If it is possible, our authors make research material and original sources available to all members. We make errors, biases and personal relationships transparent. (*Krautreporter* Web page)

Krautreporter tries to implement the norm of transparency by offering a lot of information on their Web page with regard to potential conflicts of interest. In a section entitled "newsroom guidelines", they state that all participating journalists abide by the code of ethics of the German Press Council. They also declare that articles are not paid for by third parties and that the expenses are entirely covered by the news organization. There is also a section titled, "transparency", where staff members publish information on additional employments or interests to avoid any potential conflicts of interest. Besides a description of the organizational structure and the management, the Web page offers information on how *Krautreporter* uses the generated funds.

> First of all, crowdfunding is far more transparent than the financing of traditional media outlets because everyone can see where the money comes from. Secondly, the funds

> flow before the project is actually carried out, therefore pressure is minimized. (Sebastian Esser, *Krautreporter*)

De Correspondent used this strategy previously. At the end of its first year, the journalism start-up published two reports describing in detail what happened to the world-record in journalism crowdfunding (Pfauth 2014), and the impact of *De Correspondent* on journalism and society (Wijnberg 2014). In the first report, the publisher Ernst-Jan Pfauth focused on the €60 every member paid during the crowdfunding campaign and explained in detail what the money was used for. This strategy in publishing a detailed "accountability report" was also adopted by *Krautreporter*—one of its publishers, Sebastian Esser, wrote a lengthy article on developments in the newsroom, the community and the co-operative as well as the economic situation and what has been done with all the contributions. However, while *Krautreporter* refers to the code of ethics of the German Press Council, there is no equivalent information on *De Correspondent*'s Web page—even if they have a similar newsroom statute.

> We have a written newsroom statute that was based on one very long brainstorm we had about ethics, about the way we wanted to protect our sources and also about the way we write our articles ... To be a good journalist you have to think a lot about these ethical issues, and they came up immediately. (Maurits Martijn, *De Correspondent*)

Unlike *Krautreporter, De Correspondent* offers information about company ownership and finances. Every journalist has his/her own homepage with information on their areas of expertise, specific interests and published articles. *Occhidellaguerra* does not have any specific section on the Web page with regard to transparency. Nonetheless, they publish every single cost-item for the production of every report on a special page called "glass house", and they update constantly the amount of money they raised for each project. *Contributoria* follows a similar approach, with real-time updates of the points system used to fund the different projects. They also publish the history of every article, from the idea to its publication:

> Accountability and transparency is at the very core of what we create, at the bottom of each article there is a link with the very history of the article. You see the production notes. The proposal, the comments from users, the draft they have submitted. We tried to make the openness the very core value of the process. A reader can get a sense coming back at the beginning of the story. (Matt McAlister, *Contributoria*)

The crowdfunding platform Kickstarter is somehow different given its non-exclusiveness for journalism. There are regular updates for every project, but they do not have any mission statement or code of ethics. In September 2012, however, Kickstarter attached a section called "accountability" to their FAQs, in which they address issues of responsibility, quality control or community protection. This section was added due to a critical article in the *all tech considered* blog hosted by NPR.[7] Our research has not identified any further instrument of accountability, which is why the question of transparency is mainly passed on to the creators. Kickstarter limits its own activities to the following:

> We monitor the system. Our Integrity team uses complex algorithms and automated tools to identify and investigate suspicious activity on projects. (www.kickstarter.com/press, accessed May 12, 2015)

The transformed convergence culture online, where both producers and audiences shape media content and influence—as well as challenge—how journalistic standards are understood, are reflected by specific online accountability practices such as the possibility for the public to collaborate with the newsroom. *De Correspondent* in particular (but also *Krautreporter*), due to the fact that it owes its existence to readers, offers them the opportunity to actively participate in certain production areas. Conversation and collaboration with members is therefore regarded as essential. Members can share a so-called expertise title and might end up in the "world's greatest rolodex": correspondents can highlight great contributions (comments) by tagging the author as an expert, who, in turn, may be invited to write articles. *Occhidellaguerra* is an exception, because it does not invite the audience to actively collaborate with the journalists.

Social Media and Responsiveness

Based on Domingo and Heikkilä (2012), responsibility denotes news organizations' reactions to feedback and critique about the media performance and quality of reporting coming from the audience and also through social media. When it comes to responsiveness, *De Correspondent* and *Krautreporter* have a similar approach, given that they both rely heavily on comments from their readers.

> To ask our readers what they think is important or what they would like to change was an idea right from the beginning, we do that on a regular basis. So that was goal number 1, goal number 2 was that we hope that a lot of the things we wanted to change were reflected by the members. Actually, that was the case: a lot of the things we wanted to change ourselves and make better were reflected by the members. Many things we knew ourselves could be better were also raised by approximately 70 per cent of the members. (Maurits Marteijn, *De Correspondent*)

Both *De Correspondent* and *Krautreporter* emphasize the importance of audience members in their mission statements. While *Krautreporter* states that journalists and members of the public *together* form the newsroom, *De Correspondent* declares that readers will not only be asked to contribute in terms of comments, but they will be able to discuss future investments. According to the Dutch Web page, unidirectional communication belongs to the past, while the involvement of the community is vital for a flourishing platform. But even if both start-ups stress the importance of interacting with their readers, there are some dysfunctional side-effects:

> It's hard to convince everyone that the comment section on our site is actually more than a shouting competition. (Maurits Martjin, *De Correspondent*)

Contributoria as well as Kickstarter leave responsiveness and responsibility completely to the creators and backers. Both sites do not adopt any additional instruments of media accountability, as the community acts as a self-regulating entity:

> We have a responsiveness to the article rather than dialogue with the writer ... We have a draft of a code of ethics, but we saw how the community behaved and we have thought it would be best to engage with the community to write the code. (Matt McAlister, *Contributoria*)

> Creators are responsible for their projects. When you back a project, you're trusting the creator to do a good job, so if you don't know them personally or by reputation, do a little research first. Kickstarter doesn't evaluate a project's claims, resolve disputes, or offer refunds—backers decide what's worth funding and what's not. (Kickstarter Web page, Trust & Safety)

Occhidellaguerra also allows online comments to be directly posted to the Web page. However, compared to the Dutch and the German initiatives, the number of comments is low. When it comes to the use of social media, there are different approaches used by the projects in our study. What is common to all journalism-specific projects—not platforms such as Kickstarter—is the fact that readers' donations build a strong connection between reporters and donors. It also creates a sense of responsibility in the journalists towards the backer.

> The strong relationship between the funder and the journalist is essential. (Sebastian Esser, *Krautreporter*)

The interaction with users is more important on Facebook compared to Twitter. This does not mean, however, that Facebook is not used as an additional distribution channel for articles and as a marketing tool to showcase editorial achievements.

> I think the most important goal of the social media accounts of *De Correspondent* is marketing. Marketing in the sense of reaching as many people as possible. Our Facebook account is a little bit more interactive, the tone is different, it is more focused on the reader, there are a lot of questions and we give reactions to the readers so we interact with our readers, more than on Twitter. (Maurits Martijn, *De Correspondent*)

With regard to the Twitter accounts, there are four communication types used by all accounts we have examined[8]: (1) asking to support proposals; (2) requests to collaborate to the production process; (3) publicizing published articles; and (4) community building and the sense of sharing. *Contributoria*, *De Correspondent* and *Krautreporter* all use their Twitter accounts to invite members to back specific projects and to promote already-published work. The communications include a constant invitation to collaborate at different levels including donating, providing feedback and sharing accomplished articles.

> Be sure to check out the new per-paragraph commenting feature. Use it to edit drafts together https://t.co/WyknYWqlHU http://t.co/TRFiFOT2Ww. (@contributoria, 27 March 2015)

> Our writers need your help, Members. Comment on their drafts before they submit final copy on Sunday: https://t.co/WyknYWqlHU. (@contributoria, 25 March 2015)

Occhidellaguerra has a slightly different approach using Twitter to promote features and articles, but also offer additional links pointing to information sources from third parties. The same applies to the use of the retweet function, which serves as another instrument to offer additional information from other accounts. However, the Italian crowdfunding start-up addresses the followers differently compared to the previous three projects. The difference between the collaborative tone and what we have defined as the "sense of sharing" is that the former puts contributors and writers at the same level, the latter marks the distinction of the two roles—as can be seen in the following tweet from *Occhidellaguerra.it*.

> Readers answer to @gianmicalessin in #Siria "God bless you" http://t.co/EMPWUqS6c7 #reportage #crowdfunding (@occhidellaguerra, 16 October 2014)

When it comes to the use of social media, we can distinguish two different communication types. First, there is the marketing-oriented typology, which is mainly applied in order to boost the funding of journalistic articles or projects.

> In Twitter mostly it's about encouraging backers for proposal, encourage people to make some proposals. Facebook we use just a little bit, just for our lack of experience, like a sort of broadcast … We do not do any marketing. (Matt McAlister, *Contributoria*)

Occhidellaguerra also uses their social media accounts to pass on information from journalists *in loci*, in order to let backers know how backed work is progressing. According to that strategy, followers on Twitter are also able to see videos or pictures that tell them where the journalists are—which is ultimately used as a customer (backer) satisfaction strategy.

The second typology is more interaction-oriented. It is usually linked to the recurrent topic of the community and fully incorporates the concepts of answerability and responsiveness denoted by McQuail (2003) as well as Domingo and Heikkilä (2012). Currently, Facebook is used more often to engage in (voluntary) interactions and discussions with the audience.

> Journalists, when they make a proposal they tend to take with them parents, peers, friends and followers to support them. When they become just a little bit more engaged they realize that there is a community that they can work with, as supporter and as journalist. (Matt McAlister, *Contributoria*)

Overall, a critical scrutiny of the social media communications confirms what Domingo and Heikkilä (2011, 6) found out: "despite the fact that newsrooms are using these spaces intensely, they tend to do so to promote their news products rather than to be responsive to their audiences". There are still deserted and "under-regulated" fields with regard to ethical guidelines, in particular with regard to social media and participation. The general disruption of journalism comes with specific ethical challenges, which have long been unknown in analogue newsrooms. What remains is the question whether entrepreneurial journalism start-ups have already developed an awareness of the ethical concerns and whether the specific problems of crowdfunded digital journalism are already reflected in their ethical standards.

Discussion and Conclusion

Crowdfunding-launched news outlets such as *De Correspondent* and *Krautreporter* display greater awareness in terms of accountability and transparency. They publish mission statements, link to code of ethics or publish thorough reports on how the funds have been used. If these instruments are not present, the organization outsources the responsibility to funders and proponents (Table 3).

Each of the interview participants was well aware that this particular way to finance entrepreneurial journalism entails specific ethical issues, given that entrepreneurs are constantly wearing different hats. Particularly with regard to financing there are many pitfalls that crowdfunders have to deal with, including the use of raised money and, related to this,

TABLE 3
Overview of the accountability and transparency practices

	De Correspondent	*Contributoria*	*Krautreporter*	*Occhidellaguerra*	**Kickstarter**
Actor transparency					
Transparency ownership and financing	Yes	Yes	Yes	Yes	Yes
Published mission statement	Yes	No, guidelines and terms of use	Yes	Partial	No, guidelines and terms of use
Published code of ethics	No	No	Link to the code of the German Press Council	Link to code of ethics of *Il Giornale*	No
Journalists' profiles	Yes	Partial, in campaigns	Yes, with regard to conflict of interest	No	Partial, in campaigns
Production transparency					
Links to sources in articles	Partial	Partial	Partial	Partial	Not applicable
Collaborative production	Yes, feedback and comments from members/ "experts"	Partial: comments during pre-publication	Partial, feedback and comments	No	Limited: comments
Responsiveness and use of social media					
Use of Facebook	Distribution, marketing, interaction	Distribution, marketing	Distribution, marketing, interaction	Distribution, marketing	Not applicable
Use of Twitter	Distribution, marketing, interaction	Distribution, marketing, interaction	Distribution, marketing, interaction	Marketing	Not applicable

the performance of the project and the creators' responsibilities; and the profitability and continuity of the activity. Although the interviewees never mention "ethical issues" or "ethical challenges", the concerns they raise are specifically related to issues such as autonomy, transparency and responsiveness—and thus clearly related to digital journalism ethics. However, different organizations perceive different ethical issues. The concerns change whether we look at a crowdfunded journalism start-up or a crowdfunding platform. However, our findings illustrate that start-ups with an organization similar to a traditional news outlet have indeed developed an awareness for ethical issues in the era of digital and networked journalism. Crowdfunding platforms—even if they are aware of the deficiency of ethical guidelines—are intentionally farming out such issue to their backers.

It is also interesting that—in contrast to what happens in other media industries, particularly in the field of entertainment (see Bennett, Chin, and Jones 2015a, 2015b)—there is limited criticism that comes from outside the journalistic field about the legitimacy of taking money from donors for the reason of newsmaking. On the contrary, criticism is often raised within the field, as in the case of *Occhidelleguerra*: the interview revealed that most criticism was raised by journalists working in the parent company and it was based on the idea that the publisher should guarantee a fair amount of money to assist the news production.

There is no unique way to solve ethical issues that emerge from crowdfunding. However, we can outline at least two strategies that might be adopted. Firstly, *open journalism*: in this strategy journalism is conceived as completely open to collaborations. There are many opportunities for backers and the audience in general to participate in the news production, dialogue (also through social media) with users are fostered, and there is the "willingness to see audiences on a more peer level, to appreciate their contributions, and to find normative purpose in transparency and participation" (Lewis 2012, 851). Furthermore, transparency is understood and guaranteed as openness with regard to the whole news production process and also to accountability. Social media are fully integrated into the routines of newsmaking to the extent that "the affordances and culture of social media are influencing how newsrooms are reporting the news, leading to discussions on key principles such as impartiality, verification and professional behavior" (Hermida 2012, 324).

Secondly, *journalism quality*: in this strategy, journalism remains a "closed system", not open to the public in terms of participation. It might well offer the opportunity to comment, but the audience is not allowed to participate in news production, and they are not seen as peers. Overall, it stands for the wish of professional journalists to retain complete authority. During the last 10 years, communication sciences have framed the interaction between journalists and their readers mainly in two different ways: either they emphasize the rise of citizens' voices as part of the communicative process (Gillmor 2004), or they underline the importance and the strengthening of the brand in legacy media organizations for user participation (Schäfer 2011). Crowdfunding journalism enhances a multifaceted kind of media participation, adding another meaning usually attributed to the concept (Carpentier 2011).

Within the dynamics of crowdfunding journalism, accountability itself appears to be a form of participation, particularly in its conception of responsiveness. To use the case of *Contributoria*: the British website presents some of the more traditional media accountability practices, for example, it publishes guidelines with regard to the community and backing process. At the same time, it has a less-developed system of transparency and accountability in comparison to other websites in the sample, such as *De Correspondent*. Particularly in the case of crowdfunding platforms, accountability is not only outsourced to creators and donors, but the community guarantees the transparency and accountability. The interviewees stated repeatedly that the "reactions of the community" must be seen as an implicit tool to guarantee accountability—and, on top of that, to make transparency not necessary.

From the two cases *Krautreporter* and *De Correspondent*, it emerged that money was only one aspect in crowdfunding journalism: information, dialogue and communication with the backers and potential readers are other central aspects. As Sebastian Esser from *Krautreporter* told us: "Crowdfunding creates a community, journalists and funders nearly become an editorial team". From an economic perspective, crowdfunding may help to initiate entrepreneurial projects. However, it has to be efficient and valuable enough to convert itself in an enduring news organization with a traditional business model. This is actually the case for the Dutch and German websites, which after the first year in which the crowdfunding campaign took place, switched to a traditional subscription model.

In reference to the ethical issues of crowdfunding, our paper collected several elements that show the existence of accountability practices such as mission statements or the possibility to get in touch with the media outlet through social media. Particularly independent crowdfunded start-ups have developed an awareness for ethical concerns —which derives from the fact of wearing different hats. Other aspects, such as responsiveness and participatory forms of journalism, still lack clear ethical standards. Crowdfunding platforms, on the other hand, even lack these initial building blocks, outsourcing the responsibilities to creators and backers. Kickstarter's statement in this regard is clear: "Kickstarter does not guarantee projects or investigate a creator's ability to complete their project. On Kickstarter, backers ultimately decide the validity and worthiness of a project by whether they decide to fund it".[9]

In order to decide the validity of the project, funders are advised to explore the project page and ask questions to pitchers on their own. Similarly, at *Contributoria*, the community itself is asked to judge a project, while the proposals have to be presented in detail. These platforms rely on the "community of participants" (Jenkins, Ford, and Green 2013), where the crowd itself becomes participatory, as Booth (2015, 157) states. However, not in the way Aitamurto (2011, 431) affirms—concerning the production and distribution—but with regard to accountability itself. Therefore, we can detect manifestations of participatory culture also in the case of accountability practices—or a *participatory accountability*.

Transparency and openness appear to be more important on crowdfunding platforms, while creators are looking for funds in order to get their projects financed. Once they get over the desired threshold set by themselves, the openness about what the creators are actually doing with the funds weakens—what can be described as transparency *ex ante*. It happens even if the platform supervisors are trying to convince the journalists to be completely open about their plans while implementing them:

> I think it would make a lot of sense if journalists explained how they would like to spend the money asked for in the proposal. If they do that it is much appreciated by the community, they are more likely to get support when they actually explain what they need the money for. (Matt McAlister, *Contributoria*)

Crowdfunding is becoming a relatively widespread business model in journalism, particularly among small journalism start-ups. Legacy news organizations are also using crowdfunding more often as editorial budgets decrease. Our study does not discuss whether crowdfunding is a viable business model for journalism—this was not the main question and would go beyond the scope of this article—but what can be seen is that in some cases small crowdfunded entrepreneurial projects can indeed expand into serious journalistic competitors and gain attention in the media market as the examples from the Netherlands and Germany show. However, we find that new notions of digital media ethics have to be developed with regard to crowdfunding. Particularly in the case of entrepreneurial journalism, where journalists wear multiple hats between editorial content production and commercial interests, it is of vital importance that start-ups live up to ethical standards in order to build and maintain authority and credibility.

While our research has some limitations in terms of the scope and cases we analysed, future research should focus more strongly on crowdfunding platforms and investigate how the "outsourcing" of the responsibility to the community is perceived by creators and backers. Furthermore, it would be interesting to know more about the interactions between backers, readers and journalistic entrepreneurs on social media in terms of participation or critique.

DISCLOSURE STATEMENT

No potential conflict of interest was reported by the authors.

NOTES

1. Other publications, such as Carvajal, García-Avilés, and González (2012), focus on the context of crowdfunding and what the relation between backers and journalists entails from a networking economy perspective.
2. "We typically decline to participate in academic research but if you send over the questions I'll do my best to answer them" (Justin Kazmark, personal communication with Sergio Splendore by e-mail, January 9, 2015).
3. See http://www.ilgiornale.it/sites/default/files/pdf/codice_etico.pdf (accessed November 23, 2015).
4. See http://www.tagesschau.de/inland/krautreporter-108.html (accessed November 23, 2015).
5. All quotes are taken from the following Web pages (the German and Italian quotes are translated by the authors): https://decorrespondent.nl/en; https://krautreporter.de/pages/ueber_uns; https://www.contributoria.com/about/community; http://www.gliocchidellaguerra.it/chi-siamo (all accessed November 23, 2015).
6. Source: https://www.kickstarter.com/help/stats?ref=footer (accessed November 23, 2015).
7. Source: http://www.npr.org/sections/alltechconsidered/.
8. As Kickstarter is not a journalism-specific platform, we decided not to include their Twitter account in the analysis.
9. Source: https://www.kickstarter.com/help/faq/kickstarter%20basics (accessed November 23, 2015).

REFERENCES

Aitamurto, Tanja. 2011. "The Impact of Crowdfunding on Journalism." *Journalism Practice* 5 (4): 429–445.

Aitamurto, Tanja. 2013. "Balancing Between Open and Closed. Co-Creation in Magazine Journalism" *Digital Journalism* 2 (2): 229–251.

Andersson, Ulrika, and Jenny Wiik. 2013. "Journalism Meets Management. Changing Leadership in Swedish News Organizations." *Journalism Practice* 7 (6): 705–719.

Bakker, Piet. 2014. "Mr. Gates Returns." *Journalism Studies* 15 (5): 596–606.

Benecchi, Eleonora. 2015. "L'economia del fandom tra television e cinema [The Economy of Fandom between Television and Cinema]." In *La trama dei media* [The Media's Plot], edited by Marco Cucco, 79–100. Roma: Carocci editore.

Bennett, Lucy, Bertha Chin, and Bethan Jones. 2015a. "Crowdfunding: A New Media & Society Special Issue." *New Media and Society* 17 (2): 141–148.

Bennett, Lucy, Bertha Chin, and Bethan Jones. 2015b. *Crowdfunding the Future. Media Industries, Ethics & Digital Society*. New York: Peter Lang.

Booth, Paul. 2015. "Crowdfunding: A Spimatic Application of Digital Fandom." *New Media & Society* 17 (2): 149–166.

Briggs, Mark. 2012. *Entrepreneurial Journalism: How to Build What's Next for News*. London: Sage.

Bruno, Nicola and Rasmus Kleis Nielsen. 2012. "Survival is Success. Journalistic Online Start-Ups in Western Europe." Reuters Institute for the Study of Journalism. http://reutersinstitute.politics.ox.ac.uk/sites/default/files/Survival%20is%20Success%20Journalistic%20Online%20Start-Ups%20in%20Western%20Europe.pdf.

Carpentier, Nico. 2011. *Media and Participation: A Site of Ideological-democratic Struggle*. Chicago: Intellect.

Carvajal, Miguel, Josè A. García-Avilés, and José L. González. 2012. "Crowdfunding and Non-profit Media." *Journalism Practice* 6 (5–6): 638–647.

Claussen, Dane S. 2011. "Editor's Note: CUNY's Entrepreneurial Journalism: Partially Old Wine in a New Bottle, and Not Quite Thirst-Quenching, but Still a Good Drink." *Journalism & Mass Communication Educator* 66 (1): 3–6.

Curran, James. 2011. *Media and Democracy*. Milton Park: Routledge.

Domingo, David, and Heikkilä, Heikki. 2011. "Media Accountability Online: Constraints and Opportunities for Journalistic Transparency and Responsiveness." NordMedia. http://english.unak.is/static/files/Domingo%20and%20Heikkila.pdf.

Gade, Peter J. 2008. "Journalism Guardians in a Time of Great Change: News Editors' Perceived Influence in Integrated News Organizations." *Journalism & Mass Communication Quarterly* 85 (2): 371–392.

Gillmor, Dan. 2004. *We the Media: Grassroots Journalism by the People, for the People*. Sebastopol: O'Reilly Media.

Gutiérrez, Peter. 2013. "Kickstarter: Fan Empowerment or Exploitation?" *Metro* 177: 101–102.

Hanna, Paul. 2012. "Using Internet Technologies (such as Skype) as a Research Medium: A Research Note." *Qualitative Research* 12 (2): 239–242.

Hermida, Alfred. 2012. "Social Journalism: Exploring How Social Media is Shaping Journalism." In *The Handbook of Global Online Journalism*, edited by Eugenia Siapera and Andreas Veglis, 309–328. Oxford: Wiley-Blackwell.

Hunter, Andrea. 2015. "Crowdfunding Independent and Freelance Journalism: Negotiating Journalistic Norms of Autonomy and Objectivity." *New Media & Society* 17 (2): 272–288.

Hunter, Anna, and François P. Nel. 2011. "Equipping the Entrepreneurial Journalist: An Exercise in Creative Enterprise." *Journalism & Mass Communication Educator* 66 (1): 9–24.

Jenkins, Henry, Sam Ford, and Joshua Green. 2013. *Spreadable Media: Creating Value and Meaning in a Networked Culture*. New York: New York University Press.

Jian, Lian, and Jieun Shin. 2015. "Motivations behind Donors' Contributions to Crowdfunded Journalism." *Mass Communication and Society* 18 (2): 165–185.

Jian, Lian, and Nikki Usher. 2014. "Crowd-Funded Journalism." *Journal of Computer-Mediated Communication* 19 (2): 155–170.

Karlsson, Michael. 2010. "Rituals of Transparency." *Journalism Studies* 11 (4): 535–545.

Karlsson, Michael. 2011. "The Immediacy of Online News, the Visibility of Journalistic Processes and a Restructuring of Journalistic Authority." *Journalism* 12 (3): 279–295.

Kaye, Jeff and Quinn, Stephen. 2010. *Funding Journalism in the Digital Age. Business Models, Strategies, Issues and Trends*. New York: Peter Lang.

Kovach, Bill, and Tom Rosenstiel. 2007. *The Elements of Journalism: What Newspeople Should Know and the Public Should Expect*. New York: Three Rivers Press.

Legard, Robin, Jill Keegan, and Kit Ward. 2003. "In-depth Interviews." In *Qualitative Research Practice. A Guide for Social Studies Students and Researchers*, edited by Jane Ritche and Jane Lewis, 77–109. London: Sage.

Lewis, Seth C. 2012. "The Tension between Professional Control and Open Participation." *Information, Communication & Society* 15 (6): 836–866.

Loosen, Wiebke, and Jan-Hinrik Schmidt. 2012. "(Re-)discovering the Audience. The Relationship between Journalism and Audience in Networked Digital Media." *Information, Communication & Society* 15 (6): 867–887.

McChesney, Robert W., and John Nichols. 2010. *The Death and Life of American Journalism: The Media Revolution That Will Begin the World Again*. Philadelphia: Nation Books.

McChesney, Robert W., and Victor Pickard. 2011. *Will The Last Reporter Please Turn Out The Lights? The Collapse of Journalism and What Can Be Done To Fix It*. New York: The New Press.

McQuail, Dennis. 2003. *Media Accountability and Freedom of Publication*. Oxford: Oxford University Press.

Paniagua Rojano, Francisco Javier, Marisol Gómez Aguilar, and Maria Eugenia González Cortés. 2014. "Encourage Entrepreneurial Journalism from the University." *Revista Latina de Comunicación Social* 69: 548–570.

Pfauth, Ernst-Jan. 2014. *Here's What Happened to that World-Record in Journalism Crowdfunding*. Accessed June 24, 2015. https://medium.com/de-correspondent/heres-what-happend-to-that-world-record-in-journalism-crowdfunding-cc5bac50b812.

Phillips, Angela. 2010. "Transparency and the New Ethics of Journalism." *Journalism Practice* 4 (3): 373–382.

Porlezza, Colin. 2013. *Gefährdete journalistische Unabhängigkeit. Zum wachsenden Einfluss von Werbung auf redaktionelle Inhalte* [Endangered Journalistic Independence. The Growing Influence of Advertising on Editorial Content]. Konstanz: UVK.

Schäfer, Mirko T. 2011. *Bastard Culture! How User Participation Transforms Cultural Production*. Amsterdam: Amsterdam University Press.

Singer, Jane. 2015. "Out of Bounds: Professional Norms as Boundary Markers." In *Boundaries of Journalism: Professionalism, Practices and Participation*, edited by Matt Carlson and Seth C. Lewis, 21–36. Oxford: Routledge.

Storey, John, Graeme Salaman, and Kerry Platman. 2005. "Living with Enterprise in an Enterprise Economy: Freelance and Contract Workers in the Media." *Human Relations* 58 (8): 1033–1054.

Ward, Stephen J. 2009. *Journalism in the Entrepreneurial Age*. Center for Journalism Ethics, School of Journalism and Mass Communication, University of Wisconsin-Madison. Accessed March 12. http://ethics.journalism.wisc.edu/2009/09/15/journalism-in-the-entrepreneurial-age/.

Ward, Stephen J. 2015. "Radical Media Ethics: New Wine in New Bottles." In *Neuvermessung der Medienethik*, edited by Marlis Prinzing, Matthias Rath, Christian Schicha, and Ingrid Stapf, 74–84. Weinheim/Basel: Beltz Juventa.

Wijnberg, Rob. 2014. *Dit hebben we het afgelopen jaar met jullie steun bereikt*. Accessed June 24, 2015. https://decorrespondent.nl/1692/Het-jaarverslag-2013–2014-Dit-hebben-we-met-jullie-steun-bereikt/47702556-344f690b.

"IT'S LIKE HAVING A SECOND FULL-TIME JOB"

Crowdfunding, journalism and labour

Andrea Hunter

As jobs in legacy media organizations become increasingly scarce, crowdfunding has gained some momentum as a way for journalists to raise money to start their own media ventures or bolster freelance budgets. While crowdfunding is often positioned as empowering for both the journalists and donors, what is often overlooked is the amount and type of labour involved in crowdfunding. This article examines labour in crowdfunding from three vantage points: the labour involved in the campaign itself, the labour of the donors and the type of labour crowdfunding enables. This paper argues that the amount of work is akin to having a second full-time job. Moreover, having to embrace entrepreneurial techniques and market their work is something many journalists are uncomfortable with. Further, this paper examines how donors are implicated in the labour of journalism, and how journalists are hoping to "commodify" the audience. Finally, this paper addresses how crowdfunding does afford journalists agency, enabling them to work outside of legacy news structures, which many journalists find liberating.

Introduction

As legacy news organizations struggle with cuts and closures, and journalism jobs become increasingly hard to come by (McChesney and Pickard 2011), the idea that crowdfunding may be a viable way of financing journalism has gained momentum (Aitamurto 2015; Carvajal, García-Avilés, and González 2012; Hunter 2015; Jian and Usher 2014). Much of the hype around crowdfunding is fuelled by high-profile cases. For instance, in 2012 the online science and technology magazine *Matter* raised US$140,000 on Kickstarter, over three times what was asked for. In a similarly high-profile and successful campaign that same year, a former National Public Radio (NPR) journalist raised over $100,000 to start an independent publication to cover Washington politics. More recently, in 2014, the collective Radiotopia raised over $600,000 to fund independent radio shows and podcasts. Along with these big success stories, entrepreneurial hope is buoyed by a plethora of more modest examples; journalists raising anywhere from a few thousand to tens of thousands of dollars to support freelance travel budgets, create documentaries or start online independent ventures (Aitamurto 2011; Hunter 2015). Crowdfunding has been touted as something that journalists can turn to when money is tight, jobs are scarce and becoming an entrepreneur is perhaps the best or only option (Zara 2013). While cautioning that crowdfunding is not a replacement for legacy business models, Aitamurto (2015, 203) still sees crowdfunding as playing "an important role in the emerging new business model ecosystem in journalism", not just because it can help journalists raise money, but because it is a marketing tool that can help journalists brand themselves, test story ideas and attract audiences. However, what is often overlooked amidst the hope and the possibility in crowdfunding, is the amount and the type of labour involved. This labour is often extremely time consuming and exhausting, forcing journalists to act in ways they are not accustomed to and, in many cases, not comfortable with. Moreover, although there has been some research examining the motivation of contributors to crowdfunding campaigns (Aitamurto 2011; Jian and Usher 2014; Jian and Shin 2015), there has not been critical scholarship to date that theorizes how donors contribute to the labour of crowdfunding.

Based on interviews with journalists in Canada and the United States who have crowdfunded, this article examines the labour involved in crowdfunding and journalism from three vantage points. First, it examines labour from the journalist's perspective and argues that the amount of labour involved is akin to a second full-time job. Further, it examines the type of work that crowdfunding entails, particularly the difficulties journalists experience as they try to embrace the often-conflicting values of public affairs journalism and business. Most journalists are used to pitching stories to editors or producers, but having to become entrepreneurs and sell an idea to potential funders before they can even begin the work of reporting is not something most are used to or comfortable with. In particular, they find it difficult to be publicly transparent about their story ideas before they have been fully formed and produced. They also are not used to having to market their work and justify why it is worthy of funding. Second, this article addresses the labour of donors. While crowdfunding could be characterized as empowering for the "former audience" (Gillmor 2004), drawing on Dallas Smythe's (1981) theory of the "audience commodity" and more recent theorizing of the "prosumer commodity" (Fuchs 2012a, 2012b), the article argues that one goal of crowdfunding is the commodification of audiences. Many journalists raising seed money for online publications are hoping to leverage donor interest into advertising dollars. Essentially, they hope to "sell" their donors to advertisers as proof their publication is worth supporting. Finally, the article addresses the type of work crowdfunding enables, arguing that it can be empowering, affording journalists a sense of agency in that they are able to create work outside of legacy news structures. However, I also argue that crowdfunding is a form of what Kuehn and Corrigan (2013) have called "hope labour", through which journalists are hoping to create brands, recognition and harness audience attention that they can then leverage into a more sustainable funding model.

Crowdfunding Models in Journalism

At its core, crowdfunding is a process whereby small amounts of money are solicited from a large pool of people, in order to support a project or an endeavour (Bannerman 2013). Although today crowdfunding is shorthand for online fundraising, crowdfunding is not something exclusive to the internet (Bannerman 2013; Jian and Usher 2014). It has been common practice for public broadcasters to ask audiences for monetary support. For NPR in the United States, this is a tradition that goes back decades (Aitamurto 2011). The difference with online crowdfunding is that it is easier for individual journalists who do not have large institutional support behind them to connect directly with potential funders (Hunter 2015; Jian and Shin 2015). For freelancers in particular, crowdfunding has been touted as one way to support their work in a financial climate where resources are scarce (Carvajal, García-Avilés, and González 2012). Aitamurto (2015) argues that in addition to financial support, crowdfunding also acts as a marketing tool, helping journalists build their brand and bring in audiences who will then perhaps consume and support their work in the future.

There are four main models of crowdfunding: equity based, lending based, reward based and donation based (Aitamurto 2015; Bannerman 2013; Mollick 2014). In equity- and lending-based models, investors give with the expectation, and hope, that there will be some sort of financial return on their donation. In lending-based models funders expect their money back, with interest (Aitamurto 2015). In equity-based models investors expect to share in the revenue of the project (Aitamurto 2015; Bannerman 2013). The crowdfunding models typically used in journalism are donation based, where contributors donate altruistically without expectation of compensation of any sort, or rewards based, where donors are compensated based on the amount they are willing to donate. The rewards are tier based, with journalists offering small rewards for smaller donations, such as postcards or small gifts from places they have travelled to cover a story, and larger rewards for more substantial donations, rewards such as advance copies or exclusive access to their work.

Aitamurto (2015) has identified four categories of crowdfunding specific to journalism. The first is raising funds to cover a single story; journalists turn to crowdfunding platforms to pitch a story idea with the hopes that the money raised will cover the reporting costs. Often freelance journalists who want to raise money to travel to cover a particular story will use this model. The second is crowdfunding for "continuous coverage" or a "beat". The third model is raising money for a new venture, whether an online platform or publication. The goal here is to raise seed funding. Finally, there are journalists who are crowdfunding to support endeavours that are outside of actual journalism, but will support their work. An example is a Kickstarter campaign run by *The San Francisco Public Press*—an independent online investigative magazine—that raised over $20,000 to support delivery of their newspaper by bicycle.

When audiences are directly funding the news, it raises questions about the nature of the relationship between audience and journalist. The argument can be made that with their investments donors are now, in a sense, producers of the news. While some contend donors are producers who do not have editorial control (Carvajal, García-Avilés, and González 2012), the reality is perhaps much more nuanced. Journalists who crowdfund feel a great deal of responsibility towards their funders (Aitamurto 2011), and an onus to create work their donors will be pleased with (Hunter 2015). Initial research has also found that while some journalists feel very strongly that their donors should have no editorial control over the content, others are open to more dialogue with their funders and are crowdfunding, in part, because they want input on the journalistic process (Hunter 2015). As well, outreach and community building are essential elements of crowdfunding, which can be at odds with keeping donors at arm's length from editorial content (Hunter 2015).

To date there has not been a great deal of research that looks closely at the type of labour involved in crowdfunding. Aitamurto (2015) does note that in crowdfunding journalists publicly pitch their ideas, which requires journalists to be more transparent about their work. As well, in an earlier study Aitamurto (2011) found that journalists sometimes feel uncomfortable about having to promote their story ideas through social networks. Noting that her study involved a small sample of seven journalists, Aitamurto has called this observation "initial" and "tentative" (440), and encourages that this be treated as a hypothesis and explored in further studies. Taking a cue from this research, this article will look more closely at the labour involved in crowdfunding, particularly the amount and the type of work involved.

There has been some initial research that has examined the motivations of donors and what type of journalism tends to get funded. Trasel and Fontoura (2015, 99), comparing the stories published using Spot.us with the usual coverage in the American press, found that it is "a viable alternative for publishing more different points of view, as well as subjects and themes". Jian and Usher (2014), in their study of Spot.us, found that both experienced and inexperienced journalists seem to get funded, which they point to as hopeful for young journalists who are looking for a way to start their careers. Research has also found that donors are often motivated by altruistic reasons; they want to donate to journalism that will have impact and make a difference (Aitamurto 2011; Jian and Shin 2015). This paper will look at donors from a different perspective, arguing that journalists are hoping to commodify the audience. Finally, it will look at the type of work that crowdfunding enables, particularly how journalists are able to create work outside of mainstream legacy structures, a move they find empowering, despite the sheer amount of work it entails.

The Audience Commodity and Agency

By drawing on theories of the prosumer commodity (Fuchs 2012a, 2012b) and the audience commodity (Smythe 1981), we can contextualize the role of donors in crowdfunding. While there has been some research that points to donors as investors and producers, many journalists are hoping to use the interest of donors as leverage to move into an advertising model—essentially commodifying the audience. The theory of the audience commodity goes back to Dallas Smythe (1981). As Fuchs (2012b, 695) writes, "For Smythe, the material aspect of communications is that audiences work, are exploited and sold as commodities". In other words, the commodity produced by media was not the show, or the broadcast, but rather the audience, which was then sold to advertisers in the form of ratings. Further to this, the audience was working by paying attention to advertisements—the television or radio programme is simply the "free lunch" offered as enticement to pay attention to the advertisements. As Pridmore and Trottier (2014, 139) describe, the type of work audiences engage in is an "immaterial form of labour" and by paying attention to advertisements audiences learn "to buy goods and to spend their income accordingly". Key to Smythe's theorizing was that audiences may be labouring, without explicit knowledge that they are doing so (Pridmore and Trottier 2014).

The audience commodity was—and continues to be—controversial, principally around the question of whether audiences actually work; consuming media, even advertising, is often thought of as a leisure activity. Some argue that an audience commodity analysis downplays audience agency (Caraway 2011). While it is perhaps more difficult to make the argument that consuming mass media is in fact work, with social media the argument is much more easily made, as these platforms would not exist without input from audiences. Fuchs (2012a) uses the term "prosumer commodities" to describe social media users who fill up these platforms with their creative work, whose data are then collected and sold to advertisers. Rather than positioning social media as a democratizing and empowering force, one that fosters creativity, Fuchs counters that social media, such as Facebook, is actually working towards the "total commodification of human creativity" (56).

In the case of crowdfunding, the question of whether donors are working, and what type of agency they might have, could be similarly contested. The role of the donor is often positioned as one that is empowering—audiences have the opportunity to put their money behind journalism they feel is worthwhile. They can have an impact on journalism, and by extension democracy if one believes the media to be an important part of the democratic process. However, while this may be the case during the initial crowdfunding campaign, what this article will argue is that some journalists are hoping to leverage donor interest into proof to advertisers that there is an audience for their work, effectively "selling" their audience to advertisers, with the expectations that this audience will eventually work by paying attention to advertisements and learning to become consumers.

Methodology

Interviews were conducted with freelance and independent journalists in Canada and the United States. Three Canadians and 24 Americans were interviewed. The sample included 16 women and 11 men. The interview sample was drawn from crowdfunding pitches that were accessible online between September 2013 and June 2015 on Kickstarter ($N = 19$), Indiegogo ($N = 6$) and Spot.us ($N = 2$). Although some journalists are now experimenting with continued crowdfunding from donors, either through their own websites or through platforms such as Patreon, this research is restricted to journalists who have conducted crowdfunding campaigns where the goal is to raise a specific amount of money, not secure ongoing funding. This choice was made, in part to keep the sample specific to a certain type of crowdfunding, but also because this type of crowdfunding is fairly established and well known, thus attracting a range of journalists.

Most of the journalists ran at least one successful campaign; however, one journalist had run both an unsuccessful Kickstarter campaign and a successful one. Three journalists were also only partially funded on Indiegogo, a platform that offers a "flexible funding" option where people can collect whatever they raise. The journalists who used Indiegogo were drawn to this platform because of this option, preferring to avoid Kickstarter's "all-or-nothing" policy, and the relatively low rate of success on the latter platform. As of October 2015, Kickstarter statistics show that a total of 694 journalism projects have been successfully funded, while 2294 have been unsuccessful. The crowdfunding campaigns in this study ran between 2011 and 2015, and raised funds that ranged between US$1500 and $76,000. The age range of the participants was between 24 and 56. The journalists had a range of professional experience. Eleven had worked in legacy media and were now freelancing or with independent media; eight were career freelancers; three had always worked in independent media; and five had no previous experience in journalism. The funds were used to start independent online publications ($N = 6$), support travel expenses for freelance journalism aimed at both independent and legacy media ($N = 7$), create documentaries and books ($N = 3$), fund reporting for specific stories in independent publications ($N = 9$), and purchase office space and equipment ($N = 2$).

Semi-structured in-depth interviews were conducted between November 2013 and June 2015. The interviews took place over the phone or through Skype. The interviews lasted between 20 and 90 minutes; the average length was 45 minutes. The purpose of semi-structured interviews is to explore themes or issues of interest to the research, while allowing space for participants to discuss ideas that they find particularly relevant. The interview questions were designed to draw out participants' thoughts about their motivation to crowdfund, how they found the experience, particularly the amount and nature of work involved, as well as the interactions they had with their funders. At the same time, within this flexible structure, interviewees were encouraged to expand on issues of particular interest, and bring up new ideas that the researcher did not specifically ask about. As Johnson and Rowlands (2012, 100) describe, the goal of in-depth semi-structured interviews is to understand a person's "lived experience" and particular "perspective".

The interviews were analysed using a grounded theory approach, with the goal of finding patterns from the participants' "thick descriptions" elicited in the interviews (Hesse-Biber and Leavy 2006, 119). The tool of analysis was analytic memo writing (Corbin and Strauss 2008; Lindolf and Taylor 2011). A process of open coding was used in the first step of analysis where the transcripts were first read for emergent themes, concepts and categories (Charmaz 2006; Corbin and Strauss 2008; Hesse-Biber and Leavy 2006; Holton 2007; Lindolf and Taylor 2011). As a second step axial coding was used to make connections between categories, particularly to find links and relate "minor concepts to broader level concepts" (Corbin and Strauss 2008, 193). As a final step the subcategories were integrated into analytic categories. As the focus of this article is on labour and crowdfunding, this paper will deal with the categories that emerged from the data that deal with various forms of labour. The first category is "labour and the campaign", which includes two subcategories: "design and outreach" which deals with the amount of labour involved in campaigns and "transparency and marketing" which deals with the type of labour involved. The second category is "labour and donors" which focuses on the commodification of the donors. The final category is "labour and agency" which focuses on the freedom many journalists feel that crowdfunding affords.

Labour of the Campaign

Design and Outreach

All the journalists in this research study described the amount of labour that goes into crowdfunding as extremely time consuming. First, there is a great deal of work that goes into design of a campaign, principally around writing the pitch and producing video, developing an appropriate rewards system, and designing an overall marketing plan for outreach. Second, the campaign itself is all encompassing, as successful campaigns require intensive social media outreach and contacting donors directly through email.

Beginning with the design of the campaign, many journalists said that the work involved is so intense and requires a diverse skill set that it helps to work as part of a team. The type of labour involved in designing a campaign includes not only writing the pitch, but also producing compelling video and graphics. It is often difficult for one person to do this alone. One journalist said her campaign was successful because she was working with people who had professional writing and design skills. As she described: "Fortunately, we're writers so it's not like we had to go hire somebody to write our Kickstarter for us. But it was still a ton of work … It was completely insane. I would never do it again" (Journalist, $76,000 raised on Kickstarter).

The type of labour involved also included thinking about marketing, particularly designing a system of rewards that would entice people to donate. When crowdfunding for a creative product such as a movie or a game, there are obvious rewards, such as the marketing material that goes along with the product, or the product itself. With journalism, it is more difficult to offer a "product" as a reward. First, for journalists who are crowdfunding to cover a single story, particularly an investigative story, it is not always obvious from the beginning what the end product will be. Second, for journalists who are crowdfunding to start an online publication, often the goal is for the publication to be freely available, so the "product" cannot be offered as something exclusive. Journalists said they had to think creatively to come up with incentives. The freelance journalists who were raising funds to travel would often offer postcards or trinkets from the places they were travelling. Some journalists also decided to offer exclusive content, or advance copies of their work. For the highest donors, some journalists offered their own company as a reward—either by offering themselves as a speaker for an event, or offering to go for dinner or drinks with donors. However, because many found it difficult to think about tangible rewards that would be big draws, they often decided to focus on appealing to a donor's interest in the story or the publication itself.

For example, one journalist who ran a campaign to fund a feminist online publication said she eventually decided it was best to focus on appealing to a donor's desire to see a women's magazine that did not focus on celebrity content. She said there were other people running crowdfunding campaigns for feminist magazines who were able to offer what she calls "big ticket" rewards, such as consultation with a writer for a well-known television programme. However, since she did not have these types of contacts, she had to think differently about what she could offer:

> Of course the rewards are really one of the best ways to bring people in to back your projects. So that was something I really had to sit down and think about. For me ultimately it was—"OK, well I don't really have the ability to offer these big ticket items necessarily, so I'm going to focus on offering exclusive or early access to our content and more fun rewards that are sort of related to [magazine]". But it also made me realize maybe my rewards aren't my main draw. I really need to focus on getting people behind [magazine's] mission in general and having that being our selling point. (Journalist, $15,000 raised on Kickstarter)

Essentially, some journalists decided to focus on the donor's sense of altruism; that by funding journalism they were really becoming part of the democratic process and going to bring stories to light that were not getting coverage in legacy media.

While there is a lot of work involved in designing a campaign, it is during the course of the campaign where the labour really becomes extensive. For the month of the campaign journalists have to use social media constantly to reach out to potential donors and advertise their campaign. They primarily use Twitter and Facebook to reach out to their personal networks and provide updates as the campaign proceeds. They also use their personal contacts to email potential donors individually. They spend a great deal of time thanking donors and providing updates, in the hopes that donors will make a second donation once they see that the campaign is progressing. All the journalists agreed that outreach is a key component of crowdfunding and that this process of updating social media and reaching out to contacts is the most demanding part of the process. It is not enough to simply build a site and expect people to find it. It is imperative to focus on reaching out to people who may be interested in your journalism and also able to donate. Then you have to stay plugged into social media for the month of the campaign to keep up the outreach. As one journalist observed—you cannot send one message out and think it is enough, the process of social media outreach is really about building relationships with donors.

> You have to have a solid plan for outreach. That's building partnerships, which is a lot of phone calls, a lot of emails, a lot of meetings, a lot of research and contacting people who would be interested. Social media. It's a lot of work. (Journalist, $1600 raised on Spot.us)

Similarly, one journalist said for herself—and her partner—the month of the crowdfunding campaign was about getting their names and their idea out to potential funders, rather than sitting back and watching the money come in. As she described: "The month of the campaign was really a marketing campaign more than just a money campaign. We knew we had to email people and be on Facebook and be on Twitter" (Journalist, $11,600 raised on Kickstarter). Another journalist said that outreach is so important to crowdfunding, she thinks it is essential to have a social media expert working as part of a campaign.

> A good tip would be to have someone in your pocket who knows about social media and how to promote it. Because you can write the best copy, and have the best video but if you don't have a way to promote it and get people to see it, it's not going to go anywhere. It's not going to be successful. (Journalist, $30,500 raised on Kickstarter)

Most journalists describe the process of crowdfunding as exhausting. As this journalist describes, crowdfunding at the same time that he was working his regular jobs was overwhelming. "It nearly killed me to make it happen. On top of running the site and the other jobs I do because I don't get paid enough by [current employer], it was an extraordinary effort" (Journalist, $20,000 raised on Indiegogo). Similarly, another journalist described the process as extremely time consuming and stressful. "It is exhausting. The campaign itself, from the time you hit go to the time it closes is like having an extra full-time job for a month. It's constant plugging and pushing" (Journalist, $47,500 raised on Kickstarter).

Many journalists said they were very surprised by the amount of work it was to stay on top of social media outreach, and also thanking and responding to donors. They had been drawn to crowdfunding after hearing success stories, and cautioned that these stories belie the amount of effort these campaigns take. As this journalist describes:

> I think what's happened with crowdsourced funding is people are hearing about the big stories—the movies that get made, the Planet Money NPR project which raised $500,000 to do a t-shirt. Podcasts that have raised $100,000. What they don't tell you is those people are very, very lucky. Doing a crowdfunded project takes a lot of work and a lot of personal outreach. (Journalist, $10,500 raised on Kickstarter)

Several journalists, who used Kickstarter as a platform, also said the key to their success was being singled out by Kickstarter as an interesting project and put on the site's front page. This brought a lot of visibility to their campaigns, and attracted donors who were outside of their social networks. One journalist who had run a successful campaign on Kickstarter, as well as an unsuccessful campaign, said that this type of recognition was crucial.

> At the beginning [my successful crowdfunding campaign] wasn't doing terribly well, so [Kickstarter] put it on their front page because they liked the project. Once it was on the front page then it took off. But as long as it was just counting on my own supporters

> it wasn't doing well enough. It would have failed. You could tell because when they took it off the front page it stopped doing well. Then they put it back on and it made its goal. So I think that's kind of a secret—the support of Kickstarter itself is really crucial to certain projects. I didn't get that the second time around. They didn't put me on the front page the second time around. (Journalist, $25,000 raised on Kickstarter)

Most journalists also said that another crucial aspect of their successful campaigns was reaching out to specific audiences. One journalist, who only raised one-third of the funds she asked for on Indiegogo, said that if she were to do this again she would run a more "targeted" campaign.

> In retrospect—this is kind of dumb of me—but I didn't really think about who would actually want to support something like this. What kind of people would have a vested interest in a project like this? If I were to do it again I would think about it more in that way. (Journalist, $1500 raised on Indiegogo)

This interviewee describes the way she approached her campaign as "trial and error", and feels that if she had concentrated on approaching people interested in her general topic area—in her case international human rights—she might have been better off.

Transparency and Marketing

For the journalists in this research it was not simply the amount of work that was intimidating, but it was also the type of work that was difficult to deal with. In some cases, this was a very negative experience, but for others, forcing themselves out of their typical work habits did bring what they see as positive benefits, in that crowdfunding forced them to be open and transparent about their work in a way they are not used to. However, crowdfunding also requires a degree of self-promotion that was foreign to them. Most journalists did not see themselves as primarily entrepreneurs, and the process of having to market themselves and ask for donations made them uncomfortable and, at times, felt akin to begging.

Journalists who have worked for legacy media organizations are used to having to pitch ideas to producers and editors. During the pitching process story ideas are critiqued and examined from different perspectives. This can be an intimidating process for a journalist to go through. However, some comfort comes from the pitching process taking place within a group of colleagues who often have similar values and a common understanding of workplace habits. Having to pitch your idea to a public of strangers and convince them to fund your work is something these journalists found difficult to get used to. As one journalist described, she felt very uncomfortable being so transparent about her work. It did not come naturally to her, and she had to wrestle with the idea that her idea might be rejected or critiqued in a public way.

> It was really uncomfortable at the beginning. I've never been through a public process where you put your idea out there, very publicly in front of everybody that you care about socially and professionally to be rejected. You feel a sense of that every day until it's funded. (Journalist, $3200 raised on Kickstarter)

Similarly, another journalist said having to be open and transparent about an idea before a project was even fully formed was foreign to her. She was used to pitching stories to editors and producers, but doing this in an open format was "scary" for her.

> You're opening the door to the public before you even start reporting and you're having to show proof of concept first. Those are conversations that are often held behind closed doors with just the editor or just a small team of people at the news organization. Then you go out and do the reporting and put it out in the world. That, at least, has been my experience doing big projects. So this was the first time I was really saying—"Here's an idea we have". (Journalist, $7000 raised on Kickstarter)

However, this journalist says the positive outcome of working this way was that she did get a lot of helpful feedback on her idea. First, having to defend her ideas helped her articulate her story more clearly. Second, through the feedback she was also able to find more sources for her story. Similarly, another journalist said that although he was not used to "having to justify what you're doing in a very public way", one positive aspect of crowdfunding was that it forced him to be more open and transparent about his process, which is a direction he was hoping to move in anyway (Journalist, $19,400 raised on Spot.us).

However, despite the benefits that can come from pitching an idea in a public way, asking for money and marketing their work made most journalists uncomfortable. One journalist said it felt almost inappropriate and it took some time for her to get used to the idea. She had worked for legacy media for almost two decades, where she never had to worry about the financial aspect of the business. Asking for money to support her work made her feel very exposed and vulnerable. As she described:

> I had great reservations at first. I tell my friends it felt like walking outdoors naked. Because you're putting yourself out there asking for money and it just felt like walking out in the open, unprotected in a way. Would people think this was inappropriate or not? (Journalist, $4500 raised on Kickstarter)

Another journalist said that although he has been very successful at crowdfunding, it is not something he enjoys.

> I hate social media and begging for money. It makes me kind of ashamed to hustle … It makes me feel uncomfortable. I feel like if people don't want to fund me they don't want to fund me and I don't want to be out shaking my cup on the street. It's degrading. It's humiliating. (Journalist, $26,000 raised on Kickstarter)

One journalist said it was very helpful to have people with a range of expertise working on a campaign, including fundraising, because this aspect of the process can be most difficult for people who come from a strict journalism background. She credits their success to the fact that they had a team with multiple skills.

> I think it's one of those things where we're really lucky to have a team of people who have specific skills that are really tailored to Kickstarter. I'm a graphic designer. We have a video team. We have two people who know how to shoot video. We have someone who's really good at fund development and knows traditional fundraising stuff. I think it's one of those things that can be scary for most journalists, especially freelancers or just legacy news outlets that may not have any experience in fundraising, if they're based on an advertising model, to really go into this. (Journalist, $76,000 raised on Kickstarter)

The final number of journalists in this research who had experience with marketing, or had partnered with people who had experience in fundraising, did not feel the same reservations that journalists coming from a pure journalism background did.

Labour and Donors

Much of the focus in crowdfunding is on outreach and attracting donors. Many of the journalists described this process as building a community around their project. On one hand, this is described altruistically—they want donors to be engaged with their work and start meaningful dialogues about the stories they are covering. On the other, and more pragmatically, developing a community is about getting themselves, and their work, exposure. As one journalist described: "Crowdfunding is not only about funding, but it's also building a community that will help us get our project known" (Journalist, $11,700 raised on Kickstarter).

Journalists who are crowdfunding for seed money for an online publication are typically hoping to build up a community of donors, whose loyalty will then translate into advertising dollars. Crowdfunding is a one-time endeavour that they hope will propel them into more sustainable funding through advertising. For example, for this journalist, crowdfunding was a way to get some initial content up on the Web.

> I have a bit of money to really get the site going and get content up there. I'm hoping that that will draw even more viewers and build even more of a community. Then at that point I can use those views to sell sponsorships. (Journalist, $15,000 raised on Kickstarter)

Similarly, another journalist says she ultimately wants to raise money for her publication by finding an investor. She wants to grow her publication and says this is not something she can do through crowdfunding campaigns. The key to sustainability is finding "brand sponsorships" and crowdfunding is a marketing tool that will help pave the way.

> I think this is more to get people to discover the site and when we do go and find investors, we can show them—"over 700 people backed us with over $30,000. It must mean we're doing something right". We got so much press from it, and a lot of people found the site that didn't know it existed before. So besides getting money, Kickstarter is a great place to get yourself discovered. (Journalist, $30,500 raised on Kickstarter)

At the same time, however, the relationship journalists have with their funders is more complicated than simply leveraging them into advertiser dollars. Most journalists feel a strong sense of responsibility towards their funders (Aitamurto 2011; Hunter 2015). They feel compelled to create the work they promised, and to create work that will make their donors happy they made the investment. For example, this journalist says he feels very strongly about his funders:

> I care deeply about doing a good job for them because in a very real way, they cumulatively change the way I live my life. It was this, like a deep appreciation that I probably don't feel for many other people besides my wife. (Journalist, $95,500 raised on Kickstar)

At the same time that they feel this sense of responsibility, journalists want to keep their audience at arm's length in terms of editorial control. One interviewee observed that, while very thankful for her donors, ultimately this was a business transaction:

> It's weird because on one hand they're investing in your company. But on the other hand, they're investing through a platform where that's the main purpose of the platform. So you don't really owe them anything except for what you've promised them. We want to make them [donors] feel like they're appreciated. But at the same time, once the reward has been fulfilled ... that's all the relationship is between you and them. But

> we're always going to have a reverence for them, if that makes sense. (Journalist, $30,500 raised on Kickstarter)

Trying to create editorial distance, at the same time as needing to draw in donors as part of a community, creates a strange tension for many entrepreneurial journalists. On the one hand, they feel very grateful and beholden to their funders, but on the other, this is still a professional relationship of sorts.

Labour and Agency

In this final section, we briefly examine how journalists see crowdfunding as enabling them to work outside of legacy media and typical funding structures. First, for some journalists in this research, crowdfunding was a way to get started in a business where there are not many job opportunities. One journalist said she was finding it hard to get her "foot in the door" (Journalist, $1600 raised on Spot.us). She found it difficult to get editors to take her pitches seriously because she did not have much to show in terms of a portfolio. Crowdfunding allowed her to raise enough money to produce stories on her own. For other freelancers, the motivation to crowdfund was to raise enough so that they could make money in an economic climate where freelance budgets of legacy media organizations are drying up or non-existent. For instance, one journalist says he now uses a hybrid model to finance his freelance journalism—he gets some funds from legacy media, but also raises funds through crowdfunding so that he can be guaranteed to make some money.

> They'll [legacy media] pay me for a piece but it costs me $5000, $6000 to get on a plane and stay in a hotel for weeks, hire a fixer and do all the things that journalists need to do, it costs a lot of money. If I'm getting $500–1000 for a piece it's just not going to add up to enough money to cover all my travel expenses and pay my mortgage and health insurance and food and everything else. So what crowdfunding does, is it covers my travel expenses and some extra so that I am guaranteed to make some money before I even write anything. (Journalist, $33,200 raised on Kickstarter)

Others are crowdfunding to start online publications that are independent of mainstream media. As one journalist said, they would not have been able to launch a publication on their own because "it's way too expensive" and securing a loan was not a viable option as banks do not look kindly on new media ventures (Journalist, $11,700 raised on Kickstarter). For others, crowdfunding was a way to avoid giving up control of their new venture and not be burdened by bank loans. As one journalist describes:

> [One] benefit that I saw from crowdfunding was that you could raise significant money without having to sell or give away part of your project or your business. I know there are a lot of options for investors and other types of funding, but I wasn't willing to sell off any part of [publication] at this point. I do plan on turning it into—hopefully—a profitable business. I plan to raise more money for it and sell advertisements and sponsorships and things like that. I hope that one day it will make money and I didn't want to give away any control, to be quite honest. In terms of taking out loans and stuff, I didn't want to have that hanging over my head at the beginning. (Journalist, $15,000 raised on Kickstarter)

Aside from economic independence, for the journalists in this research study crowdfunding is a way to cover stories they feel are not adequately covered in legacy media, whether it be one-off stories or publications devoted to independent journalism. As one journalist noted:

> I feel like it offers the opportunity to get the story out there that someone wouldn't report on normally. So I feel in that way there's almost a need for it. To get other things out there that wouldn't be out there. To allow writers to go down a path where maybe at the beginning there's not as much support, or there's a more open ending to it. I feel crowdfunding provides a lot of opportunities. (Journalist, $3200 raised on Kickstarter)

Conclusion

Crowdfunding through single-campaign platforms such as Kickstarter, Indiegogo and the now-defunct Spot.us is extremely labour intensive. Both the design of the campaign and the outreach involved takes a great deal of time and energy, requiring journalists to tap into their networks of families, friends and colleagues. The process of asking for money on a public platform also makes many journalists uncomfortable. Having to become entrepreneurs who are effectively "selling" their idea to a wider public is at odds with the work routines and norms most journalists are used to. As Kawamoto (2003, 23) describes: "In traditional news organizations, there is a metaphorical firewall between the advertising and editorial functions of a news medium". In crowdfunding, of course, this firewall between the money and the journalists no longer exits; what journalists are able to create depends entirely on how well they market and sell their ideas. While some journalists have embraced becoming more transparent and public about their process, seeing this as part of the move to involve audiences more in the news process, many feel very awkward about asking for money and marketing their work. Aitamurto (2011) found that younger journalists were more comfortable with the process than older journalists, however, in this research both less experienced and more experienced journalists felt awkward about marketing their work, or as one journalist described, having to "ask for permission" from the public before beginning their reporting (Journalist, $2200 raised on Kickstarter). This move towards entrepreneurial journalism goes against the norms under which most journalists are used to operating.

Alongside this sense of discomfort in the entrepreneurial space, however, some journalists do feel empowered at being able to work outside of legacy media. This affords journalists a sense of agency, a sense that they have power and can change, even in some small way, how journalism is done. Most are crowdfunding because they want to tell stories that they feel are not being reported, or are underreported in legacy media. Many journalists speak very positively about the freedom they feel crowdfunding gives them in this regard.

It may well be, however, that many of these journalists are engaging in what Kuehn and Corrigan (2013) call "hope" labour. As they describe, hope labour is "un- or under-compensated work carried out in the present, often for experience or exposure, in the hope that future employment opportunities may follow" (21). In this research study most journalists said they do not make a lot of money from crowdfunding and do not see it as a sustainable long-term way to raise funding. Rather, they are hoping that crowdfunding will be the start of full-time employment. If they are raising funds to start an online publication, many are hoping that they will be able to make this their full-time job by securing advertising or large investor funding. As argued previously, essentially these journalists are hoping to "sell" their donors to advertisers and make the case that advertisers should invest in their publication, because they have a proven audience. This process fits with theories of the audience commodity (Smythe 1981), in that key to this process is the idea that donors will become audiences, who will then "work" paying attention to advertisements. In a sense, they can also be considered "prosumer commodities" (Fuchs 2012a, 2012b) as they have helped produce the journalism in the first place, by funding it. As discussed, theories of the audience commodity are controversial, and with crowdfunding the case can be made that donors are freely giving their attention and their money to journalists. In one sense, this is empowering, but becomes murkier as journalists hope to leverage donor attention into advertising revenue. In the case of journalists who are starting their careers, and more seasoned freelancers, they are hoping that crowdfunding will bolster sagging freelance budgets and allow them to either get their start as a journalist, or continue as freelancers. While in one sense this could be characterized as empowering, in another, drawing on Cohen's (2012) research into the exploitation of freelance journalists, crowdfunding is also a way for news organizations to get more work out of freelance employees for less money. If freelancers are turning to crowdfunding, and all the labour this entails, in order to make freelancing financially viable, news organizations that use this form of journalism are profiting from unpaid labour. While crowdfunding can work well for journalists who have the energy to invest in the process, and who have small, finite projects in mind, such as start-up funds or travel funds, it is not a long-term solution to the economic uncertainty facing the field. It is, however, a place where start-ups and experiments can secure initial funding, and perhaps go on to leverage further funding through traditional advertising models or philanthropic support.

Limitations and Further Research

This research has focused for the most part on relatively well-established one-off crowdfunding sites, where norms and protocols have developed. However, further research that examines how successful journalists have been in securing on-going crowdfunding, through sites such as Patreon, would be interesting and useful. In addition, this research has touched on three crowdfunding platforms, only one of which was specifically designed for journalists. There is likely much to be learned from past experiments in crowdfunding platforms aimed specifically at journalists that are now defunct, such as Contributoria, a site for freelance journalists, Vourno, a site for video journalists, and Indie Voices, which targeted independent journalism. There are also several sites still in operation that are experimenting with different crowdfunding models, such as Beacon that has used subscriptions and donation-matching, and Byline, an invite-only platform in its beta form, that has plans to expand.

DISCLOSURE STATEMENT

No potential conflict of interest was reported by the author.

FUNDING

This work was supported by the Social Sciences and Humanities Research Council of Canada [grant number 430-2014-0426].

REFERENCES

Aitamurto, Tanja. 2015. "The Role of Crowdfunding as a Business Model in Journalism: A Five-layered Model of Value Creation." In *Crowdfunding the Future*, edited by Lucy Bennett, Bertha Chin, and Bethan Jones, 189–205. New York: Peter Lang.

Aitamurto, Tanja. 2011. "The Impact of Crowdfunding on Journalism." *Journalism Practice* 5 (4): 429–445.

Bannerman, Sara. 2013. "Crowdfunding Culture." *Wi: Journal of Mobile Media* 7 (1). http://wi.mobilities.ca/crowdfunding-culture/.

Carvajal, Miguel, José A García-Avilés, and José L González. 2012. "Crowdfunding and Non-profit Media." *Journalism Practice* 6 (5–6): 638–647.

Caraway, Brett. 2011. "Audience Labor in the New Media Environment: A Marxian Revisiting of the Audience Commodity." *Media, Culture & Society* 33 (5): 693–708.

Charmaz, Kathy. 2006. *Constructing Grounded Theory: A Practical Guide Through Qualitative Analysis*. London: Sage.

Cohen, Nicole S. 2012. "Cultural Work as a Site of Struggle: Freelancers and Exploitation." *Triple C* 10 (2): 141–155.

Corbin, Juliet, and Anselm Strauss. 2008. *Basics of Qualitative Research*. 3rd ed. Los Angeles: Sage.

Fuchs, Christian. 2012a. "Critique of the Political Economy of Web 2.0 Surveillance." In *Internet and Surveillance*, edited by Christian Fuchs, Kees Boersma, Anders Albrechtslund, and Marisol Sandoval, 31–70. New York: Routledge.

Fuchs, Christian. 2012b. "Dallas Smythe Today – The Audience Commodity, the Digital Labour Debate, Marxist Political Economy and Critical Theory. Prolegomena to a Digital Labour Theory of Value." *Triple C* 10 (2): 692–740.

Gillmor, Dan. 2004. *We the Media*. Sebastopol, CA: O'Reilly.

Hesse-Biber, Sharlene Nagy, and Patricia Leavy. 2006. *The Practice of Qualitative Research*. Thousand Oaks: Sage.

Holton, Judith A. 2007. "The Coding Process and its Challenges." In *The Sage Handbook of Grounded Theory*, edited by Anthony Bryant and Kathy Charmaz, 265–289. Los Angeles: Sage.

Hunter, Andrea. 2015. "Crowdfunding Independent and Freelance Journalism: Negotiating Journalistic Norms of Autonomy and Objectivity." *New Media & Society* 17 (2): 272–288.

Jian, Lian, and Jieun Shin. 2015. "Motivations Behind Donor's Contributions to Crowdfunded Journalism." *Mass Communication and Society* 18 (2): 165–185.

Jian, Lian, and Nikki Usher. 2014. "Crowd-funded Journalism." *Journal of Computer-Mediated Communication* 19 (2): 155–170.

Johnson, John M., and Timony Rowlands. 2012. "The Interpersonal Dynamics of In-depth Interviewing. In *The Sage Handbook of Interview Research*, edited by Jaber F. Gubrium, James A. Holstein, Amir Marvasti, and Karyn McKinney, 99–113. Los Angeles: Sage.

Kawamoto, Kevin. 2003. "Digital Journalism: Emerging Media and the Changing Horizons of Journalism." In *Digital Journalism*, edited by Kevin Kawamoto, 1–29. New York: Rowman & Littlefield.

Kuehn, Kathleen, and Thomas F. Corrigan. 2013. "Hope Labour: The Role of Employment Prospects in Online Social Production." *Political Economy of Communication* 1 (1): 9–25.

Lindolf, Thomas R., and Bryan C. Taylor. 2011. *Qualitative Communication Research Methods*. 3rd ed. Los Angeles: Sage.

McChesney, Robert W., and Victor Pickard. 2011. *Will the Last Reporter Please Turn Out the Lights*. New York: New Press.

Mollick, Ethan. 2014. "The Dynamics of Crowdfunding: An Exploratory Study." *Journal of Business Venturing* 29: 1–16.

Pridmore, Jason, and Daniel Trottier. 2014. "Extending the Audience: Social Media Marketing, Technologies and the Construction of Markets." In *The Audience Commodity in a Digital Age*, edited by Lee McGuigan and Vincent Manzerolle, 135–156. New York: Peter Lang.

Smythe, Dallas. 1981. *Dependency Road*. New York: Ablex.

Trasel, Marcelo, and Marcelo Fontoura. 2015. "Crowdfunding and Pluralisation: Comparison Between the Coverage of the Participatory Website Spot.Us and the American Press." In *Crowdfunding the Future*, edited by Lucy Bennett, Bertha Chin, and Bethan Jones, 99–115. New York: Peter Lang.

Zara, Christopher. 2013. "The Year of Kickstarter Journalism: Crowdfunding is Doing what the News Industry Can't." *International Business Times*, January 10. http://www.ibtimes.com/year-kickstarter-journalism-crowdfunding-doing-what-news-industry-cant-1007836.

DISCOURSES OF ENTERPRISE IN HYPERLOCAL COMMUNITY NEWS IN THE UK

Dave Harte, Jerome Turner, and **Andy Williams**

In recent years, a new wave of hyperlocal community news websites has developed in the United Kingdom (UK), with many taking advantage of new opportunities provided by free open-source publishing platforms. Given the trend in the UK newspaper industry towards closure and retrenchment of their local and regional press titles, it is perhaps understandable that policy-makers have shifted their gaze to these sites. This article examines the viability of hyperlocal news services with a particular focus on those that are independently owned and managed. Such operations often have a longevity that sits in contrast to a number of failed attempts by major media organisations to operate in the hyperlocal space. Yet many of the business models that underpin these sites seem precarious, often benefiting from a degree of self-exploitation. Drawing on 35 interviews with hyperlocal news publishers from across the UK, this article argues that publishers draw upon a civic discourse in order to make sense of their practice. This framing may limit the potential to develop economic sustainability and risks alienating policy-makers keen to work with an idealised "fictive" hyperlocal entrepreneur.

Introduction

"Hyperlocal" publishing in the United Kingdom (UK) has been a topic for discussion amongst media commentators (Greenslade 2007) and media regulators (Ofcom 2009, 2012) for a number of years. The growth in local news websites with a community orientation has been lauded by organisations close to media policy-makers. The civically minded consultants Talk About Local (2011) see themselves as giving "people the simple skills and support to find a powerful online voice for their community", whilst enterprise-focused investors such as Nesta have commissioned several reports about the phenomenon (Radcliffe 2012, 2015; Nesta and Kantar Media 2013) and invested their own funds in capacity-building initiatives. The more recent involvement of the Carnegie Trust has seen further investments of funds but also a more direct appeal to the British government for support and recognition to the sector, with calls for reviews to a skewed media regulatory climate in order "to start levelling the playing field on financial support" (Carnegie UK Trust 2014, 14). These interventions result in hyperlocal media being variously framed as: a potential saviour of local journalism, an emergent area of the internet economy and a mechanism to strengthen community cohesion. It is seemingly a space in which large media organisations (Guardian Media Group, Local World and Tindle Newspapers have all had endeavours in this space), individual business entrepreneurs and the amateur enthusiast can all see opportunity. To a degree, hyperlocal media sits refreshingly in contrast to the on-going "narratives of decline" (McNair 2002, 9) around the local press whereby the critical perspective on the press is almost always pessimistic. Hyperlocal's promise is articulated as an innovative, bottom-up, technology-led, alternative to the institutionalised model of news production:

> The 20th century model was for news to be gathered and delivered by institutions, very much shaped by the technologies available to them. The 21st century model shaped by new technologies is for news to be gathered and delivered by individuals and small specialist organisations and networks. (Carnegie UK Trust 2014, 2)

Given that the sector has now attracted public innovation and enterprise investment in the UK through Nesta and the Technology Strategy Board's "Destination Local" initiative (to support "sustainable forms of hyperlocal media services"; Geels 2013), it is timely that research focuses on whether hyperlocal publishing can fulfil its potential as a site of enterprise. This article examines some of the realities of running hyperlocal news media services and seeks to understand the range of motivations that fuel its practitioners' continued involvement in the space. Our focus is on the UK but the issues discussed here mirror the concerns of researchers in the United States and Europe who are investigating similar networks of community news operations. This article seeks to ask: what discourses—"institutionalised and taken-for-granted ways of thinking" (Jones 2014, 241)—of entrepreneurship do hyperlocal publishers draw upon? In what ways do they situate themselves as civic activists, digital business innovators or, indeed, both, at the forefront of a journalism enterprise revolution?

The research discussed here is part of a wider examination of the role of hyperlocal media in the UK. The "Media, Community and the Creative Citizen" project (funded by the UK Research Councils from 2012 to 2015) focused on the ways in which everyday creativity, supported by digital technologies, could enhance civic life. One of the project's research strands examined the growing phenomena of hyperlocal media in which citizens created news blogs about villages, towns or suburbs, usually about the areas in which they lived. As well as scoping the scene in general by defining the number of active sites and the volume of news it produced (Harte 2013, 2014), the project also undertook a content analysis and survey of practitioners (Williams, Harte, and Turner 2014; Williams et al. 2014).

The content analysis set out to examine hyperlocal against a similar set of criteria as had been applied to content analyses of the mainstream press. That is: Who gets to define hyperlocal news? What news is covered? What is the civic value of hyperlocal news (Williams, Harte, and Turner 2014, 6)? The analysis found that hyperlocal plays a valuable role in holding local power to account, but the results of a subsequent survey of 183 hyperlocal publishers revealed that two-thirds were paying all the costs of running their operations themselves (Williams et al. 2014, 28). Of those who did earn some funds, just over one-third were making less than £100 a month (30).

Such statistics give a glimpse into the precarious financial underpinning of hyperlocal in the UK, offering similar findings to van Kerkhoven and Bakker's (2014, 307) study of the "difficult circumstances" facing Dutch hyperlocals. But further interviews would reveal the lived experience of running news operations with such seemingly slim resources. It is these interviews that form the focus of this paper in order to discover what range of attitudes to entrepreneurship emerge within a practice so often situated as primarily a civic endeavour but one that is playing an increasingly important role in local media spheres. Specifically, we focus on the range of motivations of practitioners, the extent to which they draw on an entrepreneurial discourse in describing their practice, and explore the degree to which there is self-exploitation and precariousness within the sector.

The "Fictive" Journalism Entrepreneur

Jones and Spicer (2009, 10) have argued that the term "entrepreneur" has moved beyond the narrow Schumpeterian notion of the individual "self-made" person profiting from disrupting the market. It is now applied in a much broader sense to a larger range of individuals who might display entrepreneurial behaviours in different contexts. Entrepreneurs might be socially rather than economically focused or perhaps be from within the public sector, identifying efficiencies or improving relationships with citizens. Jones and Spicer argue that this generalisation in the use of the term is symptomatic of the way in which an enterprise culture reached into many aspects of public life in the 1980s and 1990s. Irrespective of setting, there has emerged a clear, dominant discourse of entrepreneurship: "[it] is a relatively coherent discourse which emphasises risk taking, calculation and economising, and represents these points in unfailing positive ways" (Jones and Spicer 2009, 15).

Researchers have increasingly focused on discourse as a route to explaining how such notions gain consensus. Sally Jones' (2014, 241) analysis of educational policy papers found that the "combative, status driven and all-conquering entrepreneur is still prevalent in contemporary business culture" and one that is situated in "historically masculine-framed ideas of entrepreneurship" (241). Jones argues that in education there exists the idealised "fictive" entrepreneur (drawing on Bourdieu and Passeron's [1994] discussion of the fictive student). Such a figure—gifted, responsive—is framed within policy discussion as a role model to which "only the handful of gifted, fictive students are able to achieve" (Jones 2014, 240). Luke Goode (2009) argues that this situating of such idealised "fictive" figures is common in writings on citizen- or community-led journalism initiatives, noting how much work on citizen journalism tends to "invoke a modernist, heroic narrative in which individual citizens ... serve as fitting descendants of the radical pioneers of modern journalism prior to its corruption by commerce and vested interests" (Goode 2009, 1290). Despite alluding to the political economy of citizen journalism (1289), Goode does not engage with the notion of the citizen journalist as entrepreneur, yet it is clear that the "heroic" fictive figure of the citizen as journalist also permeates the grey policy literature of hyperlocal where, empowered by digital technology and social media, such a figure is required to hold a diverse skill set, well beyond that of the traditional local "hack":

> You also need to invest time in developing relationships, promoting your site, and in some cases working to turn your operation into a viable business. As the platforms become easier to use and more commonplace, human skills are becoming as important as technical ones. Community management, sales ability and other skills in communication and content promotion are all becoming increasingly important if you want your voice to be heard. (Radcliffe 2012, 16)

Radcliffe (2012, 16; writing on behalf of the UK innovation charity Nesta) argues that embracing this diversity of skills, "can be fundamental in making hyperlocal pay". But the pressure placed on the hyperlocal entrepreneur by policy-makers and academics alike is not just a personal one but a societal one. The UK communications regulator Ofcom (2012, 103) claimed that these sites have "the potential to support and broaden the range of local media content available to citizens and consumers at a time when traditional local media providers continue to find themselves under financial pressure". Martin Moore —writing for the Media Standards Trust—argues that securing the future of local journalism is at stake: "the business model that supported news in the twentieth century no longer sustains it in the 21st. Hardest to fund has been local news reporting. This is not peculiar to the UK but symptomatic of many mature western democracies" (Moore 2014, 27).

The question of who will develop and run these sites is partly answered by the Carnegie Trust. They have given financial support to a small number of hyperlocal publishers and argue that hyperlocal offers an entrepreneurial exit strategy for those journalists made redundant from mainstream journalism. It recommends that the National Union of Journalists "should consider how it can work with employers and the government to support its members who lose their jobs in a news institution to become entrepreneurs running hyperlocal media" (Carnegie UK Trust 2014, 16).[1] Pekkala and Cook (2012, 114) draw on a set of interviews with journalism entrepreneurs participating in a development programme to claim that, "Journalists are looking to reinvent their careers". Further, the "reconfigured" journalist entrepreneur has a real chance to act "as a connector: between audiences, services and revenue streams. This triangulation requires a new emphasis on business skills to complement those already honed through journalism" (114).

The Precarious Journalism Entrepreneur

Embarking on an entrepreneurial career is inevitably precarious. Mirjam Gollmitzer's (2014, 8) study of the working lives of German freelance journalists found stress and satisfaction in equal measure within the independent context in which they carried out their profession. There was a strong desire to do justice to the normative values of journalism even if it required a degree of self-exploitation: "the complex narratives of freedom, independence, and public service ethos illustrate the will to journalistic professionalism, even as the acute awareness of economic insecurity and high stress levels relativizes those claims" (12). Gollmitzer's study contributes to the growing literature about the experiences of workers in the creative industries, which have focused on the issue of precariousness (Hesmondhalgh and Baker 2011, 2008; Ross 2008). Gill and Pratt (2008) describe the two ways in which we can understand the term: firstly, "precariousness (in relation to work) refers to all forms of insecure, contingent, flexible work—from illegalized, casualized and temporary employment, to homeworking, piecework and freelancing" (3); however, they also note how the term "embodies a critique of contemporary capitalism in tandem with an optimistic sense of the potential for change" (10). Those working in a "precarious" way have the potential to see "new subjectivities, new socialities and new kinds of politics" (10).

Hesmondhalgh and Baker's (2008) workplace ethnography of the television industry attempted to show "the specific ways in which precariousness is registered and negotiated in the lives of young workers in one media industry" (Hesmondhalgh and Baker 2008, 104). Their findings identify the vulnerability of working in the creative sector yet they also draw attention to the "symbolic nature of cultural products" (Hesmondhalgh and Baker 2008, 114) produced by workers. Like the television programmes they discuss, local journalism also has a "symbolic power" that comes with pressures and bears a certain weight of responsibility in terms of enacting the normative values that are inherent within it.

In looking across research into the motivations of journalism students, Baines and Kennedy (2010, 105) note that students are less motivated by the normative, public service ideals of journalism than they are by the promise of a career that shares the attractive features perceived to be common to other jobs in the creative and cultural sector: "independence; risk-taking; non-routine; autonomy; creativity; control (and in some cases the prospects of high earnings)". These features, they argue, are also ones that are dominant in discourses of entrepreneurship. They specifically cite the opportunity that running hyperlocal media operations offers for the enterprising journalism student: "the establishment of such an enterprise can offer the autonomy, independence and routine-free career sought by many would-be journalists and which is often no longer found in traditional hierarchical corporate media organisations" (98).

Traditional approaches to enterprise education need rethinking and instead an emphasis on experimentation and creativity can better prepare the graduate to deal with the reality of a career that might never experience secure, full-time employment in the mainstream news industry. It is better train journalists "not only to work as journalists (employed or freelance), but to establish independent enterprises" (Baines and Kennedy 2010, 98). Thus hyperlocal is situated as an ideal that not only deals with issues of precarity and scarcity of employment opportunities but is also a vehicle through which the socially conscious entrepreneur can "extend the plurality and diversity of journalism—and journalists—serving society" (109). Whilst running hyperlocal websites have now become a useful feature of undergraduate and postgraduate journalism training (in the UK at least), it is unclear how many emphasise the need for entrepreneurial skills alongside journalistic experience.

Commercial Failures

The continued emphasis on the enterprise opportunities for the individual offered in the hyperlocal space is perhaps surprising given the landscape is seemingly littered with commercial failures. *The Guardian*'s city-based "Guardian Local" experiment closed in 2011 after just over a year of running hyperlocal operations in three UK cities, claiming that it was "not sustainable in its present form" (Pickard 2011). Perhaps the largest experiment run in the UK was the "Local People" network operated by Northcliffe Media (subsequently Local World Ltd) as a franchise operation. A network of paid community publishers curated content and wrote stories in small towns across the UK. However, it gradually removed financial support with around 100 publisher roles reduced to 75 in a restructuring process in August 2012 and in turn the remaining posts were axed the following year.[2] Research by Thurman, Pascal, and Bradshaw (2011, 7) examining this network found that although "Local People" did have paid journalists (before ultimately moving to a franchise model), it suffered in comparison to sites with a more civic-minded approach:

> the reliance on community publishers from journalism backgrounds suggests that particular assumptions were made about the needs of such a community-driven project. In particular, the idea of community management as a skill distinct from traditional publishing roles appears to be, if not completely absent, then not a priority. (Thurman, Pascal, and Bradshaw 2011, 7)

Such a critique is similar to that made by St. John, Johnson, and Nah (2013, 208), whose analysis of Patch.com in the United States argued that it lacked a "community sensibility". David Baines (2012, 163) offers a case study of a major UK regional (unnamed) news publisher setting up a hyperlocal project but one that ultimately founders as a result of meeting the "Media Company's corporate needs, not the community's". Jones and Salter (2012, 103–107) also note the tensions between the need for hyperlocal sites to have an emphasis on community engagement whilst ensuring they attract advertisers that may well compromise that position. The problem of the sustainability of emergent hyperlocal media organisations is the focus of research by Kurpius, Metzgar, and Rowley (2010), who interviewed proprietors of a range of hyperlocals in the United States. They noted that whilst the form had a better chance for survival than previous experiments in civically orientated, participatory journalism, it found itself lacking a single recipe for financial success. They note that although a vibrant alternative media scene was needed now more than ever, they were unsure if hyperlocal media would survive to be part of it:

> It is not enough to declare hyperlocal media operations the antidote to the decline of traditional media outlets in the United States. None of the evidence suggests that any of these projects has developed a working model that can be easily replicated in other communities and maintained for the long term. (Kurpius, Metzgar, and Rowley 2010, 374)

Such recent discussions about the viability of alternative media forms may have a familiar ring to them. The Comedia group (Comedia 1984; Landry et al. 1985), in discussing the failure of a large number of 1970s and early 1980s alternative press titles, lambasted the sector for its lack of attentiveness to audiences and the resultant lack of appeal of their publications to advertisers:

> the "alternative" press has neither generated enough turnover from within its ranks to support itself nor consistently produced materials that are sufficiently attractive to entice floating buyers from outside its own ghetto, which could make the sector economically viable. (Comedia 1984, 100)

The upshot of the failure of the alternative press is that the workers in these small, radical organisations would "exploit their own labour to a high degree" (Landry et al. 1985, 97). Furthermore, in doing so, these organisations played an unintended role in shaping mainstream media output:

> The "alternatives" have produced something which has the chance of commercial viability, the "majors" move in and "sign up" the producers, who then leave the sector ... the alternative sector continually functions as a kind of unpaid "Research and Development" for the major commercial companies. (Landry et al. 1985, 97)

Ultimately, the potential for radical, marginal projects to develop a "Gramscian" political strategy, that is, to develop a sufficient economic base in order to navigate its own way to sustainability, is undone: "marginality becomes a self-fulfilling prophecy" (Landry et al. 1985, 98). At first glance the risk of marginality for the current wave of hyperlocal-focused alternative media operations seems remote given the scene is relatively profligate in production terms. Harte (2013) has researched the impressive collective publication rate of hyperlocal sites. Moreover, they receive welcome attention from those working to influence policy-makers and potential investors. But given the pressure on individual hyperlocal producers to be entrepreneurs who embody a diverse set of non-journalistic skills, as well as playing their part in ensuring media plurality (Barnett and Townend 2014), this requires us now to ask: "how do these 'hyperlocalists' sustain their practice and what kinds of entrepreneurs might they be?"

Method

Semi-structured interviews with 34 hyperlocal publishers were conducted in late 2013 and early 2014. The interviewees were drawn from those hyperlocals which, based on an analysis of a database of hyperlocals,[3] had demonstrated that they were publishing regularly and had been operating for at least a year. Overall, the sample can be said to be representative in as much as the balance of those working with voluntary or income-generating models, as well as the split between journalists/non-journalists, echoed that of the Williams et al. (2014) survey. The sample is certainly generalisable to the rather modest number of hyperlocals that produce content consistently and over a long (for this sector at least) period of time. In 2014, research found that there were 408 active hyperlocal sites in the UK (Harte 2014).

The degree of formal journalistic experience varied enormously amongst interviewees, ranging from experienced, formally trained journalists ($N = 18$) to those with no experience at all. There was no specific desire to target those with more or less training or indeed fill a quota that would comprise equal numbers of each, the gradations between trained/non-trained being too fine, with some having worked as journalists in the mainstream press yet having never received formal training. Others had a public relations background with first degrees that involved elements of journalism theory and practice. Clearly some could be regarded as "amateur" but Denis McQuail (2013, 92) sums up the increasing problem of trying to label journalists as either "professional" or "amateur", especially in the internet age which is: "encouraging new forms of journalism … rejecting formal organisation and with it any claim to professional status". McQuail argues that whilst journalism in mainstream organisations has become increasingly professionalised requiring higher-level qualifications, in the alternative realm such requirements do not apply but still "traditional norms and practices" (94) might be as evident in the latter as in the former.

The interviews were transcribed and then analysed thematically. On reading through the transcripts, the detailed open coding process allowed for a set of labels to be created based on the issues that arose from the interviews and allowing for the categorisation of attitudes and underlying orthodoxies. In his work on the use of Twitter in the newsroom, Stephen Barnard (2014, 7) uses the process of open, axial and then selective coding to allow a set of "frames" to emerge that "revealed the accordant values and position-takings exhibited by actors' practice in the field". Such a process was put to use here as the initial coding labels were drawn together into broader contextualising themes.

Whilst it would have been valuable to undertake a more ethnographic approach to understanding the value of hyperlocal, such an examination immediately comes up against the issue that there is rarely such a thing as a recognisable newsroom space in this sector. More likely, areas within the home, or a café, or public transport, or indeed anywhere and everywhere, become the places from which news is updated. That journalism is increasingly not produced within institutionalised spaces is something journalism researchers have recognised in recent years. Simon Cottle (2007) argues that the focus on "routine" in many earlier newsroom studies saw journalists as subjects of ideologically driven decision-making rather than having personal agency of their own. The disruption caused by technology should allow the researcher to make "a conceptual shift from 'routine' to 'practice'" (Cottle 2007, 10), heralding a "second wave" of newsroom studies (Cottle 2000). Wahl-Jorgensen (2009) recognises that the "days of the newsroom as a central ethnographic location may be numbered" (33) and the "newsroom-centric" nature of journalism research studies has marginalised particular categories of workers: local journalists, freelancers and citizen journalists amongst them (29). We are now in a period where workers are less likely to be tied to specific locations (33). That our interviews with hyperlocal publishers took place remotely (via Skype or telephone), mostly from their homes, therefore seems fitting.

Of the 34 interviewees, 28 were with men and 6 were with women. In terms of geographical spread, England ($N = 24$), Wales ($N = 7$) and Scotland ($N = 3$) were all represented in the sample. Responses have been anonymised for this article, with contributors identified by numbers. All the interviewees operated websites, with nine also publishing a print publication of some form.

Findings

Our analysis identified a set of key themes which we will discuss in turn. Although interviewees were asked directly about the economic aspects of their practice (questions posed included: "do you aim to make money from the site?"; "what is your business model?"; followed by further prompts), responses from across the whole of the interview topics revealed how dominant the issue of sustainability was even when not being directly discussed.

Civic Versus Financial Motivations

In identifying why they got started in their hyperlocal endeavours, our interviewees rarely cited what might be seen as a traditionally orientated entrepreneurial reason: that is, to create a new enterprise to make money. Only one interviewee described anything close to a "Dragon's Den" route whereby the securing of a university enterprise grant involved writing a business plan and pitching to a panel. Another chose to participate in a government-run enterprise scheme aimed at the unemployed:

> £65 a week it was at the time for six months. You had an option to get a cheap loan, and you could earn basically while getting that allowance. I kept that up and through sheer persistence, I think, I've developed a small income stream. (Int-16)

One professional journalist simply wanted to ensure their career continued as the opportunities for full-time permanent employment shrank and so therefore took matters into their own hands:

> We wanted to create jobs for ourselves. We didn't want to just sit there and go, well, the old traditional paymasters are not providing us with jobs anymore, boo-hoo, let's all go and be press officers. We decided we wanted to do something proactive about that and try and maintain ourselves in journalism in a more entrepreneurial way. (Int-22)

However, by far the majority of interviewees, particularly those without a formal journalistic background, were more likely to outline origin stories that had a more reputational/civic emphasis. They cited that starting a hyperlocal media operation came from a wish to play a greater role in participating in their community (often as incomers wishing to make their presence felt) or to address perceived reputational issues: "[we] really liked the area, and it's grown exponentially out of that" (Int-23).

> The area has got quite a bad reputation as being a kind of a chav area and we wanted to learn more about it really. So we just started with a little blog that covered the estate that we live on. (Int-2)

All except one of our interviewees lived in the place they wrote about (the exception was someone who remotely ran a hyperlocal about the town they were brought up in) so exploring the role of media in place-making was an oft-cited motivating aspect: "something like that could bring people together to some degree and it could create some sort of sense of place I suppose" (Int-6).

A desire to offer alternate representations (usually positive ones) were a very common reason to start a hyperlocal, an opportunity sometimes afforded by the shrinking coverage of local issues in the press:

> Another motivation was that the local newspaper ... has a very kind of negative slant on life as we see it and we felt there were a lot of positive things going on that basically didn't even get on the radar of the local paper. (Int-34)

That the local press seemed less able to fulfil its "watchdog" role seems to have provided an opportunity for many:

> I was aware at the time that the [local paper] had limited coverage of council business, and what business it was running was largely based on press releases and contacts within the council. There wasn't very much that was there that was actually questioning how decisions were made. (Int-20)

"Filling the gap" was a common theme but one articulated as a civic duty rather than a gap in the market from which a clear, scalable entrepreneurial opportunity existed.

One interviewee did see such a gap and in contrast to other respondents he articulated the "democratic deficit" as very much a commercial opportunity for himself: "I've always been very sure about the fact that there's no point in setting up something that doesn't have a commercial footing, because to me that's just a hobby" (Int-13).

The Entrepreneurial Skill Set

Some of our interviewees engaged in predictable entrepreneurial actions such as starting new companies (in two cases, running multiple companies), attempting to expand by extending their "brand" to other neighbourhoods and demonstrating detailed knowledge of the market potential of their operation. Yet whatever the initial motivation—civic, hobbyist or commercial—it is clear that on starting a hyperlocal there was a need to then develop a wider spectrum of skills that was not always anticipated. Many saw their operation as requiring them to learn digital skills in order to understand the degree of public engagement with their online sites:

> I've learnt a tremendous amount of actual backend stuff about blogging and SEO [search engine optimisation], and all those kind of things, which I had no clue about before. (Int-23)

> I do everything really. So there's selling and then making up adverts because I tend to do artwork for most of the people who advertise and then invoicing and chasing money for that, so that's another side of it. Writing and editing, doing techy work really. (Int-6)

The approach to picking up the required skills and knowledge was often a matter of just learning on the job: "I'm completely self-taught … I practised writing through blogging and basically picked up everything else on the way. I taught myself to video edit and shoot video" (Int-25). Learning new skills was part of the pleasure of having to (usually) manage every aspect of the operation themselves: "I do quite enjoy laying out adverts. It's another skill I'm developing, it's another string to my bow that I've learnt. I've always been a firm believer in that the more skills you have, the more adaptable you become" (Int-8).

Across the interviews no coherent sense of a connected network of practitioners emerged. This limited opportunity for knowledge exchange and it was rare to hear of skills being learned via the practices of others:

> we've picked stuff up. I think some stuff we've learned from other hyperlocal sites. We always keep an eye on other sites across the country to see what people are doing, the ideas they have, the stuff they're covering, how they're covering it. (Int-34)

Where there was attendance at networking events there seemed to be a clash of discourses: "we've been to this conference … a couple of years ago, we were commercial and we kind of felt we had a bit of a devil's eye there, how dare you be commercial" (Int-30). The value of having greater connectivity between hyperlocals was less about knowledge exchange and more about their potential appeal to advertisers:

> I think the concept is good in terms of having it as some kind of national network which would you could essentially pool page views or something like that. If you take the national outlook on hyperlocal, there is a zillion page views here and national advertisers could be interested. (Int-33)

(Not) Making Money

Although hyperlocals clearly have an entrepreneurial skill set, most are not concerned with making money from their ventures. Sometimes the reason for this was ideological:

> I'm really wary of the linkage of community stuff and money … I just think when money gets involved, it can be really tricky. I don't care if there's money involved, it's more about what people feel they want to do. (Int-27)

The resistance to asking for money was a fear of losing independence and tainting the relationship with their community; a fear of no longer being their "voice": "It's always been seen as the independent and uncensored voice of [name of area] and I think that's how I want it to continue" (Int-12). Some made a marked distinction between themselves and commercial mainstream press: "I'd say it's a community, it's about bringing a community together and being a community. If you've got newspapers, they're just about money, that's all they're there for" (Int-2). There was an element of bravado in some responses, with a sense that making money was entirely possible, just not desirable: "If I was interested in becoming a small business, I could do that, but it doesn't interest me in the slightest"

(Int-32). One described the potential of their site making "£50,000–100,000 a year" but they would rather operate it as a community venture: "I feel it's more of a community service than anything else ... I sometimes feel I'm just doing it for a labour of love. It's for the readers. So that's the part I like about it" (Int-24).

Confidence was also an issue. Indeed, some of the same people taking ideological positions also cited confidence issues. Many hyperlocals recognised that they needed funding, usually very modest amounts, to avoid the situation of having to pay for running costs themselves. Yet they simply did not feel able to approach businesses or indeed anyone for funds: "I'm terrible about going and asking people for money, just really don't enjoy it at all" (Int-29). Some waited until businesses approached them rather than seek it out: "if somebody wants to advertise and there's a couple of quid in it, then it happens" (Int-15). Those happy to accept advertising, and able to ask for it, do so within a discourse of community enterprise whereby it is fine to help local traders but less so large corporate organisations:

> [we were asked] what would you do if Tesco came along and said they wanted to advertise in your paper and we said, we wouldn't do it. And actually I hold the same view. We're about the community, we're about supporting the small businesses. (Int-31)

Many reported that they found the balance between doing journalism and reaching out to the local business community too time-consuming and often a distraction from what they felt was their core work (keeping their hyperlocal updated with content). In fact, for some it was any sense of operating in a commercial space that would be the distraction by making the endeavour much less pleasurable: "the thought of having the economic pressure of actually having to make a living through it, I think it would just totally take away the enjoyment actually and it becomes a chore" (Int-9). Occasionally the interviewees wanted to discuss what was meant by the term "hyperlocal" but only one found it a barrier to income generation:

> we found that it just took a lot of time to explain what it was we were doing, why we were doing it, how it could benefit the business and why they should do it. So it just wasn't really feasible. (Int-34)

Precarity and Self-exploitation

Perhaps the most common thread in our findings was hyperlocal producers spent more time than perhaps they wanted to on producing content and running their sites. Even where the hours were modest, the position taken was that it was too much in the light of either slim or no pay: "at least between 14 and 20 hours. It really is an unpaid job" (Int-7). "It's very rare that I'm not doing something to the paper or the site, finding articles, interacting, or whatever" (Int-28). The process of doing hyperlocal often feels like it takes over completely the lives of its producers, with one claiming that: "it's constant. We talk about [website name], it's like 24/7 pretty much" (Int-2). In this particular case it was keeping up with the social media output that took up most of the time and spilt into private domains: "we might have a missing person or a missing pet that's touched everyone, and I will check in the middle of the night to see if there's any news".

Although there was a recognition of the extent to which they were exploiting themselves, issues of exploitation extended beyond the individual hyperlocal producer and out to its network of contributors. Many described how their operations relied on sometimes quite large networks of volunteers who gave small amounts of time. The value that these volunteers gained was usually expressed in two ways. They were either seen as benefiting by gaining new skills or they were assumed to be benefiting emotionally from the act of contributing: "I think the other volunteers also feel that they're working for the good of the community" (Int-28). Clearly, without volunteers many of the hyperlocals in this study would not be operating in anywhere near the capacity they are, but even amongst those who talked up the value of the volunteerism, there were some concerns about the degree to which volunteers were being exploited.

There was much angst about the amount paid or not paid to contributors to hyperlocals and some expressed a limit to volunteerism:

> the number of people who want to blog about the neighbourhood for free, which is basically what I've been doing for quite some time, in a sustained long-term way is very, very small but what I've found is that crowdsourcing bits of content and stitching it together is a way that can bring people in. (Int-14)

Many interviewees had trouble articulating what rewards they felt should be due to others:

> I know time is money, whatever the words are. I've made a tiny bit of money out of the site … it might mean that if someone was doing some of the techie stuff, I could give them a few quid, because I'm a believer in you work, you should get paid for it. (Int-10)

For one hyperlocal there was acknowledgement that embracing a more enterprise-focused approach would solve their worries about exploiting others:

> what I'd like is I'd like to make more money, I'd like everybody who works on it to make more money. I want it to go further afield. I'd love to be able to franchise it out around the country. That would be great. I've no idea how to do that. (Int-4)

This tendency to fantasise about possible outcomes where the money issue is solved was a recurring theme. For most, the prospect of being able to pay people on a regular basis felt like a distant prospect and one in which the rewards might take various forms:

> I'd like to maybe be able to pay a retainer to some of the people who are regular contributors, on the basis that it might not be much, it might not even be NUJ [National Union of Journalists] rates, but it might be if you could post a story a week, you could have £40 a week or something, just a gesture. I'd like that. It wouldn't even have to be cash, it could be an Amazon voucher … I'd just like to somehow have something to say thanks to people, that would be nice. (Int-1)

Cross-subsidy, Grants and Alternative Economies

The tendency towards self-exploitation resulted in an informal degree of cross-subsidy whereby time was taken out of personal life to be spent on producing the hyperlocal ("I've got an understanding wife"—Int-20). But there was more formal cross-subsidising happening as well. Some hyperlocals described doing paid journalism-related freelance work as a form of cross-subsidy but others discussed how connected business ventures provided the financial underpinning for their hyperlocal. One hyperlocal cross-subsidised through producing magazines for a trade union whilst another produced a trade journal. Another ran a business "expo" that they claimed provided all the resources to employ two people to work on their hyperlocal site.

Despite the lack of desire or confidence to generate income, as detailed above, there was evidence of hyperlocals generating funds in innovative ways that demonstrate an entrepreneurial attitude. In one instance, a hyperlocal site that outwardly seems to be very successful in drawing in advertising was in fact using a bartering system:

> the adverts on there, most of those adverts you see have all been swapped. I wanted some tyres for my car so a guy from [tyre company] swapped me some tyres. I wanted my lawn doing, I've put one on for a lawncare company who's done my lawn for me. So there's no money there, I've just swapped them all for things. (Int-24)

Another hyperlocal asked for donations rather than accept advertising and uses an electronic payment system to allow readers to donate directly. However, he had instances where the donations came in a more direct form:

> a guy came up to me—this is amazing—a guy wanted to meet me, this is a few months ago, and he wanted to meet me in the community centre and he gave me £300 in cash, £150 of which were pound coins. I didn't ask where it came from. (Int-26)

But again, there was tension about how to deal with money. Some hyperlocals had not even the most basic knowledge of what might happen should they attract income: "being paranoid I rang up the Tax Office to find out what the code was for some unique tax" (Int-10). Whilst others were keen to dispose of any excess income through philanthropic means:

> any profit we make, we put into local good causes … it keeps the money circulating locally, but we don't want to bang the drum too much about it because we don't want to be too sanctimonious, be smug about it. (Int-7)

It was no surprise to see take-up of grant initiatives given the attention this sector has from public funders. For some it was a key part of their work, although securing funding was not easy: "that's another part of my job to try and find grants, and obviously they're harder and harder to come by" (Int-28). In this particular instance the grant income was not directly for doing hyperlocal work but instead was for a related activity that would cross-subsidise the hyperlocal: "I do other work with community groups doing digital media projects" (Int-28). In a similar example, the hyperlocal was happy that the funding was for other related activities rather than hyperlocal, making clear that where cross-subsidy happened it did not go towards paying individuals: "I just think when money gets involved, it can be really tricky … it's more about what people feel they want to do rather than have any money involved" (Int-27). But undoubtedly the income flowing into the sector is seeing an entrepreneurial response with those securing success noting its competitive nature:

> we were 1 of 10 projects out of 165 to be awarded that funding, and that allowed us to set up the business as a limited company and really it went from being a side project to being our main project. (Int-18)

Discussion

From our analysis, we find that hyperlocal media producers draw on a range of discourses in order to make sense of themselves as entrepreneurial subjects. This is not a sector that is internally cohesive and indeed our interviewees often talked about feeling ill-at-ease in the company of others doing the same thing:

> I went [to an event on hyperlocal] and I was the only person it seemed, it may not be true, who wasn't either a hard right-on campaigning activist or an absolute *über* geek. I seemed like the only journalist there. (Int-32)

But there is much overlap within the range of discourses that we heard expressed. Those who most closely conformed to "historically masculine-framed ideas of entrepreneurship" (Jones 2014, 241) were as likely as anyone to articulate that the decline in local mainstream media was a problem for local democracy. However, in their terms the appropriate solution to "filling the gap" was a commercial one whilst for others the "gap" allowed them to perhaps scratch a particular "itch" that they then realised had a wider benefit when their "itching" was disseminated via the internet through free-to-use open source blogging platforms or social networking sites. An example perhaps of using what Clay Shirky (2010, 176) has described as their "cognitive surplus" to create wider civic value.

In rejecting financial motives, the majority of our interviewees tended to draw on a civic discourse whereby they see their work creating other forms of value for the community they write about and engage with. In part they draw upon a kind of idealised "civic web" discourse (Banaji and Buckingham [2013, 9] offer a useful critique of utopianist positions about the civic potential of the internet), whereby internet technologies offer unproblematic routes to civic participation. Such participation is always expressed in positive terms. As one hyperlocal producer attempts to articulate, there is an underlying aim to achieve something closer to cohesion.

> Every area I think needs something like that to bring communities together, to bring people together, to share so you know what's about because otherwise you don't know what's actually going on in your area. So I think being able to do that is ... well, it's all about being a community, isn't it, I guess. (Int-2)

This view masks what is perhaps problematic for the hyperlocal sector: the widespread degree of self-exploitation amongst its workers. Interviewees almost always expressed how their input was above and beyond what was required. They find aspects of it pleasurable and burdensome in turns, and they have a clear sense of the "symbolic nature" (Hesmondhalgh and Baker 2008, 114) of their journalistic outputs. Indeed, in some examples they have a clear sense of the commercial value of their work and have resisted being exploited by mainstream organisations yet they continue to self-exploit based on their belief in the civic value of what they are doing. In turn they have a tendency to exploit others, again, drawing on a civic discourse to explain themselves.

But even within this dominant civic discourse there is certainly evidence of a wide range of entrepreneurial behaviours and attitudes, not least, as we have noted previously, a belief in the value of hard work. As tense as they are when it comes to talking about money, hyperlocal producers will try just about anything to draw in micro amounts of funding and in many cases they seem to be more than content with these small amounts. In that broad sense of how we have come to understand entrepreneurship (whereby it might be socially as well as economically focused, as discussed in Jones and Spicer 2009, 10), these are a group who fit the template: being self-starters, having a diverse skill set, taking risks and being outcome focused. That such outcomes are usually expressed primarily as being for a wider community benefit, with the desire for personal financial gain rarely foregrounded, should not detract from their value or potential impact. As John Hartley (2009, 162) has argued, such examples of "user-led innovation" have a role in reshaping and even undermining commercial models of public service journalism. However, the confines of the civic discourse mean that for many, the notion of making money is something of an anathema and potentially limits any prospect of further development of their projects. The repeated references to the motivating factor of what we might regard as hyperlocal's "warm glow" ("the big thing I get out of this is the creative aspect of it and the community aspect of it"—Int-29) is to a degree a discursive practice that prevents discussion about the complexity of the challenges facing the sustainability of hyperlocal. In some ways this research paints the hyperlocal producer as a conflicted, self-exploited figure in the entrepreneurial landscape.

Conclusion

This article has drawn on a range of interviews with hyperlocal media producers to argue that whilst the singular "fictive" hyperlocal entrepreneur, as imagined by commentators and lobbyists, does not quite exist, there is a dominant civic discourse that all our interviews draw upon to contextualise their practice. We can observe a range of attitudes to the economics of hyperlocal: at one end are those who welcome the market opportunity and are seeking to grow their operations into larger businesses; whilst at the other, there are those who have a vociferous resistance to any form of income generation. Yet the research findings offer some comfort for those who make claims about the civic value that hyperlocal creates. Academics or organisations who laud the civic activism evident in the output of many sites can feel confident that sustaining it is not dependent wholly on those hyperlocal sites generating income to survive. Williams et al. (2014) found that 62 per cent of hyperlocal publishers they surveyed raised no income at all yet 52 per cent saw no problems with sustaining their activity. Our findings have helpfully revealed that whatever position hyperlocal producers take on the issue of money, they do at least share a common set of entrepreneurial attitudes and skill sets. Almost as an inevitable consequence of their circumstances: they are multi-skilled, enjoy relatively autonomous working conditions, have a high degree of personal agency and are not averse to taking risks. Above all, they generally enjoy their work and feel valued by the communities they represent. The hyperlocal journalist entrepreneur then offers a challenge to those twin notions of the "hard-nosed" journalist and the "hard-nosed" entrepreneur.

Yet, in line with findings by Kurpius, Metzgar, and Rowley (2010) and van Kerkhoven and Bakker (2014), there is a sense of precariousness over hyperlocal's viability as either an alternative media scene or in simply "filling the gap" over the long term. For those looking to invest funding or to bring the practice to the attention of policy-makers, they can take comfort that the sector is home to some small business entrepreneurs seeking to grow media businesses that address concerns over media plurality. Yet such figures are few and far between and the risk in looking only for the "fictive" hyperlocal entrepreneur is that inevitably there will be disappointment and the policy gaze will move elsewhere. As Bourdieu and Passeron (1994, 16) point out: "if he [the "fictive" student] does not live up to being which he ought to be—his 'being-for-the-teacher'—the mistakes are wholly attributable to him, whether out of error or out of spite".

Ross, Andrew. 2008. "The New Geography of Work: Power to the Precarious?" *Theory, Culture & Society* 25 (7–8): 31–49. doi: 10.1177/0263276408097795.

Shirky, C. (2010) *Cognitive Surplus: How Technology Makes Consumers into Collaborators*. New York: Penguin.

St. John, Burton, Kirsten Johnson, and Seungahn Nah. 2013. "Patch.com." *Journalism Practice* 8 (2): 197–212. doi: 10.1080/17512786.2013.859835.

Talk About Local. 2011. "FAQ - What is Talk About Local?" http://talkaboutlocal.org.uk/faq/.

Thurman, Neil, Jean-Christophe Pascal, and Paul Bradshaw. 2011. "Can Big Media Do 'Big Society'?: A Critical Case Study of Commercial, Convergent Hyperlocal News." *International Journal of Media and Cultural Politics* 8 (2): 269–285.

Wahl-Jorgensen, Karin. 2009. "On the Newsroom-Centricity of Journalism Ethnography." In *The Anthropology of News and Journalism*, edited by S. Elizabeth Bird, 21–35. Bloomington: Indiana University Press.

Williams, Andy, Steven Barnett, Dave Harte, and Judith Townend. "The State of Hyperlocal Community News in the UK: Findings from a Survey of Practitioners." https://hyperlocalsurvey.files.wordpress.com/2014/07/hyperlocal-community-news-in-the-uk-2014.pdf.

Williams, Andy, Dave Harte, and Jerome Turner. 2014. "The Value of UK Hyperlocal Community News." *Digital Journalism*: 1–24. doi: 10.1080/21670811.2014.965932.

FREELANCING IN FLEMISH NEWS MEDIA AND ENTREPRENEURIAL SKILLS AS PIVOTAL ELEMENTS IN JOB SATISFACTION

Perspectives of masters or servants?

Rozane De Cock and **Hedwig de Smaele**

This article is concerned with a segment of journalists often neglected or marginalized in journalism research: freelance journalists. The most recent large-scale survey among professional journalists in Flanders, the Dutch-speaking part of Belgium, shows that one in five journalists is a freelancer. Only half of this group is satisfied with their job against 93 per cent of contractually employed journalists. Seen from this perspective, Flanders does not appear to be a very fertile ground for entrepreneurial journalism. Drawing on the database of the Flemish Union for Journalists (VVJ), we conducted qualitative in-depth interviews with a group of freelancers built around three main research questions: (1) What are considered the advantages and disadvantages of working as a freelancer in Flanders? (2) How satisfied are freelancers in Flanders with their work and lives, and what are the reasons for their satisfaction/dissatisfaction? (3) What are the preconditions to make entrepreneurial journalism a success in Flanders? Our results show that there is no "fixed" list of advantages and disadvantages as most features of freelance work (e.g. flexibility in working hours and assignments) can be considered as either or both.

Introduction

The majority of research on the profiles of journalists and their job careers consists of large-scale surveys conducted among employed journalists working in an editorial team. Freelancers or entrepreneurial journalists are often neglected or marginalized in these studies (Ryan 2009, 648; Edstrom and Ladendorf 2012, 711) and a qualitative research approach is even rarer in the literature. A report of the International Federation of Journalists and the International Labour Office (IFJ/ILO 2006)—that explicitly examined the situation of freelancers—still called them "atypical" workforces. Within this amalgam of unsteady employment such as temporary and occasional jobs, freelancers (71 per cent) make up the largest subset (IFJ/ILO 2006, 6). This 2006 report stresses the growing share of this type of employment within media personnel and journalists. The journalism profession is increasingly becoming more uncertain and more intense. The situation in which collectively negotiated agreements were the norm has been changed to a new reality where individuals increasingly negotiate contracts on their own (IFJ/ILO 2006, 3; Deuze 2009). As freelance journalists form an increasing subset within the professional market and since they already make up half of all journalists in some countries (for instance in the Netherlands; Hermans, Vergeer, and Pleijter 2011), the label "atypical" is no longer colleagues who work on a permanent basis. These findings are parallel to the results of research into freelance journalism in Germany where only a small professional elite of freelancers earn a high income (Henninger and Gottschall 2007, 54). The same pattern also occurs in Austria where the mean income of freelancers reaches only half that of their colleagues with fixed-term contracts (Hummel, Kirchhoff, and Prandner 2011, 5). The majority of freelancers get paid per story, while others are paid per word or receive payment in relation to time effort (IFJ/ILO 2006, 6). In general, freelancers have to produce more news stories than their employed colleagues in order to receive the same amount of money. Extra benefits such as health insurance, company car, mobile phone or luncheon vouchers are predominantly available only to employees (Paulussen and Ugille 2010, 64). In addition, self-employed journalists have less rights to sick leave and paid leave (10 per cent freelancers versus 85 per cent employees), right to maternity leave (12 per cent versus 88 per cent) and pension rights (7 per cent versus 73 per cent) (IFJ/ILO 2006, 7).

The need to devote time to financial concerns may also disadvantage self-employed journalists. Freelancers need to renegotiate on an ongoing basis so as to obtain a good salary. Many dislike this part of the job, but it is inextricably bound up with their self-employed status (Goris and Delforge 2012, 129). The situation becomes even more problematic when freelancers do not get paid for months at a time or even, do not get paid at all. In the latter regard, commercial skills and strategies for personal branding are not a luxury but rather an essential requirement for success (Gynnild 2005).

The 2013 survey in Belgium shows that only half of the freelancers (55 per cent) are very satisfied/satisfied with their job against 93 per cent of employed journalists (Raeymaeckers et al. 2013). In the literature on job satisfaction, a distinction between intrinsic and extrinsic factors of motivation emerges. Intrinsic factors such as level of creativity, variety in daily tasks, multiple contacts, intellectual challenge, autonomy and individual freedom increase internal job satisfaction and focus on the content of the journalistic work. Extrinsic elements stimulate the external job satisfaction and are related to social status, status within the professional sector, social engagement, working hours, work certainty, work pressure and wages (Deprez 2010). In general, professional journalists are more satisfied with the intrinsic than with the extrinsic aspects of their job (Deprez 2010; Hummel, Kirchhoff, and Prandner 2011).

It is clear that specific disadvantages related to a job in journalism (such as volatile working hours or job uncertainty) are more strongly experienced and felt by freelancers than by employees. However, not all of these are automatically translated into a higher degree of dissatisfaction. As far as satisfaction with working hours (45 per cent) and working pressure (35 per cent) is concerned, percentages are remarkably similar between freelancers and employees (Deprez 2010, 74–75). Differences occur when both groups of journalists are questioned about income levels (employees are more satisfied than freelancers), options for promotion (only 7 per cent of freelancers are satisfied compared to 30 per cent of employees), job certainty (only 25 per cent of freelancers are satisfied compared to nearly 75 per cent of salaried employees) and perception of social status (63 per cent of freelancers are satisfied versus 72 per cent of employees). Research by Teugels et al. (2009) has already indicated that journalists who work on a permanent basis estimate their personal competence to be higher than their freelance colleagues. A permanent job seems to be linked to greater self-esteem.

Thus, when we focus on extrinsic job factors, we see that journalists who work on a permanent basis are more satisfied than their freelancing colleagues. When we shift attention to intrinsic factors, a different image emerges. Freelancers, more than employed journalists, are satisfied with their individual freedom (83 per cent versus 74 per cent), job variety (95 per cent versus 88 per cent), and the multitude of contacts and new people they meet (90 per cent versus 81 per cent). Freelancers score higher on all but one of these intrinsic factors. The exception is individual autonomy, a variable that is mostly regarded as indicating job satisfaction in general. Individual autonomy is located in the extension of editorial autonomy, concerning which self-employed journalists are more negative than employed journalists. The differences are small, but significant (Cannie and Voorhoof 2010, 103). Freelancers indicate more often than employees that their ideas "never" or "only now and then" lead to a story. They feel that they are less able to influence editorial decisions.

Swedish research by Edstrom and Ladendorf (2012) connects the job satisfaction of freelance journalists to the condition of free and deliberate choice for self-employment. They distinguish between a portfolio model (derived from Handy 1994; see also Henninger and Gottschall 2007), in which talented, highly educated *young professionals* "are *pulled into* self-employment" and a marginalization model, in which less-talented media workers "are *pushed into* self-employment". The former is an optimistic model that stresses the advantages of self-employment, if deliberately chosen, for personal development and career structure. The latter is far less optimistic as many people are "forced" into self-employment to escape unemployment or simply because this is the way the media industry is organized.

Whereas in 2008 three out of four freelancers (75 per cent) in Flanders still indicated a deliberate choice for self-employment, this number dropped to 58 per cent in 2012. The remaining 42 per cent said they had "no choice" but to work as a freelancer (Raeymaeckers et al. 2013, 10). The former group fits in with the portfolio model, the latter with the marginalization model. The corresponding satisfaction scores confirm the importance of a free choice: whereas in 2008, 69 per cent of Flemish freelancers expressed satisfaction with their jobs, only 55 per cent did so in 2012 (Deprez 2010; Raeymaeckers et al. 2013). Together with the increased number of freelancers, the satisfaction level decreased. As 'forced freelancing' appears to be especially important among journalists below 35 years (69%), the future looks rather bleak.

Belgian journalists opt for self-employment for divergent reasons, but the longing for freedom and independence (82 per cent) is by far the most important. Other main motivations are family related (24 per cent) or financial (32 per cent) (Raeymaeckers et al. 2013, 10). Approximately 23 per cent of freelancers can be considered "big earners" for whom freelancing might be "a career opportunity for experienced workers, providing more challenges and better income than work as an employee" (Henninger and Gottschall 2007, 52). Freedom was also crucial in the discourse of Swedish self-employed journalists (Edstrom and Ladendorf 2012): both freedom *from* (managers, colleagues, assignments, working hour) as well as freedom *for* (especially family time).

Overall, we find that the choice to work either as an employed or self-employed journalist seems essential for job satisfaction but at the same time involves risk. In Belgium, a lot more journalists in 2012 saw no choice but freelancing in comparison to 2008. In the 2008 survey, 44 per cent of Flemish journalists agreed with the statement that, "media increasingly *force* journalists to work as freelancers" (18 per cent did not agree, 38 per cent were neutral) (Paulussen et al. 2010, 35). Hummel, Kirchhoff, and Prandner (2011) in Austria and, more generally, Deuze (2007, 2009) point to a steady rise in the number of freelancers, turning the formerly "atypical" workers into the future "typical" ones. This has consequences, not only for the individual journalist but also for the journalism market as a whole. A recurrent notion describing recent developments is "the loss of the collective" (Lee-Wright 2012, 23). Lee-Wright describes the disappearance of "mentoring relationships" whereby young employed journalists are taken under the wing of experienced journalists to become socialized and educated on the job. Self-employed journalists, in contrast, are isolated and are obliged to rely on their own initiative. Freelancers fall outside the collective structures such as unions and interest groups. As they are not covered by collective statute they must negotiate individually (IFJ/ILO 2006).

Methodology

In spring 2012, 71 freelance journalists were randomly selected from the database of the VVJ. Of this group, 22 freelance journalists were willing to contribute to our in-depth interview study: 14 men and 8 women in the age range 22–62 years. Interviewees were working as journalists for newspapers (quality papers, popular papers, national and regional papers), magazines, radio (national and regional), television (regional, public and commercial channels) and online media (special-interest magazines). Each interviewee signed an informed consent form. An interview guide consisting of central themes and open-ended questions was prepared. The interviews were fully transcribed and coded using the qualitative software package, Dedoose (dedoose.com). Each interview was coded by at least two coders who received coding training and discussed their work in order to reach agreement and to guarantee consistent labelling. A coding scheme was created during an inductive and iterative process. Open coding of the interviews was followed by axial coding.

Based on the literature review, our qualitative and exploratory research among Flemish freelance journalists is built around the following three research questions:

RQ1: What are the necessary preconditions for feasible freelance journalism?

RQ2: What are considered the advantages and disadvantages of working as a freelance journalist?

RQ3: How satisfied are freelance journalists with their work and lives and what are the reasons behind their (dis)satisfaction?

Results

Preconditions of Feasible Freelance Journalism

Based on the analysis of our qualitative interview results, we found three clusters of preconditions our freelance journalists mentioned during the reflective conversations. In the presentation of our results, we discuss (1) the preconditions within the professional content and context of the job; (2) the preconditions within an organizational context (time management); and (3) finally, we go further into preconditions related to the wider socio-demographic context of freelance practitioners.

Professional know how: extra competences. The freelancers in this study stressed the need to have extra professional skill competences compared to employed journalists, although they say that the purely journalistic work in itself remains the same. They need to demonstrate the capabilities of a competent entrepreneur working pro-actively to acquire orders with a long-term vision. Using personal initiative is vital, as is investing in client acquisition by offering proposals and by initiating topics for possible news items. A "sit and wait" attitude is definitely not an option within this specific segment of journalism. Some freelancers formulate "entrepreneurship" very explicitly in straightforward economic and marketing terms:

> I have always introduced myself personally. I teach my students to operate as an entrepreneur ... Make a business plan and that is: what do I need to do in order to realize my plan, my USP, my Unique Selling Proposition? First of all: what is my USP? What do I want to do? It is better to focus on to one point, something you are really good at and where there is no competition. That is better than telling yourself, "I am going to do it all". (Freelancer M)

> You have to be able to define your position. You have to place yourself in the market. Also as a journalist, wherever you are going, I mean, you have to be the one who immediately shows personality, someone they can rely on. (Freelancer F)

Next to the passion and business instinct of an entrepreneur, discipline is a constantly recurring term throughout the interviews. Freelancers state that they have the advantage of experiencing much freedom in their work (see *infra*: advantages of freelancing). But as there is no direct superior to guide and steer they must show "self-starter" motivation to succeed:

> Discipline, lots of discipline. You need to have the discipline to really say: "Look, today, I am going to work". Because, when you have no discipline and you do not work ... Well, post-poning is extremely dangerous as a self-employed journalist. And planning, planning is really very important. Because, it all falls on to your shoulders. There is no one who will do it in your place or who tells you what to do. You have no structure, you have to build your own structure. You have to make sure that you earn money and make a living. So you have to think properly in advance ... Thus, I really think we are the better planners. (Freelancer B)

Alongside this strong sense of discipline, our interviewees referenced the need to manage their working schedule in a flexible and adaptable way. Busy periods alternate with lean times and, in this respect, freelancing journalists speak of coping with uncertainty:

> I think, you need to have some peace of mind, because there are many people who would not be able to live with uncertainty. I have already gone through times during which I had loads of work to do for two months and then, suddenly, it comes to a stop. By now, I know that June, July and August are very calm months for me, months when I earn nearly nothing at all. Now, I am neither surprised nor scared by that any more. (Freelancer S)

The importance of having successful networks to obtain paid work is vital for freelancers, and more so given their status than for employed journalists. Using social media platforms to establish and develop this network was discussed with our interviewees. Yet, whatever the preferred method (online or face-to-face), networking remains a central competence:

> In the beginning, I went out to introduce myself personally. That helps. I also use Facebook a lot for that. I am more of an internet journalist. I do a lot online. I use Facebook and the

> internet as a member of associations and clubs, they offer me lots of information … Through Facebook, you can find all possible contacting information. Whatever you see when you are out somewhere, you just log in on Facebook, you send a message to someone and people always answer me, actually. (Freelancer C)

> You do need intellectual capital and a good network. It is extremely important for someone who studies communication sciences or journalism to start building their career while they are still studying. And you do so by networking. (Freelancer M)

The starting period is especially hard for freelancers. Only after a couple of years of practicing can most of them can fall back on a long and rich contact list or even a well-filled order package. This can even result in a situation in which freelancers have to decline orders and have to acquire a new competence: daring to say 'no'.

> It is hard to say "no". The first two years, it is difficult to find jobs, you have just graduated, you have no network to rely on. But after two years, you feel: "Ok, orders are coming in, and when an order is dropped or a client turns you down, there is always something new coming along to replace them". It is hard to say "no", especially in those first years, because you think: "Oh, they are not coming back" and it definitely took me about eight years to say "no" to my clients. Because now I know: they do come back. (Freelancer U)

Organizational preconditions: timetables and time management. Contrary to what may be expected, most freelancers do not complain about excessive work pressures. They mention lengthy working hours, and a number indicated that they did not want to calculate their earnings per hour for fear the sum involved would demotivate them. For the majority working overtime, and working in evenings and at weekends, is simply part of their type of job:

> I really do a lot of work during the weekends, actually, it is never finished. Occasionally, I say to myself: "This weekend, I am not going to work". But most of the time, I am preparing for an interview and doing research, or I am writing a story. Most of the time, I am doing something, but it doesn't really feel like working. That is also because, during the week, it can happen that you say to yourself: "Okay, today, I don't have a lot to do, I can go to practise my sport". (Freelancer S)

> There is no such thing as "doing overtime". Generally, I easily work 10 hours a day, on average. And then I am not even mentioning days on which you start working at 10 a. m. and have to go to a movie première in the evening or a reception, or a fashion show or the presentation of a production or the television stars awards. Then, you are working until 3 a.m. in the morning. Is that working overtime? No, that is just doing your job. It is part of the job, if you can't stand that, you shouldn't enter the profession. (Freelancer A)

More important than actual working hours is what one interviewee called "mental hygiene". Essentially, this means acquiring the mental state to avoid burn-out:

> I believe you ought to pay a lot of attention to "mental hygiene", by that, I mean you have to do other things than only working. You have to eat well, eat nice and good food, not

> only junk food. You have to drink well, nice and good drinks. You need to have good hobbies, seeing other people on a regular basis. (Freelancer M)

When freelance journalists were asked about the implications of the post-2008 economic crisis, we received a double-layered answer. The crisis has created a situation in which freelancers have to work harder to receive the same remuneration as before, but there are also freelancers who claim that the crisis period is in a way related to an "advantage" for journalists who are not fixed employees on the payroll of news companies.

> Interviewer: According to you, what makes for the fact that you have "good periods" in which you receive many orders and what causes lean periods?
>
> Freelancer U: Yes, there are times in which they make a strong appeal to salaried employees during crisis periods, but actually, it is a dual situation because … Sometimes, they also fire employees and they make a stronger appeal to freelancers because they are cheaper. Crises, they are dual: sometimes they are good news, sometimes they are not, but it hasn't bothered me yet. In the past, it went up and down. There were times that it was very quiet from June onwards until September, due to the fact that many magazines had no publications. But now, by doing specific projects, I notice that I can work throughout the whole year, actually.

Preconditions within the socio-demographic context of freelance journalists. We asked our interviewees about their education, age, job satisfaction and wage, the importance of start capital and the possibilities for financial back-up when times are lean. For most of our interviewed freelancers, it was very important to have a financial safety net at their disposal, both during the process of deciding to start working as a freelancer and during financial hard times in order to tide them over. There are regular time gaps between completing work and receiving payment for that work. In some cases, a safety takes the form of financial back-up from a partner or parents, or additional income from a part-time job, sometimes outside journalism. Freelancers also mention the importance of savings as start capital for purchasing a car, a phone, a camera, a laptop or other essential equipment to allow them to operate as an entrepreneurial journalist:

> I was very young when I started. I was still living at my parents, so that was an advantage. I did not have to pay any rent and that was a good thing, because, in the beginning, it did happen that I had only work for two days out of five … I definitely would advise people not to become self-employed when you do not have any savings. When you start from scratch, do not start as a freelancer. It is better to start doing some temporary fill-in jobs. In that way, you can save a bit because, financially, it is not so easy to be self-employed. It takes a while. The first year, well, the costs are higher than the benefits … You really need some savings. Another disadvantage of being self-employed, is the fact that some news companies are bad payers. I do not get paid every week, sometimes, it takes eight weeks before I get paid. In those situations, it happens that you need to fall back on your savings. When you have costs of your own, when your car breaks down and you have to pay the mechanics, well, then you need a nice little nest egg. (Freelancer B)
>
> During the hard times at company X, it was important that someone at home brought in a bit of cash. If I had been on my own during that time, well, then I would not have survived because I had not been able yet to build up any reserve. (Freelancer B)

Most freelancers undertake work for multiple clients. Those who work for only one client are actually the exception. Strictly speaking, journalists in Belgium who want to acquire and keep the protected occupational title of "professional journalist" are not permitted to accept any commercial non-journalistic work. The rigid application of this stipulation has long been a subject for discussion in journalism circles in Belgium, especially during depressed economic times when paid commissions may be scarce. Some of our interviewees openly admitted to accepting non-journalistic commercial work:

> From time to time, I even work for advertising companies. Simply because, unfortunately, you cannot make a living out of journalism only, you need to take in a bit of commercial work. (Freelancer J)

When asked about wage satisfaction, we noticed a difference between the so-called "entrepreneurs" (see *supra*) and those who possess these entrepreneurial skills to a far less degree. All our interviewees report that remuneration is continuously decreasing:

> When I see how much time I spend doing research and writing and when I compare it to the money I earn for it, than I can only say it is a distorted ratio. I have enough orders to make a living, so I am not complaining about my wage but, in my opinion, journalists should get better paid because there are huge differences between different customers. Some pay me 0.04 euro a sign, some pay 0.05. Others pay per page and that differs a lot. (Freelancer U)

> I really believe newspapers and media companies ought to pay more. Payment is declining and they are taking advantage of it, especially because some say you get paid under the form of copyright royalties. They tell you that you have to pay less tax on it, but in the end, this is not accepted by the tax authorities. The media companies are using this as a false argument to pay you less. For me, that is unacceptable. I used to work within the walls of a media company, and freelancers do not make up the largest cost entry, although they always tell you so. These companies are splashing around money in other ways, so they really could pay their freelancers some more. (Freelancer S)

Advantages and Disadvantages of Freelance Journalism

The answers of the interviewees show that there is no such thing as a "fixed" list of advantages and disadvantages. Most aspects of freelance work can be considered in both ways. Those who chose to work on their own see more advantages and are more satisfied than those forced into this role by market-place necessity. We described the latter as "forced freelancers" and the former as "voluntary freelancers". "Forced freelancers" are more inclined to see drawbacks.

> I had to give my resignation [as an employed journalist] because if you get fired, you are not allowed to work as a freelancer for that same company for one year. As I wanted to be sure to be able to work [for that media company] during the uncertain transition period, I resigned myself. After a while, I also started to work for other media brands. But in the start-up period, it was useful to ensure the connection with [that media company]. (Freelancer U)

Those interviewees *pulled* into freelancing consider themselves as working in an area of "entrepreneurial journalism" where their activity is more associated with independence, empowerment and self-direction.

> It is simply easier to start as a freelancer, to introduce yourself and to show what you are able to do. Afterwards, you can choose yourself whether you switch to employment or whether you stay self-employed. For example, I worked as an employed journalist for two years. Then I got tired of listening to a boss. When I left, they asked me to work as a freelancer for them. And then you get a crazy system where you earn more as a freelancer than as an employed journalist, provided you properly handle your accounting. (Freelancer F)
>
> Interviewer: Have you ever thought of doing something else, or getting an employment?
>
> Freelancer C: No, I think I will never again go for an employment. Then you are no longer your own boss. Now, I am almost not controlled by anybody … I prefer self-employment. But I am atypical, I have worked as an employee but I don't want to go back ever.

Some aspects of freelance work—for example, irregular working hours and working at home—are considered an advantage by "voluntary freelancers" but perceived as a disadvantage by the "forced freelancers". Several interviewees in the former category mentioned flexibility with personal situations including family arrangements:

> I make it a point to pick up my children from school at half past three. So then I stop working and I start working again in the evening and at the weekends. (Freelancer E)
>
> We had children, so the combination of work and family became more complicated. My wife also had a career. So I decided: "I will stay home and look after the children and work as a freelancer". (Freelancer F)

Nevertheless, having irregular working hours can be perceived as difficult to combine with family and other responsibilities:

> For example, news stories about the police, firemen … It can wreck you. With three or four hours sleep at night, you are a wreck at the end of the week and this has an impact on your social life. (Freelancer S)
>
> Actually, it never stops. You always work. It's okay for family life, but for yourself, personally, you are never done. It's very stressful. You are really never done. And if you decide not to work, you don't earn anything. (Freelancer C)
>
> I admit, I find it more difficult now than before. When I had just arrived in Brussels I was (net)working at cafés during the evenings, distributing business cards, doing interviews. In the end, you become crazy. Now, I try to do other things, going out with friends. So yes, it's not self-evident. (Freelancer E)
>
> Interviewer: To what degree are you expected to be reachable at any time?
>
> Freelancer E: For the radio, it's not too bad, but for the newspaper, it turned out to be a problem. It made me sick in the end, the feeling that it never stops. You ask yourself:

> "why are you not able to go quietly to the theater one night?" At a certain moment, it is just too heavy to bear, you know.

In several interviews, those involved mentioned the isolation produced by working from home, outside an office environment with colleagues, and the absence of regular feedback and support.

> What I lack, as a freelancer, is feedback. I don't know whether employed journalists receive a lot of feedback, but I find this a shortcoming. Feedback can also be negative. You learn from it, and sometimes I miss that. (Freelancer U)

Job and Life Satisfaction

We asked the participants to express their satisfaction with their role as a freelancer on a scale from 0 to 10 and to explain in their own words what this means to them. Furthermore, we asked them to do the same for their general satisfaction with life. On average, the freelancers in our study gave 7.6 out of 10 for job satisfaction. Individual scores fluctuated between 6 and 10. In spite of the obvious disadvantages, next to the actual crisis in media, the interviewees appear to be rather satisfied. Some participants wanted to distinguish between job satisfaction and the financial satisfaction connected to their work:

> Can I split this? Remuneration, that is 5 out of 10. But the work in itself is 8 out of 10. That makes on average 6 out of 10. The work is frustrating. You curse a lot. But it is, of course, also very satisfactory. (Freelancer H)

> Yes, that's a difficult question. It depends, financially I would only give it a 6, but with regard to amusing oneself, it's a 9. It is difficult to bring everything together in one figure. Let's make it a 7, then. (Freelancer B)

> Eight out of 10! I think that you already got the message that I like it and that I'm greatly motivated but there are some serious drawbacks: the financial aspect of the job, the lack of separation between work and private life, the lack of colleagues. So, 8 might be a good figure, I think. (Freelancer J)

> A fat 8. What lacks is appreciation for your work. With appreciation, it would be 10 out of 10 for me, notwithstanding the stress and very high work pressure. Look, when you choose this job, you know that's part of it. (Freelancer A)

The scores for overall appreciation of life ran largely parallel to job satisfaction scores. On average, respondents gave 7.5 out of 10 on both fronts although the scores did not run parallel for each individual participant.

Conclusion and Discussion

Our qualitative interview results clearly show that a "fixed" list of advantages and disadvantages for freelancing does not exist, since most features of freelance work (e.g. flexibility in working hours and assignments) can be considered as either an advantage and/or as a disadvantage. To a great extent attitudes reflected whether the choice to freelance was "free" or "forced". Those who chose freely to work on their own see more advantages and are more satisfied than those who were forced into the role. This finding confirms Edstrom and Ladendorf's (2012) distinction in Sweden between those (young) professionals *pulled into* self-employment and others *pushed into* self-employment. Free choice, therefore, is the main distinguishing precondition.

In our study, we found three clusters of preconditions articulated by freelance journalists in Belgium during the reflective conversations. First, we discussed the preconditions within the professional content and context of the job (1), then we dealt with preconditions within an organizational context (time management) (2), and finally, we focused on preconditions related to the wider socio-demographic context of freelance practitioners (3).

Freedom, or even more mastery and self-control, are frequently cited words in the interviews exploring these three clusters. Flemish freelance journalists want to be the masters of their own time, their job and their life. Freedom in journalistic work (e.g. choice of subjects, stories), however, seems more difficult to attain than freedom in work organization (e.g. working hours). But freedom has a price: the work is uncertain and seemingly never completed. Freelance journalists need to devote an important part of their time to "running their business". Essential preconditions to be successful therefore are business skills and competences with regard to budgeting, time and project management—discipline is a key element, risk-taking, negotiation and presentation (self-promotion). Journalists need to build a "unique selling proposition"—bringing a business value into the ethos of journalism. The traditional divide between the values of journalism and those of business seem to blur, and disappear, in the world of entrepreneurial journalism. It has been argued that there are considerable opportunities in journalism for those who think commercially (Laenen 2011; Briggs 2012). This reality, as mentioned previously, raises issues in Flanders given the Flemish definition of an accredited "professional journalist".

As we have seen, a successful freelance journalist is not an isolated journalist: he or she is the pivotal element within a broad social network (social capital), he or she preferably has a partner with a fixed income and gets some professional help with regard to accounting and budgeting. Again, an accredited "professional journalist" in Flanders can count on the support of the journalists' organization but as a lot of freelancers are not able to receive the title of "professional journalist", they cannot count on this support. Feedback and appreciation from the environment (e.g. colleagues, peers, clients) is often neglected but is an especially important precondition for (ongoing) motivation. Our results show the need to consider "mentoring relationships" (Lee-Wright 2012) as freelance journalists would also like to benefit from such support. In summary, freelancing in Flanders is not a black-and-white story with all entrepreneurial journalists feeling or behaving as "masters" instead of "servants". Unfortunately, due to unsuccessful preconditions and/or lack of appropriate financial rewarding and appreciation, some still feel themselves to be "slaves". Those journalists able to "master" their career structures—not least with the help of entrepreneurial skills—however, no longer wish themselves a future as a "servant".

Future research in this area could focus on the huge differences between countries as far as their proportion of freelance journalists is concerned, the reasons behind these differences, and the link with journalistic cultures and working conditions. The precise role of news companies who serve simultaneously as the "customers" of freelancers and as their "patrons", their expectations, demands and offers, need to be mapped more clearly in order to understand more fully the future of feasible entrepreneurial journalism.

DISCLOSURE STATEMENT

No potential conflict of interest was reported by the authors.

REFERENCES

Baines, David, and Ciara Kennedy. 2010. "An Education for Independence: Should Entrepreneurial Skills be an Essential Part of the Journalist's Toolbox?" *Journalism Practice* 4 (1): 97–113.

Briggs, Mark. 2012. *Entrepreneurial Journalism: How to Build What's Next for News*. London: Sage.

Cannie, Hannes, and Dirk Voorhoof. 2010. "De opvattingen van de Vlaamse beroepsjournalist." In *Journalisten: profiel van een beroepsgroep*, edited by Steve Paulussen and Karin Raeymaeckers, 99–113. Tielt: Lannoo.

Deprez, Annelore. 2010. "Beroepstevredenheid in de Vlaamse beroepsjournalistiek." In *Journalisten: profiel van een beroepsgroep*, edited by Steve Paulussen and Karin Raeymaeckers, 67–80. Tielt: Lannoo.

Deuze, Mark. 2007. *Media Work*. Cambridge: Polity Press.

Deuze, Mark. 2009. "The People Formerly Known as the Employers." *Journalism* 10 (3): 315–318.

Edstrom, Maria, and Martina Ladendorf. 2012. "Freelance Journalists as a Flexible Workforce in Media Industries." *Journalism Practice* 6 (5–6): 711–721.

Goris, Ria, and Guy Delforge. 2012. *Journalistiek: Inleiding tot het vak*. Tielt: LannooCampus.

Gynnild, Astrid. 2005. "Winner Takes It All: Freelance Journalism on the Global Communication Market." *Nordicom Review* 1(1): 111–120.

Handy, Charles. 1994. *The Empty Raincoat: Making Sense of the Future*. London: Hutchinson.

Henninger, Annette, and Karin Gottschall. 2007. "Freelancers in Germany's Old and New Media Industry: Beyond Standard Patterns of Work and Life?" *Critical Sociology* 33: 43–71.

Hermans, Liesbeth, Maurice Vergeer, and Alexander Pleijter. 2011. *Nederlandse journalisten in 2010: Onderzoek naar de kenmerken van de beroepsgroep, professionele opvattingen en het gebruik van digitale media in het journalistieke werk*. Nijmegen: Radboud Universiteit Nijmegen.

Hummel, Roman, Suzanne Kirchhoff, and Dimitri Prandner. 2011. "'We Used to Be Queens and Now We Are Slaves': Working Conditions and Career Strategies in the Journalistic Field." Paper presented at the Future of Journalism Conference, Cardiff, September 10–11.

IFJ/ILO (International Federation of Journalists/International Labour Office). 2006. *The Changing Nature of Work: A Global Survey and Case-Study of Atypical Work in the Media Industry*. Research Report retrieved from http://www.ifj.org/assets/docs/068/112/3fbf944-95ebe70.pdf.

Laenen, Ann, ed. 2011. *YoungPress.eu: Reflections on the Future of Journalism. Texts about and around the Conference 27-29.10.2011*. Antwerp: Evens Foundation and StampMedia.

Lee-Wright, Peter. 2012. "The Return of Hephaestus: Journalists' Work Recrafted." In *Changing Journalism*, edited by Peter Lee-Wright, Angela Philips, and Tamara Witschge, 21–40. London: Routledge.

Paulussen, Steve, and Tim Hoebeke. 2010. "De opleiding van de Vlaamse beroepsjournalist." In *Journalisten: profiel van een beroepsgroep*, edited by Steve Paulussen and Karin Raeymaeckers, 39–51. Tielt: Lannoo.

Paulussen, Steve, Karin Raeymaeckers, Jeroen De Keyser, and Sarah Van Leuven. 2010. "De gemiddelde beroepsjournalist in Vlaanderen." In *Journalisten: profiel van een beroepsgroep*, edited by Steve Paulussen and Karin Raeymaeckers, 23–37. Tielt: Lannoo.

Paulussen, Steve, and Pieter Ugille. 2010. "Werkvoorwaarden in de Vlaamse pers." In *Journalisten: profiel van een beroepsgroep*, edited by Steve Paulussen and Karin Raeymaeckers, 54–66. Tielt: Lannoo.

Raeymaeckers, Karin, François Heinderyckx, Sara De Vuyst, Manon Libert, Juliette De Maeyer, Rebecca De Dobbelaer, Florence Le Cam, Annelore Deprez, and Jeroen De Keyser. 2013. *De Belgische journalist in 2013. Een zelfportret*. Gent: Academia Press.

Ryan, Kathleen M. 2009. "The Performative Journalist: Job Satisfaction, Temporary Workers and American Television News." *Journalism* 10(5): 647–664.

Teugels, Marleen, Elke Van Hoof, Kristof Mory, and Hans De Witte. 2009. "Burn-out in de Vlaamse pers: een tijdbom onder de redacties." *De Journalist* 122: 9–12.

Teugels, Marleen, and Conny Vercaigne. 2010. "Burn-out bij journalisten in Vlaanderen: de slachtoffers van de nieuwsfabriek." *De Journalist* 136: 6–8.

TOWARDS A BROADER CONCEPTION OF ENTREPRENEURIAL JOURNALISM EDUCATION

Starting with everyday practice

Kirsten Sparre and **Helle Meibom Færgemann**

In this article we examine the impact of entrepreneurialism on postgraduate students of journalism at Aarhus University in Denmark. We specifically focus on a course module that students follow while undertaking a full-time internship in the media and communication industry. The module requires students to use their internship to identify opportunities for innovation, to devise innovative solutions and, where possible, to present and implement solutions. Drawing on focus group interviews and assignments, we explore how students experienced learning entrepreneurship and innovation whilst being immersed in communities of practice. The places of internship functioned as anchors for the students' entrepreneurship processes by providing access to a wide range of opportunities for development and a real-life arena for testing their own entreprenurial skills. Yet, even in this environment students did not necessarily develop a strong entrepreneurial identity. Instead, they felt the module content on entrepreneurialism made them look at their places of internship in a more critical way. Moreover, it provided them with skills for innovation and entrepreneurship that would be useful in the future.

Introduction

Over the past five years, a number of journalism educators have argued for the need to teach journalism students how to be entrepreneurial and innovative in order to navigate the challenges of a media market characterised by economic restructuring, job losses, constant technological developments, and changing relationships between users and producers of information (Kennedy and Baines 2010; Hunter and Nel 2011; Elmore and Massey 2012; Ferrier 2013). An increasing number of journalism schools in Latin America, Europe, Canada and the United States now offer modules in entrepreneurial journalism at graduate and undergraduate level (Schaich and Klein 2013). Despite the introduction of this new strand in teaching, an agreed curriculum on entrepreneurial journalism has not yet emerged.

Schaich and Klein (2013) and Ferrier (2013) have undertaken research amongst lecturers who have developed modules on entrepreneurial journalism. Both studies indicate that at this point in time modules are developed fairly autonomously in response to different local contexts. Schaich and Klein surveyed 33 lecturers from the United States, United Kingdom, France, Canada, Columbia and Mexico, including most pioneers in journalism entrepreneurship education. Only nine respondents said they had a model, or referred to an existing initiative, when developing their modules. In general, lecturers looked at and found inspiration in a number of different modules and contexts outside and inside academia (194).

Nevertheless, according to the two studies mentioned above, there is agreement amongst lecturers that the objective of entrepreneurship teaching should be to give journalism students an understanding of the business and economics of journalism, encourage the development of an entrepreneurial attitude, and provide students with skills and insights to set up and obtain funding for their own businesses. This focus on the need to develop skills for venture creation is also echoed in two studies of freelance journalists and start-up journalism entrepreneurs (Berkey-Gerard 2012; Elmore and Massey 2012).

In this article, we examine another approach to teaching entrepreneurship and innovation to journalism students. This approach is based less on skills for venture creation and more on building an entrepreneurial mindset, and giving students the skills to spot opportunities for value creation and to develop concepts that respond to those opportunities in either an entrepreneurial or intrapreneurial context. We are specifically concerned with the "Model for Entrepreneurship Education" (ME2-model) developed at Aarhus University in Denmark. Our case study shows how the ME2-model has been adapted for journalism students who are undertaking an industry internship part of completing a postgraduate module. Responding to Ferrier's (2013) call for research into the student experience of entrepreneurship education, we have undertaken research amongst journalism students at Aarhus University in 2014. In the final section of the article, we will show how the internship contributed to their learning process and how students negotiated simultaneously developing entrepreneurial, journalistic and other professional competencies.

Entrepreneurship: From Venture Creation to Everyday Practice

The number of programmes and modules concerned with entrepreneurship education continue to grow and are "reflecting a multitude of paradigms with different ontological views on the nature of entrepreneurship and different didactic approaches to education" (Blenker et al. 2011, 417). One of the very early approaches to entrepreneurship research focused on who was the entrepreneur in order to identify certain personality traits that characterised an entrepreneur. It was assumed that as the aptitude for entrepreneurship was primarily based on personality traits, it was not possible to train an entrepreneur. As a result, entrepreneurship education was considered pointless. In more recent times, this approach has been generally abandoned. Gartner (1988) argued for a behavioural approach focused on what the entrepreneur does.

The oldest and most dominant approach to entrepreneurship research that supports entrepreneurship education is the *venture creation paradigm*. According to Blenker et al. (2011), it is inspired by very early entrepreneurship theorists like Joseph Schumpeter and by traditional management disciplines (marketing, strategy and budgeting). The dominant structure for modules and programmes within this approach is the development of a business plan: students are trained in a rational planning process that primarily focuses on the relationship between the entrepreneur's new venture and its environment. The student is taught how to progress:

> through a series of stages gradually gathering and analysing relevant information and making rational informed decisions about whether—or not—to start a new venture; and if the answer is yes, how then to set up the business. (Blenker et al. 2011, 420)

Not surprisingly, this latter approach has been predominantly developed by researchers and educators at business schools (Blenker et al. 2011). Over time, a number of other paradigms for entrepreneurship education have emerged, including an approach which Blenker et al. have dubbed *facilitating an entrepreneurial mindset in everyday practice*. This approach was initiated by Steyaert and Katz (2004), who argued that a lot of more mundane types of entrepreneurship inside and outside of the market had been overlooked by previous research. More recently, Sarasvathy and Venkataraman (2011) took this point even further and argued that entrepreneurship is a method with potential for social change, which *can* be learned by everybody and therefore should be taught in all disciplines at all educational levels.

In general, this approach expands the scope of entrepreneurship from economic enterprise and profit to value creation in the broadest sense, and educational activities focus primarily on personal development of the students. Blenker et al. (2011) claim that this type of entrepreneurship education in some respects can be seen as a foundation for other forms of entrepreneurship education as it aims at creating an entrepreneurial mindset by combining a number of the following theoretical elements:

- The individual–opportunity nexus which basically postulates "that entrepreneurship involves the nexus of two phenomena: the presence of lucrative opportunities and the presence of enterprising individuals" (Shane and Venkataraman 2000, 218).
- Understanding of everyday practice in order to disclose disharmonies and create solutions for them (Spinosa, Flores, and Dreyfus 1997).
- Effectuation—a certain way successful entrepreneurs think and act (Sarasvathy 2001a).

ME2 as a Model for Teaching Entrepreneurship and Innovation

The ME2-model has been developed by academics working with entrepreneurship education at Aarhus University in Denmark. Several versions of the model co-exist under different labels (e.g. Bager 2010; Blenker et al. 2012). The model has been used as the basis for modules in different disciplines across the university's four faculties at BA, MA and PhD levels.

The rationale behind the ME2-model is that entrepreneurship is a method that can be learned and taught. Just as democracy and scientific methods cannot be said to be relevant only for a select group of citizens, Sarasvathy and Venkataraman (2011) claim that everybody is a potential entrepreneur and therefore entrepreneurship should be treated as an essential part of (basic) education. As a consequence, entrepreneurship should not only be perceived as a "career option or a fallback position in cases of employer downsizing or economic downturns; but … as a widespread driver of social change" (120). With this understanding of entrepreneurship as a method, its relevance increases for students who do not plan to embark on venture creation as a career path.

The ME2-model consists of four phases (Figure 1). The model places "means" at the centre because the means available to an entrepreneur impact on all phases of the model. Means stand for academic, professional, general and personal competencies as well as personal and professional networks. This part of the model is highly influenced by Saras Sarasvathy's (2001a, 2001b) work on how entrepreneurs think, a process she has termed

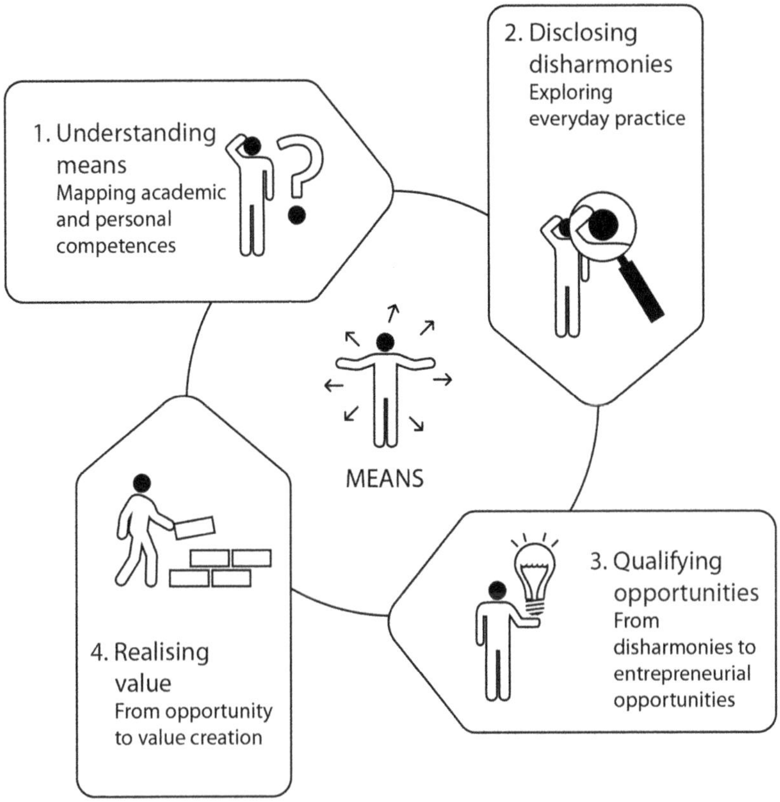

FIGURE 1
The ME2-model for entrepreneurship education

effectual reasoning. Through interviews with founders of companies of different sizes and in different industries, she found out that entrepreneurs are primarily driven by means:

> Effectual reasoning, however, does not begin with a specific goal. Instead, it begins with a given set of means and allows goals to emerge contingently over time from the varied imagination and diverse aspirations of the founders and the people they interact with. (Sarasvathy 2001b, 2)

Effectual reasoning contrasts with the predictive reasoning approach, which is causal and goal-oriented, and the traditional approach in MBA programmes that emphasise venture creation (Sarasvathy 2001b). However, it is important to mention that Sarasvathy (2008) also stresses that as start-up companies become more established and have more resources at their disposal, they should shift to a more causal approach.

In order to take a starting point in one's means—or as Sarasvathy (2001b) puts it, "who you are, what you know and who you know"—it is necessary to map preferences, interests, competencies, skills and network. This is essentially what phase 1 in the ME2-model is about. In practice, students are offered a personality-type indicator test, and afterwards establish an overview of their academic, professional and personal competencies, as well as mapping their personal and professional networks.

Phase 2 is centred on exploring and understanding everyday life and its embedded problems—so-called "disharmonies"—in order to identify opportunities for creating value in a very broad sense. This phase is primarily inspired by Spinosa, Flores, and Dreyfus (1997), who according to Blenker et al. (2012) offer a more structural and emergent understanding of how opportunities arise as opposed to Shane and Venkataraman's (2000) original view that opportunities objectively exist. For Spinosa, Flores, and Dreyfus (1997, 1), entrepreneurship is about history making which they define as changes in "the way in which we understand and deal with ourselves and with things".

The frame for history making is a so-called *disclosive space*, which is not necessarily a physical space but can encompass anything from a heavy metal fan environment to a cooking class, primary schools or a digital horse-riding community. In a disclosive space several *everyday practices* are carried out, organised and informed by *styles*. Styles are the reasons why everyday practices make sense and the way they are co-ordinated (Spinosa, Flores, and Dreyfus 1997, 17–22). If we look at the disclosive space of football we find practices such as kicking and heading the ball, running on a grass field, the referee whistling, substitutions and so forth. These practices make sense only because of the rules and traditions in football.

The opportunities for entrepreneurship come from identifying *disharmonies*. Disharmonies are practices which are not well co-ordinated with other practices (Spinosa, Flores, and Dreyfus 1997, 23). A possible disharmony in professional football could be the reliance on only one referee in games with high economic stakes. Identifying disharmonies requires a high degree of sensitivity because human beings, in general, are blind to disharmonies in our lives (15).

A prerequisite for teaching the ME2-model is that students have access to suitable everyday practices. Of course, all students have an everyday life, but at the same time we demand that they come up with a solution where they will be able to integrate some of their academic knowledge and competencies—the challenge is to match the two. Access to disclosive spaces can be established in many different ways, and once a disclosive space has been chosen, students start building an understanding of it by making observations, surveying or interviewing its stakeholders, and doing literature studies about the field. A final step in phase 2 is that students obtain evidence that their chosen disharmony is also confirmed as an anomaly by other people: "If the disharmony seems fairly pervasive—that is, if it exists for other people and in more than a few situations—it becomes an anomaly" (Spinosa, Flores, and Dreyfus 1997, 193).

In phase 3 students discover or create an opportunity.[1] In practice, they generate, develop and select ideas and finally turn them into some kind of coherent concept to create a solution for the disharmony. Equally important, students need to make sure that they have the means to implement the solution as we want students to work in an effectual way, taking a starting point in their own means (Sarasvathy 2001a).

Whereas entrepreneurship theory underpinning the ME2-model is quite clear about what this process should aim for, it is less clear about how to facilitate it: Sarasvathy and her colleagues claim that ideas are not a problem—everybody gets several ideas every day (Read et al. 2011). Spinosa, Flores, and Dreyfus (1997) present three ways of "dealing with a disharmony" but experience shows that students find it difficult to follow their approach when they are new to entrepreneurship. In this version of the ME2-model we have therefore chosen to introduce students to the difference between divergent and convergent thinking and the need for alternating between the two (Cropley 2006) during the process of ideation. Students work with a number of techniques for generating and selecting ideas, including Read et al.'s (2011) matrix for idea selection where the means of the entrepreneur play a central role in the selection process.

In phase 4, students embark on the process of realising value by demonstrating how they will turn their concept into actual value for users and/or customers. In line with Sarasvathy (2008), some of the methods and tools applied in this final phase are more causal than in the previous phases in order to create a clearer picture of how this opportunity could be realised. Most of the modules based on the ME2-model do not go far into phase 4, but in all modules students work with value propositions using Carlson and Wilmot's (2006) NaBC model and the Business Model Canvas developed by Osterwalder and Pigneur (2010). These models are focused on presenting value propositions and facilitating an iterative process of communicating with stakeholders in order to make the concept sustainable.

Adapting the ME2-model to a Journalism Module

Our module on entrepreneurship and innovation is part of the Master's degree programme in analytical journalism offered by Centre for University Studies in Journalism (CJU) at Aarhus University in Denmark. The MA in analytical journalism is one of five different Danish MA programmes in journalism (offered by Aarhus University, Roskilde University and the University of Southern Denmark, respectively). It attracts approximately 50 students each year. The MA programme is a two-year programme and consists of a number of modules on practical journalism skills, media theory, electives and a dissertation. The module on entrepreneurship is an elective module that has been developed in co-operation with the university's Centre for Entrepreneurship and Innovation,[2] and between 35 and 45 students have signed up for the module each time it has been offered. The module prepares students for entering a media market that belongs to Hallin and Mancini's Democratic Corporatist Model characterised by high newspaper circulation, professionalisation of journalism, strong state intervention with state subsidies and protection of press freedom, and strong public service ideals and institutions (Hallin and Mancini 2004).

It is a unique feature of this module that students take it in parallel with undertaking a full-time unpaid internship for a period of four to six months in the broad areas of media and communication. The need to accommodate the intern element has a strong impact on how teaching is organised, specifically:

- as students find internships all across Denmark and even abroad, the module is based on blended learning where most elements are taught online framed by two two-day seminars (camps) that all students are required to attend;
- the e-learning component is asynchronous because students follow the work schedules and routines at their places of internship and need to be able to engage with module contents at their own pace within a framework of set deadlines;
- to ensure progression through the module for students preoccupied with internship duties, assignments are short, and it is a requirement that students hand in all assignments by the deadline in order to be allowed to proceed to the exam.

Students are responsible for finding their own work placements, and whilst the module requires them to use their place of internship as the basis for an entrepreneurial innovation project, it is not a requirement that the place of internship is considered particularly suitable for innovation or is willing to participate actively in the project. Students are not required to implement their innovation concept either, although they are encouraged to do so, and several of them have been successful in doing it. Figure 2 provides an overview of the structure of the module that begins late August and concludes with an exam the following January. It consists of nine e-learning classes, two two-day camps and an exam. Below we briefly outline the contents of these modules and provide references to the texts we give students.

Four of the e-learning classes (1, 2, 3 and 7) are used to provide a media and communication context for the entrepreneurial innovation process that follows the ME2-model from class 4 onwards. Class 1 introduces students to innovation and entrepreneurship concepts and examples of media innovation (Nielsen 2009; Darsø 2011; Storsul and Krumsvik 2013) while class 2 looks at key digital forces shaping the media market (Kontrabande 2011; Ryfe 2012) as well as emerging media business models (Kontrabande and Wemind 2010). Class 3 engages students in a discussion about the value of developing entrepreneurial skills by introducing them to texts about what makes entrepreneurs entrepreneurial (Sarasvathy 2001b; Dyer et al. 2009) and texts that explain how developing entrepreneurship skills might be a way to handle the challenge of being paid to work as a journalist in the media market of the future (Hunter and Nel 2011; Berkey-Gerard 2012). Class 7 introduces students to theories and practical advice on how to develop creative cultures and capacity for innovation in a workplace setting (Keeley et al. 2013; Due 2014) as well as texts on specific challenges to innovation that arise from the way socialisation and work routines are carried out in media newsrooms (Machin and Niblock 2006; Ryfe 2009).

Learning outcomes are tested in a combined written and oral exam where students explain their own means, disharmonies, divergent and convergent processes, and proposed concept before assessing the value and viability of that concept and placing it in a wider media context. Students are also asked to reflect on what they have learned about innovation processes and their own ability to act as entrepreneurs within a communication or media organisation. Students are not assessed on the strengths of their concepts as the module is a learning process with a strong emphasis on teaching them how to act as entrepreneurs so they can repeat the process in the future.

Studying the Role of the Internship in Developing Entreprenurial Skills

As mentioned previously, it is a fairly unique feature of the module that it is taught whilst students are undertaking an internship. As educators we have little knowledge of what happens to our students during internships and how they negotiate the demands from their workplace in relation to demands made by the module. We have, therefore, undertaken research into how our students experienced the module with a particular emphasis on the role played by the place of internship in developing an entrepreneurial mindset.

In the study we asked six interrelated questions. The first three focus on understanding the contributions from the internship to the entrepreneurship and innovation project, while the latter three aim to explore the contributions made by the module itself.

RQ1: Where in the media and communication industry did students find internships and how do they characterise the innovation cultures they found?

RQ2: What opportunities for value creation did students identify?

RQ3: How were the students' projects received by the places of internship?

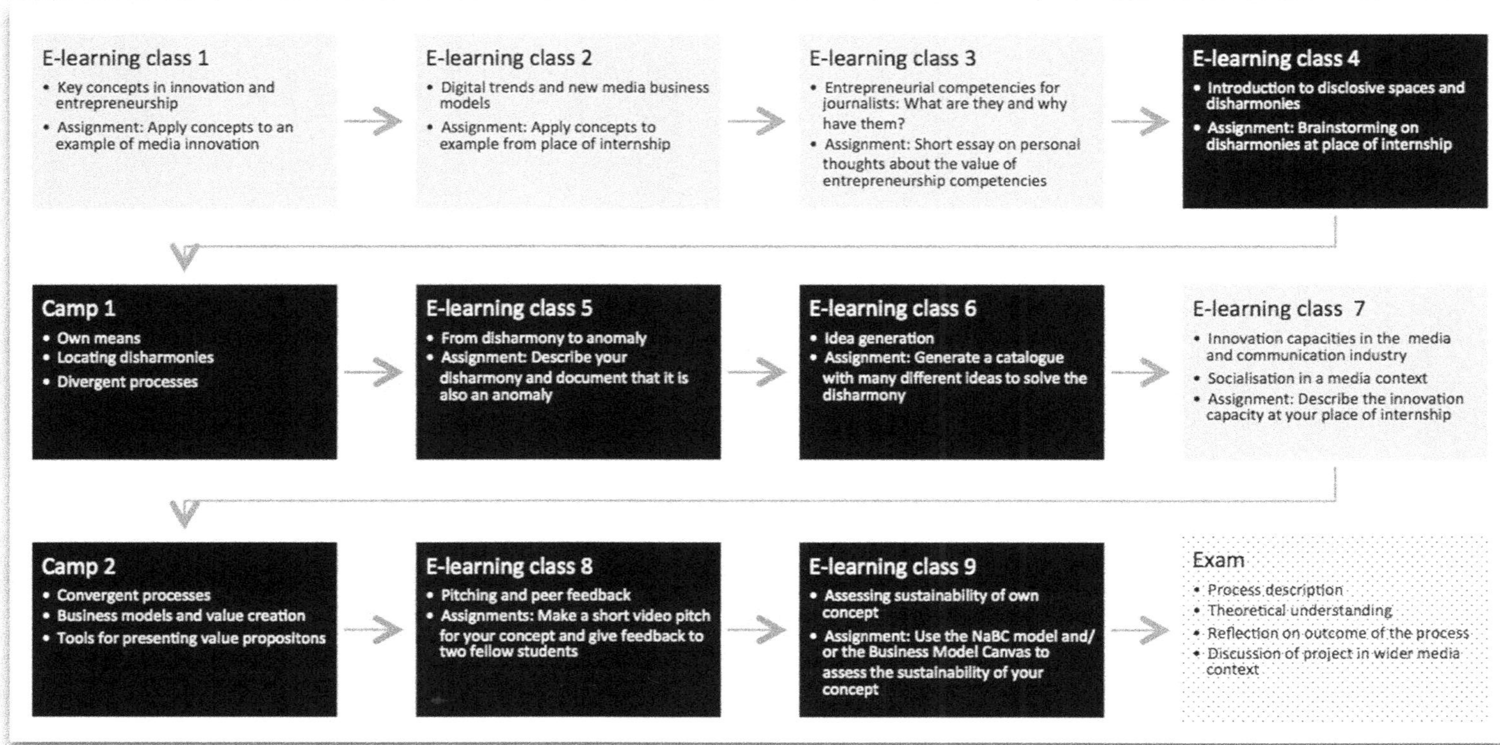

FIGURE 2
The figure shows how the ME2-model was adapted to the module on entrepreneurship and innovation for journalism students on the MA programme in analytical journalism

RQ4: Did the module motivate students to develop entrepreneurial skills?

RQ5: How did students negotiate work demands and module demands?

RQ6: Did students see any advantages to being taught entrepreneurship and innovation whilst they were doing an internship?

The research is based on two types of data. Firstly, we analysed a number of module assignments and video pitches from all 37 students (10 male, 27 female) who took part in the module in 2014 to obtain information about their places of internship, their disharmonies and concepts, and their reflections on the value of developing entrepreneurship skills as journalists. Secondly, we conducted two focus group interviews with a total of 10 students (9 female, 1 male). We had invited 14 students (11 female, 3 male) for the focus groups but in the end only 10 students were able to take part. The groups were organised according to characteristics of the students' places of internship in order to avoid that participants would be tempted to spend too much time explaining the basic set-up for their internship and instead could focus on discussing their experiences.

One group consisted of four female students and one male student who had been interning in relatively traditional journalistic roles at the Danish Broadcasting Corporation (DR), a major national newspaper, a music magazine, an art magazine and a local start-up magazine (focus group 1). The other group consisted of five female students who had all been interning at PR agencies of varying sizes working on a combination of journalistic and communication assignments (focus group 2). Each focus group lasted for 1.5 hours and the dialogue was recorded and later transcribed and coded for responses to our research questions. Before presenting our findings we would like to introduce some dynamics from research on learning and socialisation practices within journalism that are likely to have affected our students during their period of internship and created tensions for them as they embarked on their entrepreneurial innovation project.

Internship—A Complex Socialisation Process Towards Full Participation in a Community of Practice

In many countries journalism education is a combination of learning about practice at a university—or other institution of higher education—and learning through practice during an internship (Gravengaard and Rimestad 2014). This is also the case in Denmark where two different systems for journalism internships operate side by side: the majority of Danish journalism courses include paid internships of 12 or 18 months regulated by a collective agreement. Our students, however, follow a university model where they can undertake an unpaid internship for four to six months as long as the internship is part of a module where they can earn points according to the European Credit Transfer and Accumulation System—a standard for comparing the study attainment and performance of students of higher education across the European Union.

Regardless of the set-up, journalism interns are novices who enter into what Lave and Wenger have termed communities of practice when they start their internships. A community of practice is characterised by a shared domain of interest, community members that interact in relation to that interest and a shared repertoire of practices that develops through these interactions. Newcomers to any community of practice learn in practice and from practice, eventually becoming a more competent member of the group via situated learning. This is possible, because the interns are granted legitimate peripheral participation in which they are slowly introduced to the tasks of the specific community of practice until they reach the point of full participation (Lave and Wenger 1991).

For journalism students, one of the main objectives of engaging in this particular form of learning is to build the craft ethos that comes from being recognised as having the communicative competencies of a practitioner within the broad field of journalism and communication (Cotter 2010). That is particularly important for our students who are keenly aware that they will be competing for jobs with other journalism graduates who have had longer internships.

As part of the module on entrepreneurship and innovation, we ask students to identify "something" in their community of practice which can be improved using their own skills, knowledge and competencies. We also ask them to develop a solution to this problem that can create value for that community of practice. The question is whether it is natural for communities of practice to develop by being pushed towards improvement by newcomers or if we are asking too much by injecting a learning objective from outside that community?

Here it is relevant to look at what Lave and Wenger (1991) refer to as the continuity–displacement contradiction. Any community of practice is dependent on development and displacement in order to obtain continuity, and according to Lave and Wenger it is not unusual that newcomers engage in development:

> Newcomers are caught in a dilemma. On the one hand, they need to engage in existing practice, which have developed over time: to understand it, to participate in it, and to become full members of the community in which it exists. On the other hand, they have a stake in its development as they begin to establish their own identity in its future. (Lave and Wenger 1991, 115)

So in theory, equipping students with skills for entrepreneurship and innovation and encouraging them to use these skills within the context of an internship could lead to valuable development of a community of practice. However, it is unclear at what stage during the process of moving from peripheral towards full participation our students feel confident enough to bring forward suggestions for innovation of practice and whether that would naturally coincide with the dates and deadlines dictated by a university module.

Socialisation

As interns, students are also subject to processes of socialisation: part of becoming recognised as a competent member of a given community of practice involves internalising the norms, role expectations and values of that community. How journalists become socialised into workplace cultures has been an area of research interest since the middle of the twentieth century. The majority of this research has been motivated by an attempt to understand if organisational and hierarchical structures within the newsroom could be said to limit the autonomy and editorial independence of individual journalists through different forms of social control (Machin and Niblock 2006). To date, however, there has been very little research into how socialisation processes actually take place in newsrooms (Gravengaard and Rimestad 2014).

One of the earliest but still highly influential studies about social control in the newsroom was published in 1955 by journalist turned sociologist Warren Breed, who set out to explain how new journalists get to know and follow newsroom policies even though such policies are rarely written down. Breed found out that newcomers described the learning process as "learning by osmosis", and that they picked up clues about policy from praise, criticism, casual conversations, meetings, internal communications, observing executive feedback, reading their own paper and observing how their own work was edited (Breed 1955). A small study by Machin and Niblock (2006) confirmed that new journalists continue to learn newsroom policies from picking up clues in the newsroom. In addition, Gravengaard and Rimestad (2014, 83) conclude in a literature review of research on socialisation within journalism studies that "the policy of the news organization and the cultural and professional norms are tacit knowledge, seldom stated explicitly in the routinized practice in the newsroom".

The question then is how students handle the expectation that they should be sensitive to everyday practices and identify disharmonies when they are likely to operate in cultures dominated by tacit knowledge and unwritten policies? They have to engage in conversations with colleagues and management in order to obtain the information they need for their projects. Yet, getting answers might be difficult if there is no tradition for being explicit about objectives and the way things are done at the place of internship.

On top of the socialisation process at their places of internship, entrepreneurship training itself may also influence student identity. Hytti and Heinonen (2013) have identified two different entrepreneurial identities among postgraduate students after having participated in an entrepreneurship training programme hereby acknowledging that entrepreneurship education can result in new identity creation. So the question is whether students experience two parallel socialisation processes through the set-up of the module or one dominates the other?

Research Findings

> **RQ1:** Where in the media and communication industry did students find internships and how do they characterise the innovation cultures they found?

The 37 students found their internships in very different media and communication contexts: 50 per cent of students chose to do their internships at PR agencies and communication departments in non-governmental organisations, 25 per cent worked for digital and printed magazines, and only 25 per cent found internships with traditional media organisations such as printed newspapers, television and radio stations.

During the focus group interviews, students were asked to describe if they had experienced an innovation culture at their place of internship. In both groups, students reported that they had seen their organisations act in creative and relatively innovative ways when creating new content or working on customer projects, but it was their impression that their places of internship did not adopt an adequate innovative approach to developing internally.

Overall, the students interviewed wished for a more systematic approach to innovation but at the same time they also acknowledged that innovation could be happening in other parts of the organisation than where they were. Particularly in big organisations it was very difficult for interns for gain access to places where innovation processes take place:

> it is probably up there in some fancy development teams but down on the floor things are done in exactly the same way as they always were. Of course you can negotiate with your manager in editorial meetings and with your different sub-editors if something can be done differently, but it is the small things that you can influence. There are some steps before you get into this group where you can sit with your innovative hat on all day long.
>
> (A, female student, intern at the Danish Broadcasting Corporation, focus group 1)

It seems that only in very rare cases can students expect to learn about entrepreneurship and innovation in a communication or media organisation because they do not have adequate access to such processes—either because of their status as interns or because the processes do not exist. In fact, one student pointed out that without the module she would never have thought about entrepreneurship and innovation:

> This module has made me aware how little focus my place of internship had on entrepreneurship and innovation. If I had not been following this module and reading theory at the same time, I would probably not have thought about it all. (L, female student, intern at a PR agency, focus group 2)

RQ2: What opportunities for value creation did students identify?

In the venture creation tradition, entrepreneurship often focuses on developing new products or services. However, approaching entrepreneurship with a starting point in disharmonies in everyday practice produces a much wider range of opportunities for value creation. Based on the 37 students' written assignments, we have created an overview of the types of opportunities for value creation identified by the students. As Spinosa, Flores, and Dreyfus (1997) do not offer any system for categorising disharmonies, we have used an innovation thinking tool by Keeley et al. for organising the overview. Keely et al. argue that creating new products is only one way to innovate, and on its own, it provides the lowest return on investment and the least competitive advantage. A more profitable approach is to integrate multiple types of innovation, and the authors point to 10 different areas for innovation: profit model, network, structure, process, product performance, product system, service, channel, brand and customer engagement (Keeley et al. 2013).

As Figure 3 shows, students worked with a wide range of disharmonies/anomalies that spanned most of the innovation field (as it is described by Keeley et al. 2013) and their projects came in many sizes from improvements of a product or process to suggestions for changing the whole business model. Concrete examples of disharmonies picked up by students are:

- *Profit model*: The editorial staff at a horse-riding magazine does not know very much about their readers: the website states that the magazine is intended for "sophisticated persons" but when the intern wanted to know more and was willing to undertake some research for this purpose, she was not allowed to do that. Also the intern was very surprised to discover that nobody among the editorial staff (except for herself) had extensive knowledge about horses and horseback riding.

- *Process*: An upstart media company is producing live journalism shows with great success. The shows take place at theatres or other cultural venues but structures in the world of cultural producation clash with everyday practices from the world of journalism. For instance, it is difficult to find suitable venues if you work with short deadlines on current issues as venues are often booked out months in advance.
- *Brand*: A communication agency recommends their customers to be present on all platforms including social media. However, the agency itself does not have any profiles on social media and loses credibility by not showing that it can walk the talk.

RQ3: How were the students' projects received by their places of internship?

The students interviewed explained that their engagement with entrepreneurship was received in different ways in their internship locations, ranging from indifference over encouragement to present their work and, in some cases, even being given the go-ahead to implement the project. Some students found themselves in a position where they were able to influence their community of practice even though they still considered themselves newcomers. One student who had been very reluctant to present her project realised that she had been underestimating the value of her concept when her employers turned out to be very receptive to her ideas:

> Now it is done and they have received it crazily well, and they have been really happy. They are in a process, where they are trying to rethink the company and find out where they are going so the timing was perfect. I don't know if I have pushed this process forward, or I just came at the right time … but it has been received in a really positive way, so it is probably just me who finds it difficult to be the newcomer who enters totally green and suddenly wants to explain how the company should do things. (R, female intern at a PR agency, focus group 2)

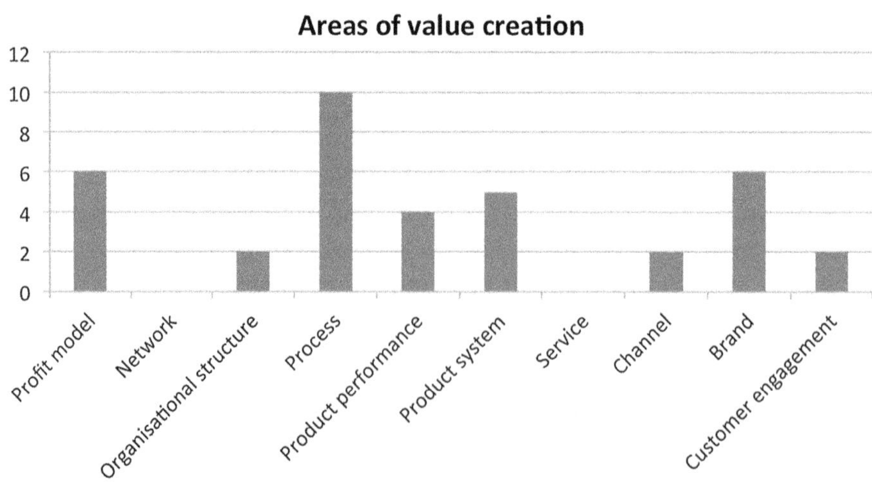

FIGURE 3
Students found disharmonies in almost all the potential areas for value creation described in Keeley et al.'s model of innovation types

Other students chose not to, or were unable to, move forward with their projects at their place of internship. But a negative reception did not necessarily deter these students or diminish their perception of the value of obtaining entrepreneurial competencies as they put the reception down to particular circumstances at their place of internship. One student attempted to set up a meeting with her editor to present her ideas several times but failed and was very frustrated. But she moved on and used her new skills in another internship:

> In my new internship, I was responsible for communication and I could use my entrepreneurial competencies. It has been a relief, to say the least. There were so many problems at the first place. They just wanted me to produce a lot of articles and there were problems if I wanted to do anything else. (M, female student, intern at music magazine, focus group 1)

RQ4: Did the module motivate students to develop entrepreneurial skills?

A few weeks into the module students were asked in a written assignment to reflect on the value of developing entrepreneurial competencies as a journalist.

All 37 students admitted to signing up for the module because it allowed them to undertake an internship that would provide them with valuable practical experience of journalism or other communication tasks. None were attracted to the module because it would give them an opportunity to develop entrepreneurial competencies *per se* although the majority did welcome the focus on entrepreneurship once they had secured an internship:

> The focus in the module seems sensible when I think about how often during our first year we have been told that the media industry is in some form of crisis where finding new ways of producing and distributing news are necessary ... But I never thought about innovation as a competency I would need to develop and nurture. (IM, female student, intern at a PR agency, written assignment)

For about one-third of students, the exposure to module texts and assignments had made an impact at this early stage and changed their motivation because they realised that entrepreneurship competencies could be relevant for their own future as journalists.

> I have always linked words like "innovation" and "entrepreneurship" to engineers and people with hard hats, so in the beginning my enthusiasm for this module was not overwhelming. However, that has changed. Time and time again we have been told that "you have to create your own jobs", and now I feel that we are being introduced to tools that we might actually be able to use for exactly that purpose. (ES, female student, intern at the Danish Broadcasting Corporation, written assignment)

RQ5: How did students negotiate work demands and module demands?

Students in the focus groups explained that they gave top priority to everyday tasks at their places of internship while module assignments were relegated to evenings and weekends. Entrepreneurship and innovation were peripheral activities in terms of time and energy, except for one student who deliberately arranged an internship at a start-up media company and spent a significant proportion of his time on developing strategies and looking for ways to fund the magazine.

Several focus group participants used the expression "two different things" when they talked about the internship and the assignments they were doing for the module.

They described how there were a number of set expectations of them as interns which mainly involved producing journalistic content or servicing clients, and meeting these expectations felt more legitimate than engaging in entrepreneurial activities. Consequently, the project lived in the shadows as students at the beginning of their projects could not see how these projects would eventually be able to contribute anything of value to their places of internship. This was reflected in the way students approached discussions with colleagues and managers when they were trying to obtain the necessary information for their projects. Such cross-over points were carefully negotiated and often happened during lunch breaks and in other informal settings because students were concerned about wasting their colleagues' time on something that they believed would not be considered relevant.

> I thought "I cannot spend their valuable time on my school assignment. I cannot book time with five senior consultants for a half-hour session to develop ideas ... ". So I asked more or less formal questions over lunch. (C, female student, intern at a PR agency, focus group 2)

> I also tried to ask questions surreptitiously. I felt very insecure about this project which perhaps is normal. I did not feel it was important enough, and I also felt a bit embarrassed. (L, female student, intern at a PR agency, focus group 2)

All students interviewed quickly internalised norms and values at their places of internship. They did not experience a similar socialisation process as entrepreneurs. The push towards building an entrepreneurial mindset mainly came from taking part in module camps and because they had to pass an exam by demonstrating that they had engaged in an entrepreneurial innovation process. Instead of becoming interns who behaved as entrepreneurs, most saw themselves as journalism students who had acquired a set of skills and methods that could be valuable in the future but for now they were mainly testing these tools for themselves.

> I think many of us felt that we could do an innovation project but it was unlikely to be implemented ... So in that way we were not socialised—it was more a set of useful tools we were introduced to for use in the future. I don't think I became an entirely different intern because I followed the module. (A, female student, intern at the Danish Broadcasting Corporation, focus group 1)

> **RQ6:** Did students see any advantages to being taught entrepreneurship and innovation whilst doing an internship?

Despite the fact that most students mainly managed to integrate their projects with their place of internship on a very tentative basis, they still welcomed the combination of learning entrepreneurship and innovation whilst working in a media organisation. Some students had been able to apply methods and tools such as ideation techniques, the Business Model Canvas and the personality type indicator test directly into their places of internship. Other students acknowledged that the module provided them with new ways of understanding dynamics in their workplace and gave them a critical perspective on their intern experience and the socialisation processes they were subjected to.

Several students pointed to the relevance of being able to draw on a real-life context when learning about entrepreneurship. It made some of the theoretical concepts easier to grasp. It was also easier to identify a real disharmony when they had inside knowledge of everyday practices in an organisation. Some students also linked the value of the internship directly to their learning outcomes in relation to taking on entrepreneurship roles:

> I think it was good to feel that it can be difficult to go out and put this theoretical knowledge into practice. Without the internship, I think it would be easy to think that I would be quite good at this and then I would have to learn later that maybe I was not that good at it after all. (J, female student, intern at a national daily newspaper, focus group 1)

> I followed a module on innovation in high school where we had to make business plans and I ended up inventing a completely useless vacuum cleaner for cars because I could not spot any real-life problems. Now I see why it is relevant to have a place of internship that can provide the frame for an innovation process: it is within this space you have to find a problem you can do something about. (C, female student, intern at a PR agency, focus group 2)

Contributions to an Emerging Discipline

In their overview of entrepreneurial journalism education, Schaich and Klein (2013, 209) concluded that "entrepreneurial journalism is new. Teaching entrepreneurial journalism is even newer". With this research article, we have introduced another approach to teaching entrepreneurial journalism based on entrepreneurship research rather than business studies and have shown how it was received by journalism students. The ME2-model has been developed and used for at least a decade at Aarhus University but we have focused on the first time it has been used on journalism students in Denmark, and also the first time that the ME2-model has been taught in a module that integrated it with an internship. The coupling was in many ways a result of circumstance and necessity but we believe it has led to some insights that can be valuable for the emerging discipline of entrepreneurial journalism education.

The ME2-model takes its starting point in the individual–opportunity nexus described by Shane and Venkataraman (2000), who argue that entrepreneurship is comprised of enterprising individuals and entrepreneurial opportunities that meet in a nexus. The model takes students through a process where they start to understand themselves as individuals with entrepreneurial abilities (phase 1), learn how to identify opportunities (phase 2), pick up methods to develop solutions (phase 3) before working on establishing a nexus in such a way that it will create value for themselves and "someone else" (phase 4) (Blenker and Thrane 2009). This approach to teaching entrepreneurship is very versatile and can lead to venture creation but does not have to. As we have shown, the ME2-model can also be used with journalism interns who almost by definition will be working as intrapreneurs if they manage to establish a nexus at their place of internship.

The key point is that the model removes venture creation as the main criterion for a successful learning process and instead allows students to explore the process of value creation and understand how they as individuals can best contribute to that process. As our students remarked several times during focus group interviews, the module gave them the opportunity to pick up tools for the future and gain a more critical perspective on their places of internship without the pressure of having to set up their own business or actually implement their project if they did not want to. It was important for them to feel safe as they were trying out these new methods—particularly as they were also trying to establish themselves as good journalists or professionals within their communities of practice.

The versatility of the ME2-model also applies to teaching methods. Based on their survey, Schach and Klein (2013) concluded that the predominant approaches to teaching entrepreneurship were learning by doing (projects), learning by listening (invited guest speakers) and learning through business-style case studies. Often the ME2-model is project based when taught in classroom contexts where students form groups to solve disharmonies from selected disclosive spaces. But as we show, it can also be adapted to a blended learning context and can use an internship or a volunteer experience to provide disclosive spaces for students to explore. The real-life setting of an internship or volunteer experience might go some way towards solving the problem raised by lecturers interviewed by Ferrier (2013) who struggled to find ways to make entrepreneurship feel real for students as they have little entrepreneurial experience themselves.

We also want to focus on some lessons from our research on the role of internships in a module on entrepreneurship and innovation. Interviews with students combined with reading of examination papers confirm that there is a strong need for teaching students entrepreneurship and innovation at university as we have seen little evidence of entrepreneurial activity in the media or communication companies where they interned, and if it is, present journalism interns are not necessarily invited to partake—mainly because of their status as newcomers in a community of practice. However, the same data also show that in some cases a nexus is established through an internship and has given a student the opportunity to create value for his or her place of internship. How such a nexus is established depends on a number of factors within the organisation as well as the personal courage and enthusiasm of the student, and is an area that would be interesting for further study. Nevertheless, the majority of students would not have learned to work systematically with the entrepreneurship method if their internship had not been combined with a university module. Similarly, if we want to see more nexuses established during internships, it will probably be necessary to help students organise internships where employers agree to make entrepreneurship and innovation part of the intern's daily practice.

Schach and Klein (2013) noted in their research that the anti-business culture of the journalism profession remains one of the key challenges when teaching entrepreneurial journalism. We have seen no evidence of an anti-business culture amongst our students and we wonder if the close coupling of an internship with a broader understanding of entrepreneurship is a possible explanation. Our students were engaged in identifying projects from everyday practice that were within their means to implement, and the value proposition of their projects often aimed at improving products or processes they cared about and were a part of. As we have shown, combining the roles of journalist and entrepreneur was not without challenges but the perception of the dangers of entrepreneurship to journalistic autonomy might change by shifting the focus from professional principles to working with everyday practices.

DISCLOSURE STATEMENT

No potential conflict of interest was reported by the authors.

NOTES

1. It is an ongoing theoretical dispute in entrepreneurship research and entrepreneurship education research whether opportunities are discovered or created or somewhere in between – something the scope of this article does not allow us to discuss further, but see Alvarez and Barney (2007).
2. In 2015, the centre was reorganised and entrepreneurship teaching has been transferred to the Centre for Teaching Development and Digital Media at Aarhus University.

REFERENCES

Alvarez, Sharon, and Jay B. Barney. 2007. "Discovery and Creation: Alternative Theories of Entrepreneurial Action." *Strategic Entrepreneurship Journal* 1 (12): 11–26.

Bager, Lene T. 2010. *Entreprenørskabsundervisning – Proces, Refleksion og Handling*. Aarhus, Denmark: Aarhus Universitet.

Berkey-Gerard, Mark. 2012. "From Student Journalists to Local News Entrepreneurs: A Case Study of Technically Media." *International Symposium on Online Journalism* 2 (2): 100–117.

Blenker, Per, Signe H. Frederiksen, Steffen Korsgaard, Sabine Müeller, Helle Neergaard, and Claus Thrane. 2012. "Entrepreneurship as Everyday Practice: Towards a Personalized Pedagogy of Enterprise Education." *Industry and Higher Education* 26 (6): 417–430.

Blenker, Per, Steffen Korsgaard, Helle Neergaard, and Claus Thrane. 2011. "The Questions We Care About: Paradigms and Progression in Entrepreneurship Education." *Industry and Higher Education* 25 (6): 417–427.

Blenker, Per, and Claus Thrane. 2009. "Whatever Happened to the Nineties." In *Strategi & Driftsøkonomi: Festskrift for Ole Ø. Madsen*, edited by Per Nikolaj Bukh and Niels Peter Mols, 205–216. Copenhagen, Denmark: Gyldendal.

Breed, Warren. 1955. "Social Control in the Newsroom: A Functional Analysis." In *Social Meanings of News: A Text-Reader*, edited by Dan Berkowitz, 107–122. Thousand Oaks, CA: Sage Publications.

Carlson, Curtis R., and William W. Wilmot. 2006. *Innovation: The Five Disciplines for Creating What Customers Want*. New York, NY: Crown Business.

Cotter, Colleen. 2010. *News Talk: Investigating the Language of Journalism*. Cambridge, MA: Cambridge University Press.

Cropley, Arthur. 2006. "In Praise of Convergent Thinking." *Creativity Research Journal* 18 (3): 391–404.

Darsø, Lotte. 2011. *Innovationspædagogik: Kunsten at Fremelske Innovationskompetence*. Frederiksberg, Denmark: Samfundslitteratur.

Due, Brian. 2014. *Ideudvikling – en multimodal tilgang til innovationens kreative faser*. Frederiksberg, Denmark: Samfundslitteratur.

Dyer, Jeffrey H., Hal B. Gregersen, and Clayton M. Christensen. 2009. "The Innovator's DNA." *Harvard Business Review* 87 (12): 60–67.

Elmore, Cindy, and Brian Massey. 2012. "Need for Instruction in Entrepreneurial Journalism: Perspective of Full-time freelancers." *Journal of Media Practice* 13 (2): 109–124.

Ferrier, Michelle B. 2013. "Media Entrepreneurship: Curriculum Development and Faculty Perceptions of What Students Should Know." *Journalism & Mass Communication Educator* 68 (3): 222–241.

Gartner, William B. 1988. "'Who Is an Entrepreneur?' Is the Wrong Question." *American Journal of Small Business* 12 (4): 11–32.

Gravengaard, Gitte, and Lene Rimestad. 2014. "Socializing Journalist Trainees in the Newsroom: On How to Capture the Intangible Parts of the Process." *Nordicom Review* 35 (Special Issue): 81–95.

Hallin, Daniel C., and Paolo Mancini. 2004. *Comparing Media Systems: Three Models of Media and Politics*. Cambridge, MA: Cambridge University Press.

Hunter, Anna, and Francois P. Nel. 2011. "Equipping the Entrepreneurial Journalist: An Exercise in Creative Enterprise." *Journalism & Mass Communication Educator* 66 (1): 9–24.

Hytti, Ulla, and Jarna Heinonen. 2013. "Heroic and Humane Entrepreneurs: Identity Work in Entreprenership Education." *Education + Training* 55 (8/9): 886–898.

Kennedy, Ciara, and David Baines. 2010. "An Education for Independence: Should Entrepreneurial Skills Be an Essential Part of the Journalists's Toolbox." *Journalism Practice* 4 (1): 97–113.

Keeley, Larry, Ryan Pikkel, Brian Quinn, and Helen Walters. 2013. *Ten Types of Innovation: The Discipline of Building Breakthroughs*. Hoboken, NJ: John Wiley & Sons Inc.

Kontrabande. 2011. "Opbrud: Strømninger og bevægelser i markederne for film, tv, bøger, musik, spil og journalistik." http://kontrabande.com/Opbrud_2011.pdf.

Kontrabande and Wemind. 2010. "Mediemodeller 2010: Nye bæredygtige eksperimenter, initiativer og forretningsmodeller for journalistik."

Lave, Jean, and Etienne Wenger. 1991. *Situated Learning: Legitmate Peripheral Participation*. Cambridge: Cambridge University Press.

Machin, David, and Sarah Niblock. 2006. "The Best Job in the World." In *News Production: Theory and Practice*, edited by David Machin and Sarah Niblock, 160–177. New York, NY: Routledge.

Nielsen, Trine. 2009. *Innovationens ABC*. Copenhagen, Denmark: Gyldendal Business.

Osterwalder, Alexander, and Yves Pigneur. 2010. *Business Model Generation: A Handbook for Visionaries, Game Changers, and Challengers*. Wiley.

Read, Stuart, Saras D. Sarasvathy, Nick Dew, Robert Wiltbank, and Anne-Valérie Ohlsson. 2011. *Effectual Entrepreneurship*. New York, NY: Routledge.

Ryfe, David M. 2009. "Broader and Deeper - a Study of Newsroom Culture in a Time of Change." *Journalism* 10 (2): 197–216.

Ryfe, David M. 2012. *Can Journalism Survive? An Inside Look at American Newsrooms*. Hoboken, NJ: Johan Wiley & Sons Inc.

Sarasvathy, Saras D. 2001a. "Causation and Effectuation: Toward a Theoretical Shift from Economic Inevitability to Entrepreneurial Contingency." *The Academy of Management Review* 26 (2): 243–263.

Sarasvathy, Saras D. 2001b. *What Makes Entrepreneurs Entrepreneurial?* Charlottesville: Darden Business Publishing.

Sarasvathy, Saras D. 2008. *Effectuation: Elements of Entrepreneurial Expertise*. Cheltenham, UK: Edward Elgar.

Sarasvathy, Saras D., and Sankaran Venkataraman. 2011. "Entrepreneurship as Method: Open Questions for an Entrepreneurial Future." *Entrepreneurship Theory and Practice* 35 (1): 113–135.

Schaich, María J. V., and Jeffrey S. Klein. 2013. "Entrepreneurial Journalism Education: Where Are We Now?." *Observatorio Journal* 7 (4): 185–211.

Shane, Scott, and Sankaran Venkataraman. 2000. "The Promise of Entrepreneurship as a Field of Research." *The Academy of Management Review* 25 (1): 217–226.

Spinosa, Charles, Fernando Flores, and Hubert L. Dreyfus. 1997. *Disclosing New Worlds: Entrepreneurship, Democratic Action and the Cultivation of Solidarity*. Cambridge, MA: MIT Press.

Steyert, Chris, and Jerome Katz. 2004. "Reclaming the Space of Entrepreneurship in Society: Geographical, Discursive and Social Dimensions." *Entrepreneurship and Regional Development* 16 (3): 179–196.

Storsul, Tanja, and Arne H. Krumsvik. 2013. "What is Media Innovation?" In *Media Innovations - A Multidisciplinary Study of Change*, edited by Tanja Storsul and Arne H. Krumsvik, 13–26. Gothenburg, Sweden: Nordicom.

THE JOURNALISTS OF THE FUTURE MEET ENTREPRENEURIAL JOURNALISM
Perceptions in the classroom

Andreu Casero-Ripollés, Jessica Izquierdo-Castillo, and **Hugo Doménech-Fabregat**

Journalism is undergoing a major restructuring reflecting the post-2008 economic crisis and ongoing technological innovation. Much discussion on future job creation is focused on entrepreneurial journalism. Spain is a paradigmatic example of this phenomenon. Between 2008 and 2014, some 454 news media outlets were created in Spain. Yet, the emergence of entrepreneurial journalism raises many questions and challenges that affect all areas of journalism. In this research study we are concerned with entrepreneurial journalism in education and, in particular, the views of journalism students. The aim of this article is to analyse perceptions regarding entrepreneurship held by current students, the journalists of the future. Our goal is test the knowledge journalism students have about entrepreneurship. We evaluate the willingness of journalism students to develop their own business project and the major barriers and obstacles they face. The methodology uses a quantitative approach based on surveys in Spain (N = 184). The results suggest an increase in the willingness of students to engage in entrepreneurship. However, students also have a negative and disenchanted view of journalism as they progress in their studies.

Introduction: The Rise of Entrepreneurial Journalism

Media companies in Spain, like elsewhere, have in recent years implemented continuous cost-reduction policies with significant job losses (Casero-Ripollés and Izquierdo-Castillo 2013). As journalism undergoes this restructuring, some openly speak about the possible disappearance of newspapers (Meyer 2009), while others argue that we are witnessing a transition, rather than the demise of journalism (Picard 2014). Spain is a paradigmatic example of the emergence of entrepreneurial journalism. Against the backdrop of a deep economic crisis and industry disruption driven by technological change, more than 11,000 jobs in journalism have been lost between 2008 and 2014. In the same period, however, 454 news media outlets have been created, mainly in the digital area and led by journalists (APM 2014). This figure illustrates the potential of entrepreneurship in journalism as a way of creating new employment opportunities. Moreover, it illustrates the importance being placed on this new form of practising the occupation.

Entrepreneurial journalism can be understood as a new form of news production in which journalists create their own media outlet in which, besides developing information content, they also play the role of entrepreneur and owner, thus making decisions for their own business. Their rise is made possible thanks to the services provided by digital technologies. The latter lower the barriers for entry into the journalism sector, markedly decreasing the financial investment needed to develop a news media outlet. This, in turn, simplifies the possibility of developing new journalism projects to an extraordinary extent, particularly in the online environment.

The rise of entrepreneurial journalism raises many questions and challenges for all areas of journalism. One of the most notable is the introduction of entrepreneurship in journalism education and the views of journalism students regarding this phenomenon. The aim of this article is to analyse perceptions regarding entrepreneurship held by those who will be future journalists and who are now receiving their education in the classroom. Our goal, specifically, is to find out what knowledge journalism students have about entrepreneurship, in general, and about entrepreneurial journalism, in particular. At the same time, we examine the skills that are deemed essential for entrepreneurial journalism. Additionally, we evaluate the willingness of journalism students to develop their own business project in the field of journalism. Finally, we explore the major barriers and obstacles, as well as the main opportunities and advantages, that students associate with entrepreneurial journalism.

The main contribution of this research lies in the focus on the perceptions held by journalism students regarding the phenomenon of entrepreneurship. So far, the literature that addresses students' views has focused on other aspects such as news media roles, political motivations, future job expectations, or professional values and skills. Research on this aspect applied to entrepreneurial journalism is still emerging. Initial studies have demonstrated a low willingness by students to engage in entrepreneurship. This article shows a change in this view although students also have a negative and disenchanted view of journalism as they progress in their studies. This finding concerning disappointment offers an important contribution because it poses a challenge to educators and universities, as well as journalism schools. Moreover, this research reveals how students rate the main skills associated with entrepreneurial journalism. Finally, it allows us to identify the main obstacles and major opportunities that students perceive in entrepreneurship. These data provide information that should prove useful in the improvement of journalism education and introduce the topic of entrepreneurship into the curriculum.

The Elements of Entrepreneurial Journalism

Entrepreneurial journalism is a relatively new area of research although the academic literature has revealed, across a variety of different sources, several of its characteristics. The first is connected to the type of media associated with this phenomenon. These are small-scale media linked to individual initiatives or small co-operatives formed by journalists (Hoag and Seo 2005; Quinn 2010; Picard 2014; Kelly 2015). They are the very opposite of the large media corporations, which arose from the concentration processes that have dominated the media industry in recent decades (Rae 2004). The small size involved means these projects generally require reduced infrastructure and resource needs.

A second aspect of entrepreneurial journalism is its connection to the creation of a business of one's own. Different authors define this as "employing yourself" (Ferrier 2013; Kelly 2015) and associate it with the discovery of new opportunities and new business niches (Mellor 2009). We see a different way of working as a journalist, a way whose emergence and momentum has been forced by the current market, characterised by the increasing loss of jobs in mainstream media due to the effects of the economic crisis and the job reductions in the sector (Quinn 2010). Entrepreneurship is conceived as an employment opportunity for journalists, arising as a response to a fast-changing environment. It emerges as the by-product of macroeconomic changes and not as their cause (Anderson 2014). It is a reactive phenomenon in response to the financial weakness of journalism, the destruction of employment, and loss of job security (Neff 2012).

A third element connected to entrepreneurial journalism, and derived from the previous element, involves the perception of the journalist as an entrepreneur (Briggs 2012; Picard 2014). This phenomenon is characterised by tearing down the wall that traditionally separated the creation of content from business management. Entrepreneurship enables journalists to become the owners of their own businesses (Elmore and Massey 2012). For this reason, they not only produce the news, but must also make decisions regarding the business. This implies not only a form of self-employment but also an entrepreneurial autonomy, since it involves the establishment of independent enterprises. In this sense, it differs from freelancing (Baines and Kennedy 2010), a traditional activity linked to journalism. Freelance journalists, when collaborating with news media, maintain their status of employment by the company, although they are technically not on the payroll. Entrepreneurial journalists are the owners of their own media outlet, which is an independent business.

From this latter viewpoint, entrepreneurship involves overcoming the concept of media worker (Deuze 2006), which has led to the perception of journalists as news industry employees. This pattern has been predominant within the hegemony of the media company model that has existed since the beginning of the twentieth century (Hunter and Nel 2011). Entrepreneurial journalism is linked to the emergence of new industrial forms of news production. It is also the result of the non-existence of a viable business model in the digital environment and of the current dominance of the "trial and error" formulas experienced by journalism (Campos-Freire 2010; Casero-Ripollés 2010; Berman, Battino, and Feldman 2011). In this context, entrepreneurial journalism has been labelled "craft production mode" (Picard 2014), as the journalist assumes responsibility for all the stages of the business process and news production.

The literature reviewed attributes two qualities to entrepreneurial journalism: innovation and creativity. This connection goes back to the seminal definition provided by Schumpeter (1936), who understood entrepreneurship as a form of innovation based on creative destruction. Since then, innovation has been identified as a key element in entrepreneurship both in general (Drucker 1985; Zampetakis and Moustakis 2006), as well as in its application in the field of journalism (Jarvis 2010). Innovation is related to a new idea, device, product, or service, but this does not automatically imply the development of entrepreneurship. Although the two concepts are complementary, synergic, and interrelated (Zhao 2005), innovation and entrepreneurship are different. Not all new ventures are innovative, and not all new knowledge generates viable business opportunities (Landström et al. 2015). One important difference is that innovation is related to opportunity identification and entrepreneurship is linked to opportunity exploitation. Innovation is the source of entrepreneurship and entrepreneurship allows innovation to flourish (Zhao 2005). Several authors claim that entrepreneurial journalism involves venturing into new territory and topics, and incorporating new techniques (Hunter and Nel 2011; Lassila-Merisalo and Uskali 2011). This is why journalists who pursue this path must have the capacity for risk-taking (Mellor 2009).

All of these characteristics are the reason why, generally speaking, the literature presents entrepreneurial journalism from a positive perspective. The beneficial elements that it provides to both journalism and society are emphasised, and the criticisms or objections are diluted. Among the positive factors, it is suggested that entrepreneurship facilitates economic growth and the creation of jobs for journalists (Hoag and Seo 2005). Additionally, it is said that it constitutes a reinvention of journalism in business terms (Briggs 2012). It is also credited with promoting the free flow of information and people's access to news (Kelly 2015). In this regard, it encourages democracy (Quinn 2010) since it introduces new voices that generate a better and healthier democracy (Hoag and Seo 2005). Consequently, entrepreneurial journalism is characterised by its social function, its ethical standards, and for considering the news as a public good (Vázquez Schaich and Klein 2013).

Entrepreneurial Journalism and Education Practice

The emergence of entrepreneurial journalism has led to a debate about how this concept should be introduced into journalism education. Several authors have called for its inclusion in the curriculum in universities and schools of journalism as a key element in the journalist's toolbox (Baines and Kennedy 2010; Jarvis 2010; Quinn 2010; Claussen 2011; Hunter and Nel 2011; Lassila-Merisalo and Uskali 2011; Kelly 2015). The education of journalists who take advantage of the opportunities provided by entrepreneurship is one of the main topics of discussion in this field. This has intensified another long-standing debate about journalism education in the light of changes brought about by digital technologies (Dates et al. 2006; Deuze 2006; Mensing 2010; Drok 2013). One of the main pillars in this debate is that universities and journalism schools should become laboratories of innovation by adopting an active role in the media industry. In this context, we see the teaching hospital model, based on learning-by-doing, and the entrepreneurial journalism programme, as innovative formulas so that journalism studies may adapt to the current fast-changing external environment (Anderson 2014).

The literature reviewed has shown that the curriculum for journalism studies is only slightly aimed at entrepreneurship (Baines and Kennedy 2010; Hunter and Nel 2011; Ferrier 2013). What prevails is a vision in which journalists are educated to be media workers (Deuze 2006). For many, the incorporation of entrepreneurial journalism in core curricula remains a pending issue. This is why, in part, journalism students tend to have a low willingness to launch their own media companies (Delano 2001; Casero-Ripollés and Cullell 2013). However, several studies indicate that the introduction of entrepreneurship in education generates positive stimuli both in business in general (Charney and Libecap 2000; Lange et al. 2011; Mueller 2011), as well as in the field of creative industries (Rae 2004) and journalism (Aceituno-Aceituno et al. 2014; Paniagua-Rojano et al. 2014). In this way, the incorporation of entrepreneurship in the education of journalists may assist the emergence of entrepreneurial journalism projects.

In this context, several authors mention the training competencies linked to entrepreneurial journalism which should be incorporated into the curriculum. Thus, Mellor (2009) states that media entrepreneurs must acquire two essential skills: professional knowledge about their niche and the new techniques, and business knowledge about their audience and the possible market challenges. Quinn (2010) insists on offering courses to understand and investigate audiences and their consumption habits. On the other hand, Hunter and Nel (2011) claim that an enterprising journalist should have five great competencies:

(1) creativity and innovation; (2) business skills; (3) essential journalism skills related to the creation of news content; (4) technical skills (Web design, video editing, etc.); and (5) writing skills for various types of media. Jarvis (2010) stresses the importance of multimedia skills in entrepreneurship. In any case, the connection between entrepreneurial journalism and innovation requires that its practitioners be permanently attentive to new techniques and the incorporation of new skills.

The literature in this area includes research on perceptions of some of the interest groups related to entrepreneurial journalism, including the opinions of educators (Ferrier 2013; Vázquez Schaich and Klein 2013) and the views of journalists who choose to start their own businesses (Elmore and Massey 2012). The educators who lead entrepreneurial journalism courses have a three-fold motivation: industrial (in order to show changes in the sector), institutional (to renew the curriculum offered by their university), and mentality (to promote innovation) (Ferrier 2013). Vázquez Schaich and Klein (2013) point out that the main obstacle to activating these courses is the reduced background and expectations of the students according to the educators. They consider it important to teach entrepreneurial skills to journalists so they may create their own work, so that they may identify and exploit journalism and business opportunities, and because it is the future of the media industry (Vázquez Schaich and Klein 2013). In general terms, these educators believe that entrepreneurship in journalism is specific and differentiated, and that entrepreneurship should be incorporated into journalism studies (Ferrier 2013). Meanwhile, enterprising journalists emphasise that, for their colleagues, entrepreneurship was not presented as a career option. In their view, a journalist's education should include business skills together with media skills. They see entrepreneurship as an employment opportunity that universities and journalism schools should not ignore (Elmore and Massey 2012).

Research on students' views has, to date, focused on issues such as their perception of news media roles (Hanna and Sanders 2012), their professional attitudes (Bjørnsen et al. 2007), their professional skills (Casero-Ripollés et al. 2013), their political motivations (Hopmann et al. 2010), their career motivations (Hanna and Sanders 2007; Sanders et al. 2008), their degree motivations and life values (Carpenter et al. 2015), or their future job expectations (Hanusch et al. 2015). Some of these papers argue that education in journalism has little or no impact on the perceptions held by students (Bjørnsen et al. 2007; Carpenter et al. 2015). On the other hand, others argue that there is a shift in students' views as they progress in their studies (Hanna and Sanders 2012; Hanusch et al. 2015).

In any case, none of this growing body of research focuses on studying the perceptions that journalism students, and future professionals, have of entrepreneurship. Indeed, this remains a poorly addressed issue. Only a very small number of studies have broached this topic by analysing the willingness of journalism students to become entrepreneurs. These studies highlight the low level of interest evidenced by students towards this end (Casero-Ripollés and Cullell 2013; Goyanes 2015). In light of this general absence of evidence in this area, this research article aims to fill the gap in the academic literature by analysing how journalism students view the phenomenon of entrepreneurial journalism. The main objective is to find answers to the following research questions:

> **RQ1:** What do journalism students perceive as entrepreneurship in general, and what are their views on entrepreneurial journalism?

RQ2: Which are the major skills they perceive as necessary to become journalism entrepreneurs?

RQ3: To what extent are they willing to become more entrepreneurial in the field of journalism?

RQ4: Which are the obstacles and opportunities they perceive with respect to entrepreneurship in journalism?

Methodology

Our methodology uses a quantitative approach based on surveys. A questionnaire was designed based on a population comprised of a total of 374 students whose objective is to obtain a degree in journalism. All the students were enrolled in any of the four years of study offered at the Universitat Jaume I (UJI) in Spain. The probability sample is composed of 184 students. This number ensures a sufficient representativeness since it covers 49.2 per cent of the total population. The test statistic t takes the value −0.992 with 183 degrees of freedom ($n - 1$) and a significance of 0.322. The value of significance ($p > 0.05$) indicates that there are no statistically significant differences between the tested sample and the population. Therefore, the sample is representative of the population. The margin of error is equal to ±3 per cent (0.03) with a confidence interval of $2\sigma = 95.5$ per cent.

A sample stratification was applied with the use of educational level as a variable to analyse the results of the survey. Thus, there are two differentiated levels of studies: the first cycle (corresponding to first and second years) composed of 97 people; and the second cycle (corresponding to third and fourth years) composed of 87 people. The stratification between stages corresponds to an educational intervention. During the first cycle the students attend modules with a general focus on journalism studies. During the second cycle, the degree programme becomes more specific and introduces subjects such as Media Management and Media Systems, which are based on the development of knowledge and skills related to entrepreneurship.

For the creation of the content of the questionnaire, there was an initial qualitative phase, conducted through two focus groups. The first was composed of six students, three women and three men, enrolled in the first and second years of journalism studies at the UJI. The second group was composed of third- and fourth-year students, four men and four women. As it was a qualitative technique, the symmetry in the gender variable was maintained. The goal of this initial stage was to obtain information for the design of the subsequent phase, which would be based on a survey with a quantitative questionnaire given to the sample population. The results obtained from the focus groups allowed us identify the key and decisive topics related to the sample population's perceptions about entrepreneurship. With this information, the variables of the survey were constructed. The results obtained from the focus groups were used to select and refine the options for the closed-ended questions of the questionnaire designed for the survey. This questionnaire combined dichotomous questions with multiple choice or forced selection questions. The study was conducted during the second semester of the 2014/15 academic year. The focus groups were held in February 2015. Once the information gathered in this phase had been processed, the questionnaire was designed and the field work began, which took place between April and May 2015. The processing of the data was carried out with SPSS software.

Results

Perceptions of Entrepreneurship: General Ideas and Specific Views

The survey results reflect a significant link between entrepreneurship and innovation. More than half of the student body (55.4 per cent) associated entrepreneurial initiatives with projects that address any type of innovation in the field (Figure 1). However, this idea loses strength as students progress in their studies. This perception reflects a commonly held belief in journalism, where "one of the most striking effects of this conjunctural and structural crisis affecting the media industry is the generation of strong restructuring processes and the flourishing of intensive innovation dynamics" (Campos 2010, 14). On the other hand, the link between entrepreneurship and employment is also significant. As seen in Figure 1, 53.8 per cent of the students perceived this phenomenon as a job opportunity, as a form of self-employment. Moreover, this conviction increases as they advance in their studies, up to 60 per cent in the second cycle corresponding to the final years of study.

The figure of the entrepreneur is still somewhat confusing for students, and there is some dispersion when it comes to associating entrepreneurship with specific forms of business or figures. For example, 33.2 per cent linked entrepreneurship to the figure of the entrepreneur and 32.6 per cent linked it to the self-employed. However, the most significant finding is the association of entrepreneurship with the freelance journalist. As seen in Figure 1, 36.4 per cent of the students made this connection. The traditional role of the freelancer is based on one-off collaborations with media outlets; they are not on the company's payroll. However, this is not the same as entrepreneurship (Baines and Kennedy

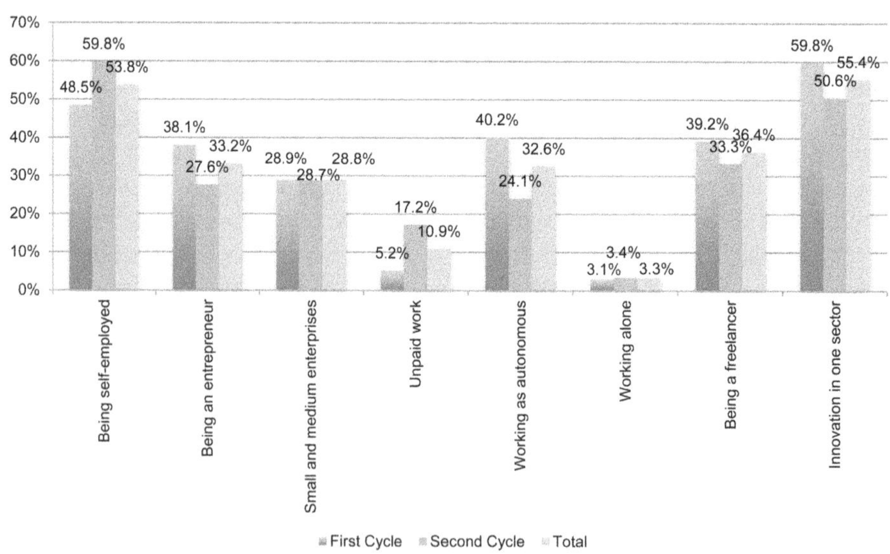

FIGURE 1
Ideas associated with entrepreneurship

2010). In business terms, freelancing does not create an independent business, as the person is still employed by the company, albeit in a temporary way. This shows a certain level of confusion in the perceptions held by students regarding entrepreneurship. This is also seen in the fact that 10.9 per cent associated entrepreneurship with unpaid work (Figure 1). This places entrepreneurial journalism within the realm of job insecurity, on the one hand, and equates it to a hobby, on the other. It is disconcerting to note that this figure increases as students progress in their studies, from 5.2 per cent in the first cycle to 17.2 per cent among students in the second cycle. This reveals that the current curriculum of journalism studies does not contribute to improving knowledge about entrepreneurship among students.

Therefore, the results reflect a certain lack of knowledge regarding the figure of the entrepreneur and their position within the job market. A noteworthy point is the practical unanimity in the rejection of the identification of entrepreneurship as solitary work (3.3 per cent of the total). For students, this activity is performed under the parameters of collective work and is, therefore, linked to relationships with other agents in the sector.

In relation to how entrepreneurship is perceived specifically in connection with journalism, students agree in associating this phenomenon with the creation of one's own media outlet, irrespective of its support. As seen in Figure 2, 77.2 per cent believe that the start of a media outlet, whether it is offline or online, may be considered entrepreneurial journalism, provided that it is developed through a private initiative. This perception held by the student body goes against the thesis defended in most of the literature linking entrepreneurship with digital technology as a key area where new journalistic projects of this nature are developed. Only 34.8 per cent of students directly link entrepreneurship with the creation of a media outlet on the internet. Moreover, this dissociation between journalistic entrepreneurship and digital technology occurs widely among all students, regardless of their level of studies. However, it is more pronounced among those in the

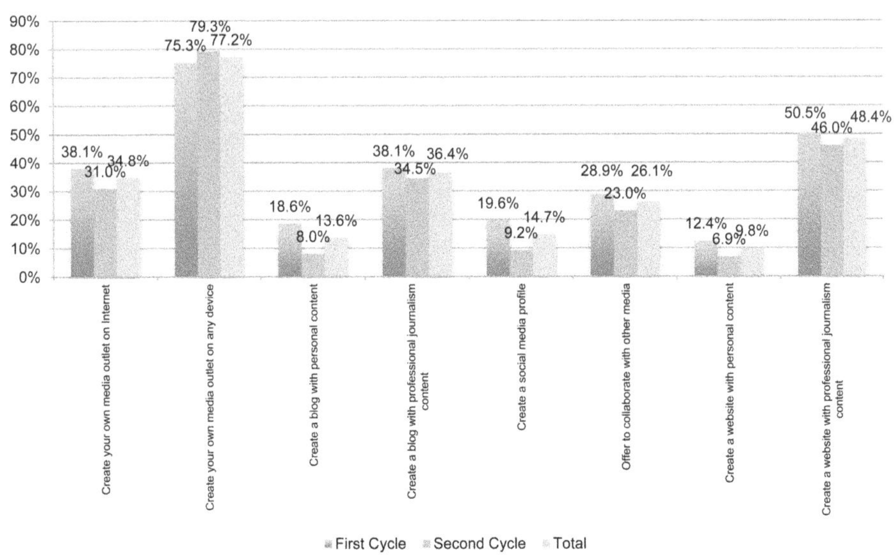

FIGURE 2
Views related to entrepreneurship in journalism

second cycle, that is, those who have advanced further in their studies. Therefore, the innovation that is associated with entrepreneurship is not necessarily related to the use of digital technologies in the perceptions of students, although this is one of the key factors enabling the growth of media entrepreneurs.

Students also linked entrepreneurship in journalism to professionalisation. In this sense, the content becomes a differentiating factor. Students associated entrepreneurship with the result of the work of journalists, regardless of whether they do that work on a website (48.4 per cent) or a blog (36.4 per cent). This also vindicates professionalisation in an entrepreneurial environment, although some of the students (14.7 per cent) contemplate non-professional options, such as the dissemination of personal content through different outlets (website, blog, social networking). In this sense, there is some confusion or ignorance with regard to the identification of an entrepreneurial journalism project, which occurs mainly in the first years, where television programmes or YouTube channels are erroneously given as examples of entrepreneurial projects.

Perceptions Regarding the Competencies and Skills Necessary for Entrepreneurial Journalism

Our results show the assessment carried out by students of a series of competencies linked to entrepreneurship in journalism. The data show the assessment of each competence on a scale of five levels (Likert scale), from "completely agree" (5) to "completely disagree" (1). The analysis reveals a difference between a group of general competencies and others that are more specific to the practice of journalism. In the analysis of this aspect, there are no significant differences between students in the first cycle (early years) and those in the second cycle (final years).

The results present interesting findings (Table 1). The competence that is most valued by students is the use and knowledge of digital technologies with a mean of 4.6 (SD = 0.59). This is followed by creativity (mean = 4.6, SD = 0.62) and the ability to take the initiative (mean = 4.5, SD = 0.69). These are skills that connect directly with the innovative and

TABLE 1
Degree of importance of each competency in entrepreneurial journalism

Skills	Mean	SD
Expertise in the use of digital technologies	4.6	0.59
Creativity	4.6	0.62
Ability to take initiative	4.5	0.69
Knowledge of the activity of the communication system, exploring its problems, challenges, and opportunities	4.4	0.74
Knowledge of the operation and management of a media company	4.1	0.82
Ability to lead teams	4.1	0.82
Knowledge of areas of specialisation in journalism	4.1	0.77
Ability to work autonomously	4.1	0.89
Knowledge of the information consumer market	4.1	0.76
Leadership skills	3.9	0.87
Knowledge of legal, ethical, and historical aspects as they pertain to the practice of journalism	3.8	0.90
Knowledge of economics and finance	3.3	0.90

Ascending scale: 1 = completely disagree; 5 = completely agree.

creative side of entrepreneurship. These results support the idea that students identify entrepreneurial journalism as a phenomenon associated with innovation. In the same way, this association is mentioned in the literature that highlights the importance of creativity as a core competence in entrepreneurship (Zampetakis and Moustakis 2006), as well as digital technologies in the promotion of independent and self-employment (Handy 1995).

This belief remains strong, and creativity and innovation are skills that students directly associate with entrepreneurship. In relation to the prioritisation of technological skills, 94.5 per cent of students considered that it was important or very important to know and work with digital technologies to practise entrepreneurial journalism (Figure 3). This figure is significant in that it contradicts our previous results, where students did not associate entrepreneurship with the creation of a media industry on the internet as a priority. This is an outcome that once more reveals confusion among students when it comes to defining and knowing more about the profiles associated with entrepreneurship in journalism.

A second block of skills that received a remarkable rating by students are those related to knowledge of the media industry and the management of media companies. Knowledge of the issues, challenges, and opportunities in the sector, which allow us to identify niche markets to create enterprising media, reached an average of 4.4 (SD = 0.74) (Table 1). Moreover, skills necessary for the management of a media company in general received a mean rating of 4.1 (SD = 0.82). This represents an increase compared to the data obtained in previous studies (Casero-Ripollés, Ortells-Badenes, and Doménech-Fabregat 2013). The ability to lead teams also achieved a high mean score (mean = 4.1, SD = 0.82). The high rating for this final competence supports the idea, already revealed

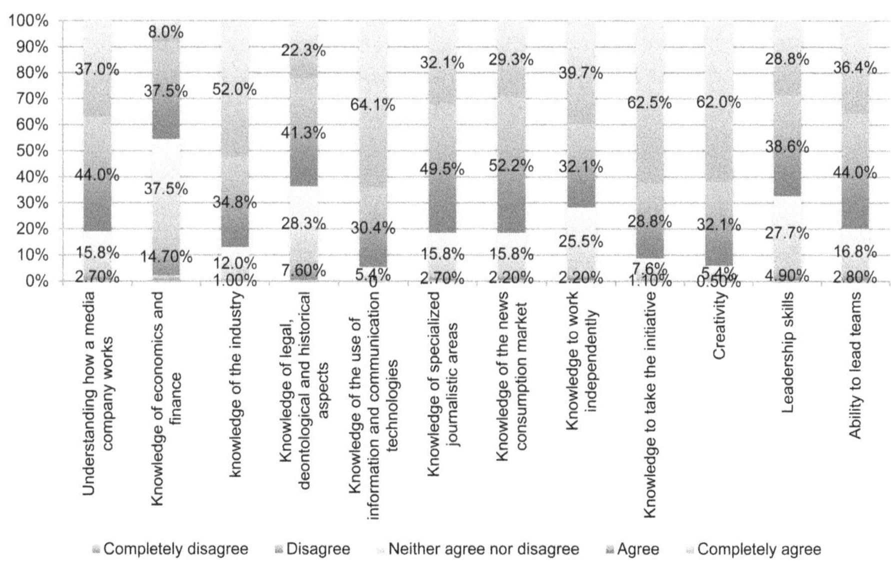

FIGURE 3
Degree of relevance, as perceived by the students, of the skills necessary for entrepreneurship

by the results of the previous section, that students perceive entrepreneurship in journalism as a collective effort where management and leadership skills are very useful.

What stands out from our findings is that competencies related to audience knowledge did not receive a higher rating despite the importance that the literature attributes to them in the development of enterprise media (Mellor 2009) and in the renewal of the business models for journalism in the digital environment (Campos-Freire 2010). Students gave a mean rating of 4.076 (SD = 0.7644) to knowledge of the news consumer market, placing this skill in ninth place out of the 12 that were rated in total. Equally, it is worth noting that knowledge of economics and finance in general is perceived as unhelpful in entrepreneurship in journalism, as this skill achieved a mean rating of 3.3 (SD = 0.90) (Table 1). Only 8 per cent of students considered it important to acquire economic and financial knowledge (Figure 3). These results raise two issues. First, those students understand entrepreneurship as a phenomenon associated specifically with journalism. This is why they highly valued media company management skills and appreciated knowledge of general economics less. Secondly, students did not only associate entrepreneurship with its economic and financial aspects.

Perceptions Held by Journalism Students Regarding the Feasibility of Entrepreneurship in Journalism: Willingness, Obstacles, and Opportunities

The results indicate that 65.2 per cent of journalism students would be willing to undertake their own business project. This figure shows an increase in relation to the above literature that identified a small student interest in entrepreneurship (Delano 2001; Casero-Ripollés and Cullell 2013). However, this willingness diminishes as students progress in their studies. Thus, in the second cycle, corresponding with the final years of study, the percentage of those willing to undertake their own business is 59.8 per cent, compared to 70.1 per cent of those in the first cycle (first and second years) (Figure 4).

Despite the difference in interest towards media entrepreneurship between students in the first cycle and those in the second, there are few significant differences in the identification of barriers and opportunities to carry it out. For example, 73.4 per cent identify the

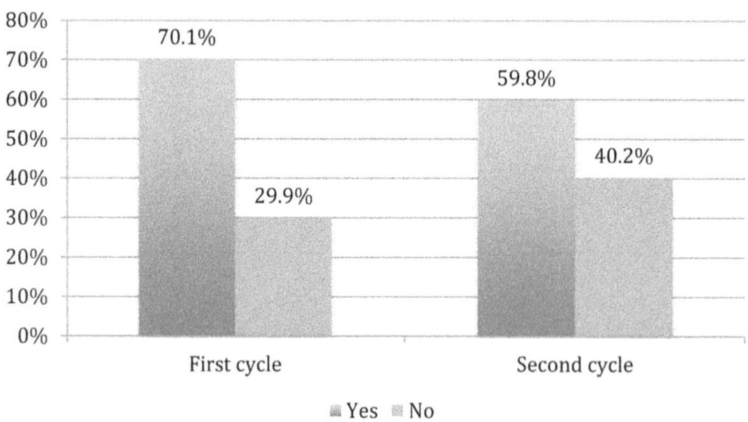

FIGURE 4
Willingness on the part of journalism students to start their own business in journalism

difficulty in enabling the company to generate profits as the main barrier to entrepreneurial journalism (Figure 5). Wage insecurity appears as the second obstacle perceived by students (65.8 per cent). Advancement in the level of study has an effect on these perceptions, as it causes an increase in the percentage of students who perceive it as a drawback, of up to 73.4 per cent. The difficulty in obtaining financing, at 63 per cent, comes in third place.

High competition in the media industry, at 58.2 per cent, ranks as the fourth obstacle to entrepreneurship in journalism according to students (Figure 5). The generalisation of digital technologies and flexibility in content distribution has led to the disappearance of barriers to traditional entry into journalism, promoting entrepreneurship. However, this has paradoxically led to the emergence of a new barrier, associated with the difficulty in differentiating oneself in a highly competitive environment, characterised by a rich media offering. This is something that students perceive clearly.

There are four aspects that students associated less with barriers to entrepreneurship in journalism. Not having a fixed work schedule is not perceived as a problem, since only 16.3 per cent perceived it as a disadvantage (Figure 5). Also, difficulties in knowing all of the areas of the business (20.1 per cent), finding and retaining an audience (33.7 per cent), and designing the perfect media product (25 per cent) are not perceived as significant barriers to entrepreneurial journalism. These data reflect a high level of confidence in students both in terms of their knowledge and elaboration of strategies that allow them to perform and position themselves in the media market.

In terms of the opportunities evident in entrepreneurship, it is worth noting the perceived editorial and ideological freedom. A resounding 82.1 per cent of the students consider that the creation of their own entrepreneurial project guarantees freedom from any compulsion in terms of the selection of news topics, sources, and approaches (Figure 6). The possibility of having a high degree of professional autonomy and independence is the main positive attribute linked with entrepreneurial journalism. In this regard, the practice of this

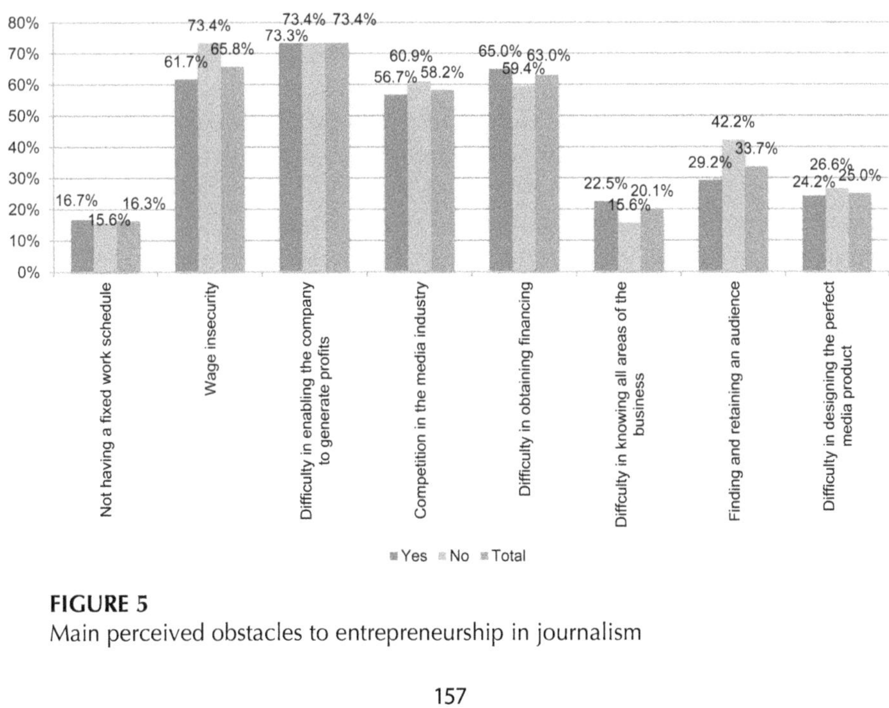

FIGURE 5
Main perceived obstacles to entrepreneurship in journalism

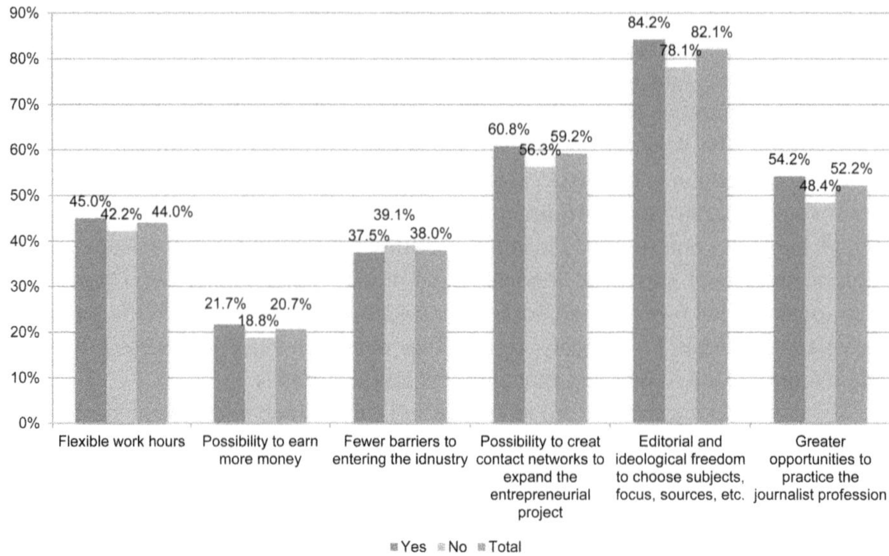

FIGURE 6
Main opportunities perceived in entrepreneurship in journalism

type of journalism is linked with a high margin of manoeuvre in the elaboration of the news content that gives the journalist control over the production process, thus keeping external interference to a minimum.

Another positive aspect linked to entrepreneurship is that it allows the creation of networks of contacts, which may contribute to extending the business project or to generating different ones. Overall, 59.2 per cent of students see this possibility as an opportunity. This view supports the literature finding that seeking contacts and networking plays a decisive role in the viability of entrepreneurial journalism (Mellor 2009). In addition, 52.2 per cent of students considered that entrepreneurship offers the advantage of greater job opportunities in the field of journalism (Figure 6). This perception views entrepreneurship as a window of professionalism that is an alternative to the incorporation of future journalists as media workers in mainstream media, which are increasingly less able to hire journalists. This idea emphasises one of the positive characteristics of entrepreneurship, namely that it is understood as a job opportunity. These results show that the perception of future journalists, now students, coincides with that of active journalists who associate entrepreneurship with the invention of their own work (Anderson 2014). Interestingly, students do not perceive entrepreneurship as offering employment benefits to journalists. The ability to earn more money as a media entrepreneur than as a media worker is only seen as an opportunity by 20.7 per cent of students (Figure 6). Moreover, although with a slightly higher rating, neither is the option of having a flexible schedule (44 per cent) identified as an advantage of entrepreneurship.

In the analysis of the results linked to the opportunities that entrepreneurship offers to journalism, there are no significant differences in regards to the level of studies. However, what does stand out is that, in general terms, the percentages obtained by the main opportunities are clearly smaller than those achieved by the main obstacles. The comparison between Figures 5 and 6 shows that, globally, the barriers obtain higher values. These data suggest that students perceive obstacles with a greater intensity and clarity than the opportunities provided by entrepreneurial journalism.

Conclusions and Discussion

Our results identify a number of significant issues related to perceptions held by journalism students regarding entrepreneurship. The first concerns the high degree of confusion in terms of knowledge of entrepreneurship, in general, and of entrepreneurial journalism, in particular, which corresponds to RQ1. The data indicate that students do not clearly identify the figure of the entrepreneur, as they associate it with freelancing in a significant percentage. Additionally, a significant number of students link entrepreneurship to the universe of unpaid work by associating it with a lack of job security or the world of hobbies. These results suggest that the limited introduction of entrepreneurship in journalism education, mentioned in the literature (Baines and Kennedy 2010; Hunter and Nel 2011; Ferrier 2013), might be a contributing factor in this confusion and one that prevents a greater understanding of entrepreneurial journalism.

Journalism students associate entrepreneurship with innovation and creativity, and barely connect it to economic and financial issues, on the one hand, and to the need to gain more in-depth knowledge of the audience and their habits of consumption, on the other. This identification of skills is related to RQ2. In this regard, this research offers elements for the introduction of entrepreneurial journalism in the curriculum of journalism education. The strengthening of technical skills, the introduction of knowledge about the audience and market challenges, and lastly, the importance attributed to innovation and creativity in the creation of media products seem to be appropriate strategies in the promotion of entrepreneurship.

In addition, the results allow us to identify the main obstacles and major opportunities that students link to entrepreneurial journalism (considered in RQ4). We can highlight the economic and financial aspects (economic volatility, difficulty in obtaining profits, wage insecurity, and funding problems). Among the advantages, it is worth noting the preference over independence and editorial freedom in the creation of news content. We also see networking and the increase in the possibilities of obtaining work as a journalist. However, globally, the opportunities receive lower percentages than the obstacles. This suggests that students perceive barriers with a greater intensity and clarity than the advantages offered by entrepreneurial journalism.

In contrast to previous studies (Casero-Ripollés and Cullell 2013; Goyanes 2015), the data indicate the existence of a high willingness among journalism students to venture into entrepreneurship. This is seen in the 65.2 per cent who claim to have an interest in creating their own business in the form of an enterprising media outlet. This shows the journalism students' willingness to become entrepreneurial, corresponding to RQ3. However, the results show a new and highly significant aspect: the increase in the level of study goes hand-in-hand with the appearance of a disenchanted and cynical view towards entrepreneurship among journalism students. Four items of empirical evidence support this statement: (1) willingness to undertake a new business is reduced among students in the second cycle (more advanced studies), (2) the identification of entrepreneurship as unpaid work increases among students in the second cycle, (3) the association of entrepreneurship with innovation is lower among students in the second cycle, and (4) the perception of a lack of job security as an obstacle increases among students in the second cycle. We can therefore conclude that the perception of entrepreneurship is more positive among students who are beginning their studies than those who are in the final stages.

This finding has important implications. The first is that we may confirm the change in perception among journalism students as they progress in their studies, as suggested by some of the literature (Hanna and Sanders 2012). However, the main implication lies in the fact that journalism education tends to increase the negative view held by students regarding journalism. This trend matches, in part, that detected by Hanusch et al. (2015), who found that, in a sample of eight countries, students' desire to work in journalism decreases as they progress in their studies. Our contribution applies this idea to the field of entrepreneurial journalism, which would also be affected by the thesis of disappointment among journalism students. The reasons behind this attitude cannot be stated with certainty yet. The lack of job security and employment in journalism, on the one hand, and the failure to meet students' expectations throughout their education, in terms of what they expected and what their training is providing, on the other hand, might be some possible reasons. In any case, this trend poses a great challenge for journalism educators, as well as universities and journalism schools. If skills, courses, and training content on entrepreneurship are not introduced into the curriculum, there is a risk of missing the opportunities afforded by entrepreneurial journalism for the future of journalism.

DISCLOSURE STATEMENT

No potential conflict of interest was reported by the authors.

FUNDING

This research was supported by the Universitat Jaume I de Castelló [grant number PI11A2013–12].

REFERENCES

Aceituno-Aceituno, Pedro, Carlos Bousoño-Calzón, José Joaquín Escudero-Garzás, and Francisco J Herrera-Gálvez. 2014. "Formación en emprendimiento para periodistas [Entrepreneurship Training for Journalists]." *El Profesional de la Información* 23 (4): 409–414.

Anderson, C. W. 2014. "The Sociology of the Professions and the Problem of Journalism Education." *Radical Teacher* 99: 62–68.

APM (Asociación de la Prensa de Madrid - Press Association of Madrid). 2014. *Informe annual de la profesión periodística 2014* [*Annual Report of the Journalistic Profession* 2014]. Madrid: APM.

Baines, David, and Ciara Kennedy. 2010. "An Education for Independence: Should Entrepreneurial Skills be an Essential Part of the Journalist's Toolbox?" *Journalism Practice* 4 (1): 97–113.

Berman, Saul J., Bill Battino, and Karen Feldman. 2011. "New Business Models for Emerging Media and Entertainment Revenue Opportunities." *Strategy and Leadership* 39 (3), 44–53.

Bjørnsen, Gunn, Jan Fredrik Hovden, and Rune Ottosen. 2007. "Journalists in the Making: Findings from a Longitudinal Study of Norwegian Journalism Students." *Journalism Practice* 1 (3): 383–403.

Briggs, Mark. 2012. *Entrepreneurial Journalism: How to Build what's Next for News*. Los Angeles, CA: Sage /CQ Press.

Campos Freire, Francisco. 2010. "Los nuevos modelos de gestión de las empresas mediáticas [New Management Models for Media Companies]." *Estudios sobre el Mensaje Periodístico* 16: 13–30.

Carpenter, Serena, Anne Hoag, August E. Grant, and Brian J Bowe. 2015. "An Examination of how Academic Advancement of US Journalism Students Relates to their Degree Motivations, Values, and Technology Use." *Journalism and Mass Communication Educator* 70 (1): 58–74.

Casero-Ripollés, Andreu. 2010. "Prensa en internet: nuevos modelos de negocio en el escenario de la convergencia [The Press in the Internet: New Business Models in the Scenario of Convergence]." *El Profesional de la Información* 19 (6): 595–601.

Casero-Ripollés, Andreu, and Cristina Cullell. 2013. "Periodismo emprendedor. Estrategias para incentivar el autoempleo periodístico como modelo de negocio [Entrepreneurial Journalism. Strategies to Promote Self-employment in Journalism as a New Business Model]." *Estudios sobre el Mensaje Periodístico* 19: 681–690.

Casero-Ripollés, Andreu, and Jessica Izquierdo-Castillo. 2013. "Between Decline and a new Online Business Model: The Case of the Spanish Newspaper Industry." *Journal of Media Business Studies* 10 (1): 63–78.

Casero-Ripollés, Andreu, Sara Ortells-Badenes, and Hugo Doménech-Fabregat. 2013. "Las competencias profesionales en periodismo: Una evaluación comparativa [Professional Skills in Journalism: A Comparative Evaluation]." *Historia y Comunicación Social* 18: 53–64.

Charney, Alberta, and Gary D Libecap. 2000. *Impact of Entrepreneurship Education*. Kansas City, MO: Kauffman Center for Entrepreneurial Leadership.

Claussen, Dane. 2011. "CUNY's Entrepreneurial Journalism: Partially Old Wine in a New Bottle, and not Quite Thirst-quenching, but Still a Good Drink." *Journalism and Mass Communication Educator* 66 (1): 3–6.

Dates, Jannette L., Theodore L. Glasser, Mitchell Stephens, and G. Stuart Adam. 2006. "Does Journalism Education Matter?" *Journalism Studies* 7 (1): 144–156.

Delano, Anthony. 2001. "The Formation of the British Journalist 1900–2000." PhD thesis, University of Westminster.

Deuze, Mark. 2006. "Global Journalism Education: A Conceptual Approach." *Journalism Studies* 7 (1): 19–34.

Drok, Nico. 2013. "Beacons of Reliability: European Journalism Students and Professionals on Future Qualifications for Journalists." *Journalism Practice* 7 (2): 145–162.

Drucker, Peter F. 1985. *Innovation and Entrepreneurship*. New York, NY: Harper and Row.

Elmore, Cindy, and Brian Massey. 2012. "Need for Instruction in Entrepreneurial Journalism: Perspective of Full-time Freelancers." *Journal of Media Practice* 13 (2): 109–124.

Ferrier, Michelle Barrett. 2013. "Media Entrepreneurship: Curriculum Development and Faculty Perceptions of What Students Should Know." *Journalism and Mass Communication Educator* 68 (3): 222–241.

Goyanes, Manuel. 2015. "Apoyo estructural en la intención emprendedora de estudiantes de periodismo y comunicación audiovisual en España [Structural Support in the Entrepreneurial Intentions of Spanish Journalism and Audiovisual Communication Students]." *El Profesional de la Información* 24 (1): 55–61.

Handy, Charles. 1995. "Trust and the Virtual Organization" *Harvard Business Review* 40–50.

Hanna, Mark, and Karen Sanders. 2007. "Journalism Education in Britain: Who are the Students and what do they Want?" *Journalism Practice* 1 (3): 404–420.

Hanna, Mark, and Karen Sanders. 2012. "Perceptions of the News Media's Societal Roles: How the Views of U.K. Journalism Students Changed during Their Education." *Journalism and Mass Communication Educator* 67 (2): 145–163.

Hanusch, Folker, Claudia Mellado, Priscilla Boshoff, Maria Luisa Humanes, Salvador De León, Fabio Pereira, Mireia Márquez Ramírez, Sergio Roses, Federico Subervi, Vinzenz Wyss, and Lyuva Yez. 2015. "Journalism Students' Motivations and Expectations of their Work in Comparative Perspective." *Journalism and Mass Communication Educator* 70 (2): 141–160.

Hoag, Anne, and Sangho Seo. 2005. "Media Entrepreneurship: Definition, Theory and Context." Paper, *NCTA Academic Seminar*, April 2005, San Francisco. http://www.smeal.psu.edu/fcfe/research/fcfe/more/white/mediaentre.pdf/.

Hopmann, David N., Christian, Elmelund-Præstekær, and Klaus Levinsen. 2010. "Journalism Students: Left-wing and Politically Motivated?" *Journalism* 11 (6): 661–674.

Hunter, Anna, and François P. Nel. 2011. "Equipping the Entrepreneurial Journalist: An Exercise in Creative Enterprise." *Journalism and Mass Communication Educator* 66 (1): 9–24.

Jarvis, Jeff. 2010. "Teaching Entrepreneurial Journalism." *BuzzMachine*, last modified January, 11. http://buzzmachine.com/2010/01/11/teaching-entrepreneurial-journalism/.

Kelly, Sara. 2015. *The Entrepreneurial Journalist's Toolkit: Manage your Media*. Burlington, MA: Focal Press.

Landström, Hans, Fredrik Åström, and Gouya Harirchi. 2015. "Innovation and Entrepreneurship Studies: One or Two Fields of Research?" *International Entrepreneurship and Management Journal*, 11: 493–509.

Lange, Julian E., Edward Marram, Ajay Solai Jawahar, Wei Yong, and William Bygrave. 2011. "Does an Entrepreneurship Education have Lasting Value? A Study of Careers of 4,000 Alumni." *Frontiers of Entrepreneurship Research,* 31 (6): 210–224.

Lassila-Merisalo, Maria, and Turo Uskali. 2011. "How to Educate Innovation Journalists? Experiences of Innovation Journalism Education in Finland 2004–2010." *Journalism and Mass Communication Educator* 66 (1): 25–38.

Mellor, Noha. 2009. "Journalism and Media Entrepreneurs." In *Entrepreneurship for Everyone: A Student Textbook*, edited by Robert Mellor, 166–181. London, UK: Sage.

Mensing, Donica. 2010. "Rethinking [again] the Future of Journalism Education." *Journalism Studies,* 11 (4): 511–523.

Meyer, Philip. 2009. *The Vanishing Newspaper*. 2nd ed. Columbia, MO: University of Missouri Press.

Mueller, Susan. 2011. "Increasing Entrepreneurial Intention: Effective Entrepreneurship Course Characteristics." *International Journal of Entrepreneurship and Small Business* 13 (1): 55–74.

Neff, Gina. 2012. *Venture Labor: Work and the Burden of Risk in Innovative Industries*. Cambridge, MA: MIT Press.

Paniagua Rojano, Francisco J., Marisol Gómez Aguilar, and Maria Eugenia González Cortés. 2014. "Encourage Entrepreneurial Journalism from the University." *Revista Latina de Comunicación Social* 69: 548–570. http://www.revistalatinacs.org/069/paper/1024_UMA/RLCS_paper1024en.pdf

Picard, Robert G. 2014. "Twilight or New Dawn of Journalism. Evidence from the Changing News Ecosystem." *Journalism Studies* 15 (5): 500–510.

Quinn, Stephen. 2010. "Opportunities for Journalism Education in an Online Entrepreneurial World." *Asia Pacific Media Educator* 20: 69–80.

Rae, David. 2004. "Entrepreneurial Learning: A Practical Model from the Creative Industries." *Education + Training* 46: 492–500.

Sanders, Karen, Mark Hanna, Maria Rosa Berganza, and José Javier Sanchez Arand. 2008. "Becoming Journalists: A Comparison of the Professional Attitudes and Values of British and Spanish Journalism Students." *European Journal of Communication* 23 (2): 133–152.

Schumpeter, Joseph A. 1936. *The Theory of Economic Development*. Cambridge, MA: Harvard University.

Vázquez Schaich, Maria José, and Jeffrey S Klein. 2013. "Entrepreneurial Journalism Education: Where are we Now?" *Observatorio (OBS*)* 7 (4): 185–211. http://obs.obercom.pt/index.php/obs/article/view/715.

Zampetakis, Leonidas A., and Vassilis Moustakis. 2006. "Linking Creativity with Entrepreneurial Intentions: A Structural Approach." *The International Entrepreneurship and Management Journal* 2 (3): 413–428.

Zhao, Fang. 2005. "Exploring the Synergy Between Entrepreneurship and Innovation." *International Journal of Entrepreneurial Behavior & Research*, 11 (1): 25–41.

Index

www.ingramcontent.com/pod-product-compliance
Ingram Content Group UK Ltd.
Pitfield, Milton Keynes, MK11 3LW, UK
UKHW050754180926
475701UK00007B/1035
* 9 7 8 0 3 6 7 2 6 4 6 2 8 *